Taj Nathan is a medical doctor who has [...] as a forensic psychiatrist. In his clinical p[...] and treat the perpetrators and victims of v[...] hospitals, prisons and the community. Alongside his clinical work, he has carried out extensive research in many areas of forensic psychiatry (including aggression and its causes), and he has led the development of innovative services for offenders with psychiatric difficulties. Drawing on both his clinical and academic expertise, he is frequently asked to provide expert evidence in criminal and family law courts. Having authored numerous scientific papers and academic book chapters, he turned to writing for a wider audience and in 2018 he won the John Murray and Spectator Essay Prize for a piece on the origins of violence. This is his first book.

Praise for Dangerous Minds

'An eye-opening journey into dangerous minds . . . This exceptional book by a forensic psychiatrist explores what drives people to commit reprehensible acts . . . This thoughtful and engrossing book is as much about law as it is about minds. John Major once said that "society needs to condemn a little more and understand a little less" when it comes to crime. Nathan reminds us that we do not necessarily have to choose. It's possible to condemn actions, and individuals, while seeking to comprehend what produced them. Attempting to do both might be the only way to achieve something like justice'
Sarah Ditum, *The Times*

'Not only a fascinating read but it was one of the most compassionate, thoughtful and thought-provoking books I have read in a long time'
Kristina Reed, Barrister

'A unique text in explaining to a lay readership what a forensic psychiatrist does – clinical and medicolegal, and within the clinical hospital and prison work . . . A great service to the profession and to the public'
Professor Keith Rix, Honorary Consultant Forensic Psychiatrist, Visiting Professor of Medical Jurisprudence, Mental Health and Intellectual Disability Lead, Faculty of Forensic and Legal Medicine of the Royal College of Physicians

Dangerous Minds

A forensic psychiatrist's quest to understand violence

TAJ NATHAN

JOHN MURRAY

First published in Great Britain in 2021 by John Murray (Publishers)
An Hachette UK company

This paperback edition published in 2022

3

A CIP catalogue record for this title is available from the British Library

Paperback ISBN 978-1-529-39293-7
eBook ISBN 978-1-529-39294-4

Printed and bound in Great Britain by Clays Ltd, Elcograf S.p.A.

John Murray policy is to use papers that are natural, renewable and recyclable products
and made from wood grown in sustainable forests. The logging and manufacturing
processes are expected to conform to the environmental regulations of the country of
origin.

John Murray (Publishers)
Carmelite House
50 Victoria Embankment
London EC4Y 0DZ

www.johnmurraypress.co.uk

For Saffron, Sadie, Keir and Lindsay

Contents

Dangerous Minds

Beginnings

THERE WAS NO reason for Edward Drummond to believe this January day was going to be different from any other Whitehall working day. Having completed his civil service chores and visited the bank, he set off back to Downing Street where, as the prime minister's private secretary, he had an apartment. He was passing a Charing Cross coffee shop when, without any warning, he felt a searing blow to his back and, according to a witness, his jacket burst into flames.

The sharp bang drew the attention of a quick-witted police officer, who dashed across the road as a man prepared to shoot at Mr Drummond again. But even with the assistance of passers-by the officer struggled to disarm the shooter, who violently resisted and managed to discharge a second shot, though this time without causing injury to anyone. Eventually overpowered, the shooter – a man named Daniel M'Naghten – was arrested and detained in police custody for questioning.

Drummond's initial prognosis seemed hopeful. Reeling from the gunshot wound, he had staggered back to the bank and, following medical attention, was able to return to his own home. The bullet was later successfully extracted and it was reported to the press that his surgeons, Mr Guthrie and Mr Bransby Cooper, 'have every reason to believe that Mr Drummond is doing very well'. However, in the following days Drummond's condition worsened and within five days of the shooting he died of septicaemia. M'Naghten's crime had become a capital offence.

After the shooting M'Naghten was taken to the police station at Gardener's Lane, where he was charged with attempted murder. But despite his resistance to police at the scene, M'Naghten was surprisingly cooperative under questioning. However, it wasn't only this willingness to admit to the shooting that surprised the police; as the interrogation proceeded it became apparent from M'Naghten's responses that his intended target had been the prime minister, Sir Robert Peel.

Daniel M'Naghten was a Scottish craftsman who, following a brief, unsuccessful acting career, set up his own woodturning workshop in Glasgow in 1835. An industrious and frugal man, M'Naghten ran his workshop for five years and was able to save a considerable sum of money, teaching himself French and attending lectures on anatomy and philosophy in his spare time. But despite his financial success, his behaviour over the years preceding the shooting pointed to unusual tendencies. M'Naghten had, he explained to the Metropolitan Police, for years been terrorised by the ruling elite. He was known to be eccentric and evasive and this was not the first time that he had made such claims; back in his native Scotland he had complained to both the Glasgow commissioner of police and an MP that he was being followed by Tory spies. His landlady in Glasgow observed a remarkable change in M'Naghten's manner. She thought 'his eyes wore a strange appearance' and she came to feel fearful of him. He would moan and groan in his sleep and protest that devils were haunting him. Once, she found pistols in his room, pistols that he explained were for shooting birds.

During the murder trial that followed the killing of Drummond, the court learned that the shooting had formed the denouement of a remarkable conspiratorial tale. M'Naghten's trial started on 3 March 1843 in front of a packed courthouse. The prosecution called a series of witnesses, including an anatomy teacher, to testify that in their dealings with M'Naghten they had observed no signs of mental derangement. M'Naghten seemed to many of the people who knew him to be a functioning member of society. But, using the testimony of eight medical experts, the defence persuaded the jury otherwise. To these eminent physicians and surgeons it was obvious that M'Naghten had accepted unquestioningly a fiction invented by his psychotic mind. Their statements proved compelling. In the absence of medical evidence to the contrary, the jury was directed to reach a verdict and, without even retiring, the foreman announced on 4 March that they found the prisoner not guilty on the grounds of insanity.

The public was aghast, convinced that criminals and violent madmen would be encouraged to commit terrible deeds because of the lenient response to the homicidal actions of a lucid man. To the press, the verdict was an outrage that besmirched the reputation of the legal and medical establishments. This was a carefully plotted and fully confessed crime, and yet M'Naghten was being found not guilty.

Queen Victoria, reminded of the attempt on her life three years earlier by a man also deemed by the courts to be insane, was moved to intervene and in correspondence with Sir Robert Peel she asked Parliament for a tighter definition of insanity. In response, the rattled criminal justice system laid the foundations for an enduring approach to understanding the mental origins of criminal behaviour. Although the details of his crime have been largely forgotten by psychiatrists and lawyers, M'Naghten's name has since become part of legal history – the M'Naghten rule stipulates that the defence of insanity should rest on clear proof that the accused was labouring under such a defect of reason from disease of the mind as not to know the nature and quality of the act he was doing. This rule placed reason and disease centre stage in the law's assessment of the criminal mind.

Far from 'getting away' with his crime M'Naghten spent the next twenty-one years confined to the Bethlehem Hospital and then, shortly after its opening, the Broadmoor Criminal Lunatic Asylum, until his death in 1865.

Human nature is nothing if not contrary. My father was a psychiatrist so, sharing an interest in the medical profession but desiring a specialism that was more tangible, I was determined to become a surgeon. With a reckless propensity to sustain injuries on the school rugby field, my regular attendance at the local hospital as a patient stimulated an interest in orthopaedic surgery. The conventional medical model relies on the process of diagnosis to identify underlying pathology (or disease), which is then treated by either reversing or removing it. In simpler terms, identify what is broken and fix it. If a tumour is discovered by a patient's doctor, a surgeon will cut it out. I found the mechanistic simplicity of the surgeon's trade immensely appealing. As a teenage contrarian, to me psychiatry felt as if it lacked the certainty of 'real medicine'.

Now, having practised forensic psychiatry for twenty-one years and acted as an expert witness in many hundreds of cases, I see that this quality that led me to initially resist psychiatry was the very thing that later drew me to it. The more I have examined the criminal manifestations of the human mind, the more I have seen the limitations of medical diagnosis. To me, reducing types of consciousness to broad-brush diagnostic labels obscures rather than reveals the fascinating patterns created by a constant swirl of interacting thoughts, perceptions, feelings and impulses.

Although the last few decades have seen a remarkable increase in our awareness and understanding of mental health, physicians studying the mind are not a new phenomenon. In ancient Greece, the school established by Hippocrates, the father of medicine and supposed author of the oath I recited on completing medical training, advanced an account of madness based on bodily substances in contrast to the supernatural explanations pervasive in the fourth century BC. Yet the formal establishment of psychiatry as a distinct profession is much more recent.

The term 'psychiatry', which was introduced in the early nineteenth century, combines the Greek words for soul or mind (*psyche*) and healing (*iatros*). 'Mind healing' was medicalised on an industrial scale in the 1800s, with the building of vast institutions to incarcerate the mad. One such asylum in the south of England became home to Daniel M'Naghten: Broadmoor Asylum was specially designed for the incarceration of 'criminal lunatics'. It was the first, and for many decades the only, forensic psychiatric hospital in England. Meanwhile the extensive programme of ordinary asylum building was well underway across Europe and the United States. These grand structures hidden away 'round the bend' of long driveways were places to be fearful of for many people well into the late twentieth century. They were the settings of horror films and the places wayward children would be threatened with.

I would know; I grew up in one. In 1972, when my father was appointed consultant psychiatrist to an asylum in rural North Wales, my family and I moved into the doctors' accommodation in its sprawling grounds. Turning off a country lane, we would drive through the entrance gates and along a broad road, flanked on one side by a tennis court and on the other by a bowling green, up to the front of the three-storey limestone facade, which spanned out on either side of the central clock tower. The wide stone staircase we climbed led into the entrance hall of what was originally known as the North Wales Counties Lunatic Asylum, which opened in 1848. Even after we moved to our family home in Denbigh – a town that was defined to many across North Wales by its asylum – I would often accompany my father when he went to work at the weekend. I had no sense of the problems inherent in the institutional response to mental suffering; instead these visits were an opportunity for me to bask in the respect and fondness the hospital staff and patients appeared to have for my father.

Neither was it my father's original intention to pursue a career in psychiatry. In 1962 he left Kochi in south India alone on a liner with 300 US dollars, which to avoid confiscation by the Indian customs were concealed between two glued-together pages in *Savill's System of Clinical Medicine*. Without an iota of bitterness, he has told me that following his arrival he read the signs instructing him that on account of his skin colour he would not be welcome to apply for any decent accommodation in London, and it soon became clear to him this was also the main reason why he was repeatedly turned down for many posts in his favoured speciality of paediatrics. Needing to find employment, he accepted the offers of less sought after junior doctor jobs in psychiatry and then fully embraced this as his career with his eventual appointment to the post of consultant psychiatrist in Denbigh. During my weekend trips to the hospital, I recall often seeing patients walking either along the unending corridors or around the expansive grounds. To me, then, their eccentric demeanour and brooding countenance was part of their psychiatric disorder. Now, I recognise that their appearance may have been just as plausibly explained by the stuporous effects of commonly used psychiatric medications. At the time, I knew nothing about the conditions of the many more people who were incarcerated inside the Victorian-built wards.

Twenty years after moving out of that asylum, I moved into another; this time a forbidding Gothic edifice, which had opened in 1888 as a pauper lunatic asylum on the outskirts of Leeds. My decision to apply for the post there, as a junior psychiatrist, was a last-minute decision, made only a few weeks before I fully qualified as a doctor. Up to then I had planned to move to London where I had already accepted a post in an Accident and Emergency department, but then just before committing to a completely different type of medical career, I impulsively succumbed to the draw of psychiatry and relocated to the accommodation block of High Royds Hospital in West Yorkshire.

Today's system of diagnostic classification of mental illness can be traced to the attempts to organise and simplify the confused psychiatric terms that prevailed at the time of M'Naghten's trial. An influential broad dichotomy of insanity was introduced by the German psychiatric empiricist Emil Kraepelin in the 1890s, which split insanity into two classes: episodic manic-depressive insanity (later updated to bipolar disorder) and a progressively deteriorating psychotic condition that he called *dementia praecox* or 'a precocious madness', a label that was to fall out of fashion in favour of schizophrenia. With repeated subdivisions over the following 120 years, there are now over five hundred diagnoses within the current iteration of the controversial *Diagnostic and Statistical Manual of Mental Disorders*. Despite these refinements, hair-splitting debates over a patient's diagnosis remain a regular feature of psychiatric case conferences.

Early in my training, I watched a heated discussion between two senior psychiatrists about whether a patient, whose case had just been described to them by a nervous junior doctor, was suffering from one or another type of schizophrenic psychosis. Even as a psychiatric novice listening to these debates, I had some scepticism about the extent to which identifying the specific diagnosis would help me reach a good understanding of what my patients were telling me. I was drawn to thinking about the origins of their experiences and I did not find making a diagnosis particularly helpful to developing these thoughts. In preparing for my professional exams during my training I had to learn the lists of causes for each of the major psychiatric diag-noses. I memorised those factors – under the broad headings of 'genetic', 'other biological' and 'environmental' – which had been found from studies of groups of patients to have a more likely than chance association with the diagnosis in question. This type of research consistently found, for example, that birth complica-tions or maternal influenza during pregnancy were some of many possible causal factors for schizophrenia. Accordingly, it was (and still is) something that we routinely ask in our psychiatric assess-ment – whether there had been any obstetric or birth problems. But I did not feel satisfied with explaining the patient's problems in the form of a list of causal factors.

Later in my training years, I began specialising in forensic psych-iatry, a branch of medicine that deals with the assessment and treatment of offenders in prisons and secure hospitals, many of whom exhibit violent behaviour. Forensic psychiatry deals with the interface between medicine and the law, and so I began hav-ing to articulate my opinion in an arena that was much more testing and combative than those medical case conferences. Not only are criminal courts adversarial by design, but the questions are far more challenging since lawyers often do not accept the basic assumptions that psychiatry takes for granted. My opinion that a homicide is the result of the killer's diagnosable condition is not enough for their lawyers to present a defence of insanity to a charge of murder; the court needs to know more specifically how the condition affected the defendant's mind to cause him or her to kill. Paradoxically, anticipating the legal questions meant that I needed to start thinking more about the patient's mind than my psychiatric training had prepared me for. The court may be willing to take account of my evidence about the role of an unfortunate upbringing, or birth trauma, on the actions of the defendant at the material time (that is, the time when the offence is said to have occurred), but they would also need to hear how those particular factors are relevant to the violent actions carried out by this particular person – why their mental processes led them to commit this particular crime.

Similarly, once I began working in other types of court proceedings the limitations of an explanation based on a diagnosis or a list of causal factors became clear. It would be of little assistance to the family courts in reaching a decision about the safe care of a child if I were to just present symptom names and the associated diagnostic label. From my assessment, I need to acquire an understanding of that person's subjective experience – their thoughts, feelings, emotions, beliefs, impulses, urges, perceptions – so that I can try to explain not only why they had behaved as they had, but also the circumstances that may increase the chances they would behave in that way again; and most importantly the circumstances where they would be less likely to.

For about a decade I regularly delivered an introductory lecture to medical students at the University of Liverpool on the basics of the psychiatric examination. Because this was the area I worked in and because I knew it would grab their attention, I illustrated my lecture with forensic psychiatric cases: stories of patients who had committed acts of serious violence. Before starting the talk, I emphasised that these cases were not typical of patients with mental health problems. I did not want the students to leave the lecture theatre holding the common assumption that mental health problems are equated with dangerousness. Similarly, I must stress that the people whose stories I have told here are by virtue of their referral to me not typical – the majority of people who require psychiatric treatment are not dangerous, they pose no threat to society.

The cases I have described in this book, which are taken from my work both as a treating psychiatrist and as an expert witness before the courts, have been part of my journey in developing an explanatory understanding of the minds of my patients and their dangerous behaviour. In all but one of the case studies I am offering an examination of the perpetrator of a crime, and while my focus is on them we should not forget that their actions caused harm to real people; there is a victim, or victims.

I

Seb

Each morning in the prison, the officers call out the names of prisoners who have prearranged commitments later that morning. Those expecting visits from their solicitors or family members make their way to the visiting area, and those with appointments to see the doctors get ready to go to the health-care wing. But the prisoner I was due to see would not be leaving the building where he was being held; his assessment would only go ahead if I went to him.

Even before Seb had arrived at the prison five weeks earlier, the staff had received a notification that he ought to be subject to close monitoring. Such had been the concern about his mental well-being that while still in police custody, an out of hours forensic psychiatric assessment had been requested. Seb had been compliant with the arresting officers, but he had given the impression that he was unconcerned by what had happened – it seemed as though he didn't mind at all that he was being arrested. More bizarrely there were flickers of apparent self-satisfaction. A nurse and the on-call doctor from the local forensic unit travelled to the police station, but Seb declined to come out of the police cell to speak to them. Accompanied by police officers, the clinicians went to his cell to speak to him directly, but whatever they said Seb stuck to the same line: he had nothing to say to them. He even resisted attempts to be drawn into casual conversation. And so the clinicians, along with the on-call consultant, agreed that Seb did not require admission to hospital. Having said that, this reticence, along with the particulars of the crime Seb had committed, left the assessors reluctant to rule out psychiatric issues completely. Seb had been arrested on suspicion of murdering his mother.

The next morning the doctor who had assessed Seb in the police station called the prison mental health team to recommend that, on arrival, he was admitted to the health-care wing for further monitoring. From their observations, the officers and nurses also felt that Seb was not quite right, though they found it difficult to put their finger on precisely why they felt that way. He kept a distance from everyone. When he spoke, he used as few words as possible to make his point, which was either a specific request – such as for clean towels – or more often to decline offers of help or support from the staff. He did not want to come out of the cell for meals or to relax in the day room. He seemed to be eating and sleeping well and although he avoided contact, if they spoke to him he was not noticeably irritable and there had not been any aggression. That was, until the second night.

Just before the end of her long shift, one of the nurses went to check on Seb. She found him leaning on his sink looking into the small wall-mounted mirror. At first glance there was nothing unusual. During the debrief later, the nurse recalled that it was slightly odd that he did not react at all to her presence, but at the time she thought there was a mundane explanation; he seemed lost in his own thoughts. With only one foot in his cell, the nurse tried to get Seb's attention by calling his name. Then it was a bit of a blur. He must have sprung towards her and, as she made to leave the cell, wrapped his forearm around her neck, pulling her back. The staff heard her shout out and the sound of her alarm, which she had activated by pressing the red button on her belt radio. Fortunately, it was only a few steps from the nurses' office to Seb's cell, but they were not expecting the strength with which Seb fought against their attempts to release his arm from their colleague's neck. A prison officer who arrived at the scene admitted that he felt he had no choice but to hit Seb on the head, which explained the facial bruising that surfaced over the subsequent hours. With the help of officers who had run from other wings in response to the alarm, they were able to free the nurse and lock Seb back in his cell.

Segregation units are used to house particularly disruptive or dangerous prisoners. They impose tighter restrictions within conditions of greater security. It is a modern version of the punishment cell, which in a Victorian prison was commonly found in the basement. The prisoners colloquially shortened the 'segregation unit' to the 'seg' or referred to it as the 'block', which I have always assumed is derived from 'punishment block'. Under present-day rules, transfer of a recalcitrant inmate to the segregation unit can be authorised to maintain the good order and discipline of the prison. After what was regarded as an attempted hostage-taking incident on the health-care wing, Seb was assessed as too dangerous to remain there, and so when I visited him for his assessment, I made my way to the 'seg'.

A junior doctor was due to accompany me on this assessment. I knew that once through the initial security checks we would have to wait in the prison lobby for our escort, and I used this time not only to brief my trainee about Seb's case, but also to set the scene for her first visit to a prison segregation unit. As a regular visitor I knew the atmosphere on the unit was completely unpredictable; it could at times be eerily quiet, but frequently I had arrived in the 'seg' to a cacophony of screams, shouts, howls and shuddering bangs that were made all the more unnerving by the sources of the noise being out of sight. The only opportunity for the residents of the bleak single-man cells to interact face to face with their fellow inmates was during their brief allotted time for exercise in individual caged pods running outside half the length of the building. Otherwise, communication was mostly by shouting indiscriminately across the central space of the unit. Sometimes these were calls to welcome a new arrival who was in their fold or to threaten ones who were not. Alternatively, the focus of their attention could be the officers; either to plead for something or announce their aggressive intentions.

Visitors to the unit often provoked renewed excitement. I used to wonder how the prisoners who already knew me could tell when I came on the wing, despite the doors and hatches being firmly shut. They'd yell, 'Dr Nathan, come here a minute, I need to speak to you,' just after I passed their door. I realised later that they could spy through the narrow slit between the heavy metal door and its frame. When other prisoners heard about the presence of a doctor, they would shout out that they were ill and needed to see me urgently. Some probably required medical attention. Most were suffering due to extreme isolation and craved any sort of interaction. The calls tended to subside once I had passed along the unit, or they would turn into other pleas and threats, as if the existence of other people also reminded them of their desires and grievances. As we walked through the 'seg' that day, I warned the junior doctor that she may be the target of misogynistic abuse.

True to form, our arrival stirred the occupants of the segregation unit. My trainee walked beside me as we headed towards two officers talking by a standing workstation about two thirds of the way along the wide central landing. I caught her stifling a flinch at the unexpected bang and piercing shout of 'go fuck yourself' as we passed one cell door. The officers, who I knew from many visits to this unit, anticipated that

I'd come to see Seb, and helped me to find a small office where we could speak without being overheard by the other prisoners.

Once the four of us had squeezed into this rarely used room, the officers told me that what surprised them more than anything was that Seb showed no desire to leave the segregation unit. It was not a realistic option yet, but when there had been an informal discussion about the progress he would need to make to move off, Seb said he should not be moved. The officer who was there when he made this comment sensed from his assured tone that it veiled a threat.

Seb was on what the officers call a 'three-officer unlock'. All segregation unit residents are only allowed out of their cells one at a time, but those who are considered particularly unpredictable, like Seb, require at least three officers to be on hand before the door to the cell can be opened. Indeed, Seb's attempt at hostage-taking warranted the imposition of this precaution. Puzzling over how long it had remained in place, I asked why. The senior officer explained that after easing the supervision requirements for allowing Seb out of his cell, within twenty-four hours there were grounds to reintroduce them, though not because of actual aggression or even a threat. An officer had opened the cell door to allow Seb access to the shower, and as Seb crossed the spacious lobby between his cell and the shower room, he stopped in his tracks and fixed the officer with a steady stare. The officer firmly ordered Seb to keep moving. He did, but when this moment of strange and unexplained conduct was seen in light of the incident on the health-care wing, they took the precautionary approach of reinstating the three-officer unlock system. Assessing risk was all the more tricky when the nurses and doctor, who had carried on seeing Seb on the segregation unit, had not been able to make any headway in getting him to talk about the first incident.

I was accustomed to using the adjudication room for assessments. Its primary purpose was to hold formal reviews of prisoners' recent transgressive behaviour but, as long as it was not in use, it provided a relatively safe place for my assessments of the segregation prisoners. The prisoner would sit on a single seat that was connected by a steel arm to a sturdy table that was in turn anchored securely to the ground, and that was large enough to impede an angry prisoner intent on lashing out at an officer – or myself – sat on unfixed chairs down the length of the table or at the governor seated at the head. There were two doorways at either end of the same wall, which allowed the prisoner and the governor to enter and exit the room without getting close to each other. I enquired what the officers thought about me starting a discussion with Seb in his cell and then, if he seemed able to focus calmly, moving him to the adjudication room, which was more conducive to a clinical assessment. The officers agreed to the plan as long as the blind on the main window into the adjudication room remained open so that they could watch closely from outside.

It turned out that we did not need to implement the plan. Peering over the officer's shoulder as he checked on Seb through the hatch, I saw a body shape on the bed. There was no response to the request for him to sit up; Seb had covered himself entirely with his blanket and remained still. When the officer opened the door and announced why we were there, there was still no sign of a response. Through an exchange of glances and nods, we all understood that we would try the next option, which we had agreed beforehand. The two officers in front of me stepped apart to allow me to stand at the threshold of the cell with the lead officer just ahead of me. If necessary, they were ready to pull me and their colleague back from the cell and slam the door shut. Feeling self-conscious about talking to a blanket in front of an audience of three officers and a trainee doctor, I introduced myself to Seb and said that I was there to see if there was anything else that could be done to help. In the silence waiting for a response, I scanned his cell for anything of significance. During assessments of prisoners in the segregation unit, I have often found their cells to be in a state of disarray. The floor may be sodden after the occupant has blocked their lavatory as an act of dissension. Messages may be scrawled on fragments of paper or other surfaces. On occasion, faeces have been smeared on the walls in what is understatedly called a 'dirty protest'. There were no such signs in Seb's cell. The very few possessions were arranged tidily on the floor against the furthest wall.

As a last attempt to get his attention, the lead officer told Seb that soon there would not be another chance to speak to a doctor. It had no effect. Maintaining the direction of my gaze towards Seb, I carefully stepped backward out of the cell. The officers tried again to get a response, asking whether there was anything he wanted while they were there. Seb remained motionless.

Seb's solicitor had requested an opinion on whether his client's mental state at the time of the offence amounted to insanity according to the M'Naghten rules. The day after my unsuccessful assessment of Seb, I called his solicitor to explain that Seb's mutism would frustrate my attempt to understand his state of mind at the time of the killing. Although all the signs pointed to a 'disease of the mind', I was unable to determine if that caused him to not know what he was doing when he attacked his mother. The solicitor and I went on to agree that there was a separate issue that needed resolving before the court could be asked to consider a potential defence of insanity.

In March 1831, Justice James Park was sitting in a court set up periodically in York, the York Spring Assizes. The courtroom was crowded due to interest excited by the case of Esther Dyson, a young woman in her early twenties. She had been 'indicted for the willful murder of her bastard child by cutting off its head'. She appeared unmoved by the reading out of the indictment, and when the clerk asked whether she was guilty or not guilty, she did not respond.

Since the establishment of the jury trial in twelfth-century England, an unresponsive defendant was a potential challenge to the legitimacy of the court. A ritualistic exchange had to be completed before the defendant could be tried. He or she would first be prompted to announce whether they were guilty or not guilty of the alleged crime. An answer of 'not guilty' triggered a second question: 'Culprit, how wilt thou be tried?' If they responded by agreeing to be tried by God and their country, the trial could commence. This opening ritual depended on the participation of the defendant. In theory, a conviction could be avoided by standing silent. The motives for unresponsiveness varied from avoiding forfeiture of property that otherwise would pass to their heirs, to sparing one's family and reputation the shame of a conviction. The Statute of Westminster in 1275 permitted the court to take measures to make the uncooperative defendant think again. These 'felons refusing lawful trial' could be detained in a hard prison – prison *forte et dure* – until they had a change of heart. To further discourage defendants remaining mute, an element of torture was added to their punishment, hence the change of terminology to *peine forte et dure*. Extra pressure was applied, literally. Lying naked and on their back in a dark cell, the prisoner had ropes tied to their arms and legs which were pulled so that they were splayed across the floor. Then heavy irons or stones were placed on their body. Being pressed under increasing weights together with the food and water restrictions caused the mute defendant either to reconsider their position or to perish. While imprisonment, pain and hardship may undermine a stubborn defendant's resolve to stay quiet, it could not cure a person's mutism if they had never possessed the capacity to speak in the first place.

Fortunately for Esther Dyson, the practice of *peine forte et dure* had been abolished some sixty or so years before her court appearance in York. But entering a plea prior to initiating the trial remained a necessary part of the ritual. Justice James Park ordered that a jury should be sworn in to try whether she stood mute 'of malice or by the visitation of God'. To put it another way, was she stubbornly silent or genuinely unable to speak? A witness, Mr James Henderson, a supervisor in the cotton mill where Dyson had worked over the previous eleven years, testified to the court that she had appeared during that time not to have the ability to hear or speak. To his knowledge, she had been born both deaf and dumb. Having heard this evidence, the jury found her mute by visitation of God. Mr Henderson was then employed by the court to interpret for Dyson through the use of signs. She indicated a plea of not guilty. Her interpreter began to explain to her that it was her right to challenge a juror she objected to, a right still possessed by defendants in today's jury trials. The proceedings faltered again when Mr Henderson notified the court of the considerable difficulty he had in making Dyson understand her entitlement. The court was to hear that although she was intelligent enough to understand everyday events, she could not be made to understand the more technical yet critical elements of a criminal trial.

The test I apply when assessing a defendant's fitness to plead to criminal charges has its origins in the next course of action Judge Park chose. He ordered that a fresh jury was sworn in to try whether Dyson was sane. The gentlemen of the jury were instructed that they were not being asked to determine whether she was 'labouring under lunacy'. The question for them to resolve was whether 'she has at this time sufficient reason to understand the nature of this proceeding, so as to be able to conduct her defence'. By this definition, Dyson was found by the jury to be insane. She then fell within the purview of the Criminal Lunatics Act 1800, which stipulated that a defendant found insane should be kept in strict custody. Mindful of the evidence he had heard that Dyson was amenable to education, the judge advised that she should receive the recommended help to improve her understanding in case of reinstatement of the proceedings. It seems she did not receive this help, or if she did the matter was not returned to court, because Dyson was sent to the West Riding Pauper Lunatic Asylum and she remained there until her death thirty-eight years later.

In 1836, five years after Dyson began her indefinite detention, a Mr Pritchard appeared at the Shropshire Assizes on a charge of bestiality. Like Esther Dyson he could neither hear nor speak. The judge, Baron Alderson, turned to the ruling in the Dyson case and used that approach to develop a set of specific questions for determining his fitness to plead. R v Pritchard became and remains the leading case. Rather than mutism, the common reasons I am called on by lawyers to answer these questions involve the defendant's impaired understanding due to acute mental illness, learning disabilities or dementia.

Seb was not completely mute, but there was good reason to doubt his ability to make a proper defence to the charge of murder. My impression was that he was not being deliberately obstructive. Although the present-day test still rests on the R v Pritchard ruling, the procedure has changed since the 1830s. The evidence of two doctors must be presented to the court and the final decision rests with the judge, rather than a jury. I filed my report to the solicitors stating that he was, in my opinion, unfit to plead. The fitness to plead hearing was scheduled for six weeks hence, to allow time for a second medical opinion to be sought. Before then, I had other priorities to attend to.

Until Seb agreed to speak I was not going to be able to understand his mind. All the same, I was not content for him to stay in prison. There was enough evidence, I thought, to make a case for assessment and treatment in hospital. Following liaison with a suitably secure forensic hospital and written recommendations to the Ministry of Justice, a warrant was issued for transfer.

By the time we next met, six weeks later, Seb had been moved to hospital. Unlike Esther Dyson, Seb would not be indefinitely detained, and I believed – based on what I could tell from his history – that he was likely to be suffering from a condition that would respond to treatment.

In the forensic hospital, I was reintroduced to Seb by a ward nurse who escorted him to the interview room. Before even having a chance to check whether he was any more communicative, I could see a change in his appearance. Many, but not necessarily all, of my patients who experience distressing psychotic experiences seem to gain significant benefit from antipsychotic medication. Unfortunately, most have also suffered from the undesired effects of drugs of one kind or another. The antipsychotics in common use when I entered psychiatry almost thirty years ago were prone to inducing involuntary movements that could bring the patient unwanted and stigmatising attention. Fortunately these neurological side effects are much less likely with more modern antipsychotics, though the newer tablets have been found to cause metabolic changes. A common overt manifestation is weight gain. From Seb's heavier appearance, I suspected that he had been started on antipsychotic medication.

Seb confirmed this was the case; he had been taking anti-psychotics and, though he had difficulty satisfying his appetite, there was an evident change for the better. While by no means chatty, Seb was now a willing participant in our discussion. He told me that several months before his arrest he started to feel overcome with waves of disconcerting unease, which developed into a more relentless sense of foreboding and dread. Things around him didn't feel right. People had a dreamlike aura about them. He questioned whether they were who he thought they were. Then Seb's thoughts crystallised. It dawned on him that he was surrounded by imposters. The woman masquerading as his mother looked and behaved like her in every respect, but he could not shake his conviction that she was a charlatan, and that this imposter was involved in the abduction of his real mother. The usurper, who had cleverly adopted all his mother's characteristics, vehemently repudiated his allegations. He explained to me that he interpreted her protestations as a sign of how desperate she was to maintain the fraud. His tone became more earnest as he spoke about the offence, but he did not become overtly emotional. (It was as if his memory was not yet fully infused with emotion – whereas his words acknowledged responsibility for carrying out the offence, his tone was that of an objective spectator.) Seb's options seemed to be narrowing. He could not leave the charade unchallenged, but revealing to the imposter that he knew the truth could imperil his true mother. He wrestled with himself before the final night when he stabbed the woman he believed was not his mother while she slept.

Seb took the failure of his real mother to reappear to be a sign that the conspiracy ran deeper than he had previously thought. He decided that the best course of action was to avoid talking to anyone about what he knew. On the whole, he could suppress signs of his simmering frustration, but occasionally it became too much to bear, such as after the first couple of days on the health-care wing when he grabbed the nurse.

The way Seb spoke to me showed that he was able to stand back from his former conspiracy-obsessed existence and question the veracity of his beliefs. I asked him when his perspective changed. He said he had acquired his new insights several weeks after his admission, around the same time that he started taking medication.

There was agreement about Seb's diagnosis. The presence of delusions in the absence of other psychotic symptoms such as voices or visions encouraged a diagnosis of delusional disorder; a diagnosis that falls within the same category as schizophrenia. There was also a term for the specific type of experience he had: Capgras syndrome, named after Joseph Capgras, who described the case of a middle-aged woman from Paris who in June 1918 visited the local police commissioner to ask for two officers to accompany her and witness the evidence of a widespread crime. She reported that children were being illegally confined across Paris, including in the basement of her house. The police took her to an infirmary from where she was admitted to Sainte-Anne mental asylum. After about a year she was transferred to another asylum, Maison Blanche. There she came to the attention of Capgras, a psychiatrist who was interested in the themes of substitutions and disappearances that ran through her delusional beliefs. She believed she had been the victim of an abduction, and that she and others had identical doubles. She thought that 'the theatre played out by these doubles is unbelievable'. With a colleague the psychiatrist published a report on this case, which they termed *illusion des sosies* or illusion of doubles.

My medical training had taught me that, having found a term for a patient's condition and one for his symptoms, I had achieved sufficient understanding and the assessment was complete. But these terms only describe, they do not explain. To get to the underlying mechanisms that explain why Seb experiences symptoms, we should listen in detail to exactly what he is saying. If we accept that the unique nature of a person's mental experiences is the product of the workings of their mind (which is uncontroversial), then paying careful attention to what they are saying is likely to throw light on the way their mind generates those experiences. So, instead of asking my patients just enough to know whether a false belief they hold is a delusion, I am interested in encouraging them to tell me as precisely as they can how the belief came about and why they continue to hold it.

Knowing a little about the workings of the brain can also help us interpret Seb's words. Seb claimed that the woman he killed appeared to have the same form as his mother but a different identity. He acknowledged that he could not detect any difference in appearance between the imposter and his mother, but even so, he was sure this was not his mother. How can that be? We know from brain scans on both humans and other primates that recognising other people relies heavily on facial images and involves a number of different brain pathways. Essential to facial recognition is a neural network that processes the physical representation of the face: individual neurons respond to different features or characteristics – such as the distance between the eyes or the shape of the mouth – and these neurons work in concert to recognise a particular face. However, disruption in this network can interfere with a person's ability to recognise the face of a familiar person, a condition that is known as prosopagnosia, literally meaning 'face ignorance'.

Seb's problem was not prosopagnosia. He could recognise the form of his mother's face. It was her identity that he questioned. I was interested in his description of how his experiences started to go awry. Before the definable paranoid beliefs took hold, his perception of the world was accompanied by a general sense of doubt. He emphasised feelings of unreality; he was sure of nothing. This suggested to me that Seb's problems started with a non-specific interference in the emotional significance of his perceptions. To put it more straightforwardly, Seb could not grasp a clear meaning, but there was an undertone of danger.

Seb spoke of a jump from this early feeling of ambiguity and nebulous threat to the arrival of certainty. An idea came to him that helped resolve his confusion about the reality of the world around him (including his mother's identity) and to him it was consistent with his conspiratorial feelings. But while this idea – that his mother had been replaced by an imposter – matched his reality, it was out of kilter with everyone else's. And so, instead of rejecting the idea, Seb interpreted others' actions in a way that supported this idea. The belief that his mother's replacement was part of a wider plot gave meaning to his experiences and then he selected evidence consistent with that meaning. In reaction to a loss of the sense of familiarity that had previously accompanied the visual image of his mother, Seb accepted a coherent yet false narrative.

Neurobiological studies that have identified the neural networks used for recognising others and for evaluating our beliefs have undoubtedly improved our understanding of the origins of psychotic distortions of the sort experienced by Seb. It is not completely outlandish to assume that at some time in the future we will have sufficient brain-imaging power to produce an electrical and chemical portrait that corresponds to an individual's thoughts, feelings and behaviour. But advocates of this future overlook the fundamental limitation of neurobiology as an explanation of human behaviour. The neurobiological discipline can complement our understanding of the patient's subjective account of troubling psychic events, but using only the language of brain chemicals and neuronal pathways does not give us an understanding of what is troubling or psychic. We have to retain the subjective perspective to truly understand human experience and behaviour. To explain violence, we must contextualise the physiology with psychological abstractions, such as impulses, urges and motives.

The narrative that Seb had created was obviously a delusional one, but what happens when the narrative that supports a violent act is more difficult to judge?

> We attribute the social and psychological problems of modern society to the fact that that society requires people to live under conditions radically different from those under which the human race evolved and to behave in ways that conflict with the patterns of behavior that the human race developed while living under the earlier conditions.

These words were penned by Theodore 'Ted' Kaczynski, a former professor of mathematics who, for more than seventeen years, was also the author of an extensive campaign of indiscriminate homicidally motivated violence. Driven by hostility towards modern technology and the destruction of the natural environment, Kaczynski posted and hand-delivered incendiary devices across the United States that caused the death of three people and injured another twenty-four.

Known to the police and the press as the 'Unabomber', due to his particular targeting of universities and airlines, Kaczynski was a complicated figure. He was raised in a family where intelligence was highly valued, and his brilliant mind was conspicuous from an early age. Scoring 170 on an IQ test in fifth grade led to him skipping a year. In high school he was moved ahead another year. Later Kaczynski expressed his resentment at the isolating effect of being with older peers who did not accept him. However, academically he continued to shine. At just sixteen he became an undergraduate at Harvard University, and went on to earn a master's and then a PhD in mathematics at the University of Michigan. He joined the Mathematics Department at UC Berkeley in 1967, but then – without explanation – abruptly resigned after two years. Frustrated by the rapidly changing world, Kaczynski had shunned academic life and moved to Montana, where he began building a cabin in the woods. He lived there as a hermit, completely cut off from the modern world.

It was from that cabin in the wilderness that, between 1978 and 1995, Ted Kaczynski hand-manufactured and delivered sixteen increasingly sophisticated bombs. Eventually, having evaded police detection for nearly two decades, he wrote to the press offering to bring his revolutionary actions to a halt if his manifesto, 'Industrial Society and its Future', was published. The 35,000-word manifesto was published in the *Washington Post* and the *New York Times* in September 1995. Ted's brother, David Kaczynski, who already had suspicions about his brother being the Unabomber, noticed content and stylistic similarities in the manifesto with his older brother's letters from the 1970s and went to the FBI. In the spring of 1996 Theodore Kaczynski was arrested at his cabin in Montana.

During the subsequent trial, a court-appointed psychiatrist's assessment was that Kaczynski was likely to be suffering from a mental illness. Interpreting Kaczynski's assertion that technology threatened the survival of humanity as delusional satisfied one of the fundamental criteria for a diagnosis of schizophrenia. Had present-day diagnostic approaches been in use in the 1800s, Daniel M'Naghten would undoubtedly have received the same diagnosis. But M'Naghten's preoccupations had a quite different quality to Kaczynski's. M'Naghten's beliefs that he was being constantly followed and hounded by disguised malefactors were objectively false, but, while it was bizarre and dangerous in parts, 'Industrial Society and its Future' contained well-articulated sentiments and ideas to which large sections of society would subscribe. The central thesis in Kaczynski's novella-length manifesto could not be rejected out of hand. After its publication, Professor James Q. Wilson of the University of California wrote in the *New York Times* that the manifesto was 'a carefully reasoned, artfully written paper' and that 'if it is the work of a madman, then the writings of many political philosophers – Jean-Jacques Rousseau, Tom Paine, Karl Marx – are scarcely more sane'. Is it simply his willingness to act on these beliefs – and to cause harm to members of the public – that separates Kaczynski from Rousseau, Paine and Marx?

Most patients with a diagnosis of schizophrenia are not violent. By chronicling forensic psychiatric cases there is a risk of reinforcing the media cliché of the violent schizophrenic. On the contrary, my view is that such stereotypes are broken down by sympathetically examining real-life cases while emphasising their rarity. The diagnosis of schizophrenia relies in part on the identification of psychotic experiences such as delusional beliefs or hallucinatory voices. It comes as a surprise to many that these experiences are not uncommon among the general population. A clinical diagnosis additionally requires the unusual experiences to be accompanied by high levels of distress and dysfunction. Some individuals suffering in this way may have periods when to the observer their behaviour appears bizarre.

What has become increasingly clear to me in my practice is that diagnosis is not a particularly informative way of understanding behaviour. I have been involved in too many trials in which the central issue has been whether the criteria for a specific diagnosis were met. In one murder trial I testified in, the victim had sustained forty-nine knife wounds, and was found with 'long carvings' across his chest and abdomen, salt rubbed into the wounds and cleaning fluid in his eyes. I was one of three forensic psychiatrists called upon to assess the defendant, who had a history of psychosis. The judge concluded that the prisoner had been acting out a scene from an Australian horror film with which he had a fascination. But after our evidence was heard in court, the news coverage concentrated on the diversity of professional opinions about how to interpret the killer's psychotic mental state. It was reminiscent of the diagnostic disagreements I used to watch between my early career mentors.

I would not dispute that the discourse of mental illness and psychiatric diagnosis can serve a purpose. Representing Kaczynski as mentally ill would not only counter the evil monster narrative and stimulate a desire for understanding rather than condemnation, it could also be the foundation for a legal defence, which would prevent the imposition of the death penalty. But the debate over whether Kaczynski suffered from a serious mental illness exposes the fallacy of the categorical divide between normality and mental illness. I can see how the defence-instructed psychiatrists could agree with the view that Kaczynski showed features associated with schizophrenia. Even before his bizarre belief system and fulminating ramblings became known to the world, residents living in the vicinity of his shack saw him as a shambolic curiosity. The severity of his pathology could be accentuated by lining up the many anecdotes of odd behaviour from his younger days. But the alternative view is that Kaczynski was at risk of being diagnosed with schizophrenia just on account of his eccentricity and nonconformity. The American Psychiatric Association states that beliefs cannot be designated delusional unless they are so extreme as to defy credibility. Having drawn incorrect inferences about his external reality, M'Naghten arrived at a patently false conclusion and so could be said to be delusional. Kaczynski, however, had come to reject society through a considered analysis of the direction that society was taking.

But does it help our understanding of the cause of their criminal behaviour to know whether or not Ted Kaczynski or Daniel M'Naghten suffered from schizophrenia? To encourage trainee psychiatrists working with me to think about the problems with a diagnosis of schizophrenia, and for that matter most mental illness diagnoses, I pose two simple questions. Firstly, I ask them to define schizophrenia in one sentence. They confidently respond by talking about psychotic symptoms such as hallucinations and delusions. I then ask these doctors, who have recently completed their medical training, to use one sentence to define a physical health condition such as asthma. They answer using phrases such as an inflammatory airway disease resulting in bronchospasm. The doctors, bemused by my line of questioning, may include symptoms (wheezing and shortness of breath) in their answers, but they do not rely on symptoms alone to define a disease; they know that one particular symptom can be caused by different bodily disease processes. Complaints by a patient of wheezing and shortness of breath hint at an asthmatic condition and lead the physician to undertake further diagnostic investigations. If the diagnosis of asthma is confirmed, then the doctor is confident about the location and nature of the disease (or pathology), i.e. a chronic inflammatory process in the airways. I emphasise to my trainees that mental illness diagnoses do not direct us to a pathology that explains the symptoms and behaviour. Even experienced psychiatrists often forget this in their day-to-day practice. Pondering whether the diagnosis is schizophrenia or not, which we spend so much time doing in clinics and court, takes us down an explanatory blind alley.

In the case of Ted Kaczynski, the matter was never resolved. Midway through proceedings, the trial was brought to an abrupt halt when, faced with the prospect of a humiliating trial in which his legal team would portray his philosophy as the ravings of a madman (he claimed that his attorneys launched a mental health defence against his wishes), Kaczynski changed his plea to guilty of murder. It was no longer necessary to demonstrate that the responsibility for the Unabomber's actions was lacking due to a psychiatric condition.

Delineating these driving forces is central to eliciting the origin of violence. Ted Kaczynski was motivated in his belief that the forces of technology needed to be halted; studying the nature of his beliefs is more important than deciding whether or not we label them delusional symptoms of schizophrenia. At the core of most motives for violence are assumptions about the intentions of others. Daniel M'Naghten's ideas of being followed and persecuted gave him his reason to act; Seb believed that a sinister collective was intent on keeping his mother hidden against her will.

Understanding motivation is certainly important, but it is only half the story. Counter-cultural beliefs, such as those in Kaczynski's 'Industrial Society and its Future', are not uncommon and very rarely lead to violence. To understand the other half of the story, we need to think about why hostile feelings are so seldom translated into homicidal actions. For most of us, even a flickering awareness of the consequences of our imagined aggression automatically triggers negative feelings that prevent us from going through with a violent act. And since we are programmed to avoid negative feelings, we are inclined to suppress or resist the thoughts that cause them. If you were to imagine being the perpetrator of a violent attack on the person you love or care for most in the world, it is likely that you are immediately repulsed by the thought – that you imagine the horror in their reaction, the pain they would feel, the feelings of shock, betrayal, confusion. Even imagining such an act of violence is uncomfortable. Thus adopting the emotional perspective of the victim is, for most people, enough to stop a violent impulse in its tracks. This is because when we imagine a violent act from the perspective of the victim, we are demonstrating a type of empathy – we are imagining the mind of another.

Empathy is a critical human ability and, when it comes to violence, it is powerfully inhibiting. So crucial are these processes that they do not even require conscious effort: they run behind the scenes, constantly inhibiting a myriad of counterproductive impulses. Violence is a consequence of an interplay between emotional forces driving the aggressive urges and the countervailing mental processes resisting aggressive action. Without being able to explore their subjectivity with them, I can only speculate in the cases of M'Naghten and Kaczynski. However, given the opportunity to assess Daniel M'Naghten, I would have tested my hypothesis that, as well as the paranoid misinterpretations of the actions of others, M'Naghten became consumed by an overwhelming hypervigilant fear. (This was certainly evident in Seb's history.) For survival reasons, fear shifts the balance of our concern from both self and others towards just the former. As a consequence, the influence of inhibitory predictions of the victim's suffering is diminished. I am only speculating but it might be the case that M'Naghten was so in fear for his life that the assassination of a representative of his persecutors seemed like the only way to protect himself – subjectively, this may have been an act of self-defence. If it were possible to interview Ted Kaczynski, I would explore the extent to which he was already emotionally disconnected from others even before he physically took himself away by moving to the cabin; he may not have possessed strong socially influenced inhibitory faculties anyway.

The improvement in Seb's mental functioning meant that he was able to pass the test of fitness to plead. Despite the court accepting the central part played by Seb's disturbed state of mind in his actions, he did not reach the very high bar set by the rules for defining legal insanity introduced after M'Naghten's trial. (Many have questioned whether even M'Naghten himself would have reached it.) The alternative and more recent defence of diminished responsibility, only available for charges of murder, was advanced on Seb's behalf and was not challenged by the prosecution. This resulted in a conviction of manslaughter rather than murder, which allowed the court to accept the recommendation for Seb to be sentenced to hospital rather than prison.

2

Drew

DIPPING MY HEAD into the general office, I hoped there would be no messages. I had an overdue report to finish. As I made to turn away, my secretary called out: the nurse in charge on the admissions ward needed to speak to me. The report would have to wait. It was about Drew, my secretary explained. 'Didn't you hear the racket?'

Drew, the nurse told me, was in seclusion. A bit like a secure box, the seclusion room is a common feature of many mental health wards. It has no fixtures or fittings; nothing that a patient can hurt themselves with. It is the location of last resort for a patient who is otherwise considered unmanageable. The featureless surfaces surrounding the confined space are interrupted only by a light, almost flush with the ceiling, and a strengthened mattress and an anti-rip sheet on the floor. From my office I could feel, as well as hear, Drew's powerful kicks of protest through both the walls and the handset. Brief pauses in the rhythmical thudding were filled with screaming and though the individual words were difficult to grasp, I was left in no doubt about the sentiment.

Such signs of uncontrolled rage might, you'd think, induce a narrowing of attention on the source of the potential threat – a state of psychological and physiological preparedness for attack. But we on the psychiatric ward are inured to it. This scenario was not especially unusual; Drew was not the first patient to demonstrate this kind of behaviour and experience had taught us that the door was able to withstand an onslaught of this sort. In recounting what had just occurred, the nurse in charge, Tina, was hardly ruffled – in fact, in psychiatrist speak, I'd say she conveyed an emotional disconnection from events. Paying more careful attention, I could sense subtle signs of the recent instinctual burst of adrenaline that had allowed a focused and dynamic reaction to the incident moments before. Her speech was slightly speeded up and breathless; there was a faint quiver. Perhaps not completely un-rattled then. Without comment, we would pause in mid-sentence in our conversation, drowned out by Drew's screams. Maintaining an emotional distance from many of the things we experience in forensic psychiatry protects us and better enables us to deal objectively with what we face. To not be driven by our emotions alone. There is a risk, though: we need to guard against becoming unfeeling.

Drew had smashed the television. This took some doing, I thought – it was housed in a strengthened box with a perspex cover fixed to the wall. Glance around the ward and you would see other similar safety measures. The couches were too heavy to pick up and throw; too well built to break into pieces; and covered in a material that would not burn or rip. The doors and windows were reinforced, there was an airlock to enter and exit the building and a perimeter fence of a prescribed height; these were the physical elements of a hospital defined as 'medium secure'. It was more than just the tangible structure. The staff would oversee a gamut of safety procedures – the procedural security – ensuring prohibited items did not make their way onto the ward, carrying out perimeter checks to detect potential breach points, and counting cutlery in and out. The third type of security relies on familiarity with the patient – not just a matter of knowing the diagnosis and the patient's history, but keeping each other up to date on what is in the patient's mind? How are they getting on with those around them? What news might they be about to receive? Anything that could provoke a reaction. This is relational security.

The medium secure hospital that was my base for over fifteen years was one of the earliest in a modern-day asylum building renaissance. Up to the 1970s, the only forensic hospitals in England were the three 'special' ones. The first, and home to Daniel M'Naghten until his death in 1865, was Broadmoor. It was hoped that the excessive demand for places in Broadmoor would be eased with the opening of a second criminal lunatic asylum in rural Nottinghamshire (Rampton) in 1912. However, the pressure did not abate and on the outskirts of Liverpool a third special hospital (which became Ashworth) was opened in 1933.

In the process of isolating a small group of patients from society, the cultural remoteness of these institutions isolated the staff who worked in them. The ever-present gap between the prison-like special hospitals and the county asylums yawned wider with the liberalisation of regimes in the non-forensic mental health services. Beset by revelations of patient mistreatment and mismanagement, their demise has often been falsely heralded. The need for more accessible forensic hospitals was recognised in the 1960s. Following a familiar pattern in forensic psychiatry, change did not occur until a tragic case exposed the problem to the public.

Unlikely as it sounds, the impetus for the development of the type of forensic hospital where I worked can be traced back to a mysterious illness that struck the workforce of a small optical and photographic company in the south of England. In 1971, the Bovingdon Bug, as the malady came to be known, caused sickness, hair loss and numbness. After the painful death of a second employee, something had to be done. A meeting was convened in the canteen by the company doctor.

Dr Anderson explained that they had eliminated two possible causes – exposure to radiation and heavy-metal poisoning – so the illness was most probably viral. To Dr Anderson's surprise and annoyance there was a dissenting voice in the audience. A 24-year-old employee, Graham Young, who had been with the company for no more than a few months, challenged Dr Anderson. He said that hair loss was the critical symptom – a telltale sign of poisoning. At a later meeting with Dr Anderson, Graham Young's interest in toxicology allowed him to confidently back up his thesis. He did not anticipate that sharing his knowledge would attract suspicion. The company owner, John Hadland, spoke to his solicitor, who reassured him that he could notify the police. John Hadland's actions were vindicated when a search of Graham Young's bedsit in Hemel Hempstead found the surfaces crammed with phials of unknown substances, the walls covered with Nazi imagery and, under the bed, the diary of a poisoner. A routine enquiry early in the investigation revealed an even more startling finding.

The police check showed that three years short of a century after Daniel M'Naghten had died there, Graham Young had become one of the youngest residents of Broadmoor. Young had begun working at Hadlands some months before after eight years in the psychiatric hospital. A boastful display of his knowledge of toxicology was also his undoing on his first offence, when Young was a schoolboy.

Young's school chemistry teacher, Mr Hughes, felt uneasy about his fourteen-year-old pupil's narrow interest in poisons, and decided to investigate. When one night he looked in Graham Young's desk, he had expected to find potions, but what he uncovered were macabre poems and drawings. What was even more unsettling was that Young's friend suffered from a recurring and unexplained illness. The school decided to investigate further, and appealing to Young's vanity arrangements were made for him to meet with in an undercover psychiatrist. Young shared his secrets and the conversation was reported to the police.

Young's family had always had their suspicions about the death of his stepmother and the violent sickness suffered by his father, sister and aunt. With hindsight Young had shown early signs of eccentricity: while at primary school he became interested in chemicals and explosives and had developed a fascination for the Nazis – though Hitler competed for Young's hero-worship with the nineteenth-century Rugeley Poisoner, Dr William Palmer. Having tested the effects of poisons on animals, when he was thirteen Young began experimenting on humans, buying chemicals from local chemists and slipping them into the food and drink of family members and his only school friend.

In 1962, at the age of fourteen, Young was convicted of malicious administration of a noxious thing to inflict grievous bodily harm. Dr Donald Blair, a consultant psychiatrist, examined Young in Ashford Prison. During a hearing at London's Old Bailey, Blair shared his pessimistic prognosis with the court. 'There is no doubt in my mind that this youth is at present a very serious danger to other people. His intense obsession and almost exclusive interest in drugs and their poisoning effect is not likely to change, and he could well repeat his cool, calm, calculating administration of these poisons at any time.'

Mr Justice Melford Stevenson sentenced Young to a hospital order and directed that he be admitted to Broadmoor. Early in his hospital stay, Young did not disguise his morbid passions. He delivered impersonations of Hitler, endlessly played Wagner, and took to wearing a swastika pendant he had handcrafted in the hospital workshop. Within weeks of Young's arrival at the hospital, a prisoner was found on post-mortem to have ingested cyanide, although it was never determined if Young was responsible. Suspicions of a continued tendency to inflict harm by poison were aroused when a cup of coffee and a tea urn were found to contain cleaning substances. There was then a period of improved behaviour, though what was interpreted at the time as sufficient improvement to move him to a parole ward may be seen in light of subsequent events as Young hiding his interests.

After eight years in Broadmoor, Young was twice granted leave to his sister's home and then on 4 February 1971 he was discharged back into the community. In those first few weeks he took up a training place as a storekeeper. He was noticed to have a sympathetic attitude to a fellow trainee, who later developed acute abdominal pains, followed by violent vomiting and then a loss of control of his legs. On the day he submitted his application to Hadlands in Bovingdon, he signed the chemist shop's poisons register for a purchase of thallium. Following his arrest on suspicions of the poisonings at Hadlands he was remanded to Brixton Prison and, on 29 June 1972, he was found guilty of two charges of murder, two of attempted murder and two of administering poison. This time he was sentenced to life imprisonment.

Forensic psychiatrists would now baulk at the thought of a patient moving from a special hospital straight to the community. We have come to realise that behaviour in a highly supervised, secure psychiatric hospital tells us very little about the way someone will be when living on their own, with occasional contact every few weeks with a representative of the authorities. Throughout the period of Graham Young's detention in Broadmoor, there were no other forensic services. The public inquiry into the failures that allowed Young to kill again recommended the building of a new type of forensic hospital. The plan was one for each health region, which explains the original name – regional secure unit – often shortened to RSU. The first opened in 1980 in the north-east of England. Since then security measures have been standardised across these units. Now known as medium secure units, they sit within a security hierarchy below the 'high secure' (the term that replaced 'special') hospitals and above the low secure units. Although the total number of patients detained in secure psychiatric hospitals is difficult to establish, one recent estimate was about 8,000 in England and Wales.

I later learned that, having smashed the box and the television, Drew had dug a shard of the broken screen into his forearm as the ward nurses rounded on him. They managed to fix his arms still and prevent any further injury to himself. Colleagues shepherded other patients away from the immediate area. For most patients this was to protect them; for others it was to ensure that they did not exploit this moment of distraction. At this point Drew had dropped the piece of glass and two nurses held each arm. Rather than calming the situation, it seemed to infuriate him. His body writhed violently and he flicked his head aggressively to the side. He was about to free himself from the nurses' grip. Three other nurses promptly stepped in to immobilise his butting head and flailing legs. What initially looked like a messy scrum transformed into a synchronised movement as Drew was eased to the floor. Once securely held, the nurses loosened their grip while trying to talk him down but it did not have the desired effect. He would tense his limbs in an attempt to shake off the nurses. He singled out one of the nurses by name – one he had been particularly close to – and spat out the unimaginable horrors he intended to inflict on him and his family. As his strength waned, the staff eased their grips again and tried to get him to discuss how they could end the conflict safely. This seemed to increase his indignation.

The staff could not be sure that letting go would be safe. Paradoxically, moving him to the seclusion room would give him greater freedom, since he would not have five nurses restraining him. Once the decision was made, they exited the room in a carefully planned operation to avoid anyone being hurt.

While in most circumstances attacking someone is un-acceptable, we can see how some people in certain situations may resort to violence. It is a way – albeit a maladaptive one – of achieving a particular goal. It may be a means of dissipating an intense angry emotion, dominating another person, repelling perceived threat, or acquiring someone else's property. Self-directed violence, on the other hand, is far more puzzling. What purpose can a savage attack on one's own body ever achieve? But even though the motivation may not be imme-diately obvious, self-harm and suicidal behaviour are among the common reasons for people going to hospital emergency departments.

I questioned Tina about why Drew might have smashed the television. We both knew that he had mutilated his body many times before, but why again now? Tina said that Drew had asked for lorazepam, but had been turned down. Lorazepam is one of the most ubiquitous types of medication on inpatient prescription cards, yet it does not treat any psychiatric illness. It is to be taken as needed, or *pro re nata* (Latin: 'for the affair born'), which is shortened in the ward-based dialect shared by patients and staff to PRN. Acting on the same brain receptors as alcohol, lorazepam induces a sense of calm. Like alcohol, it can depress the mind and, as with alcohol, it can disinhibit. Also like alcohol, it can be addictive.

Drew had said he was anxious, but when he was denied the drug he 'kicked off', Tina said (her tone did not disguise the frustration). 'He's got it now,' she added (and this, I could tell, was said for a wider audience). Like a number of her colleagues, Tina had questioned me about what we were achieving by keeping Drew in hospital. Maybe we are making him worse, she suggested. Indeed, three months earlier I had overcome such objections to successfully make the case for transferring Drew from prison to our hospital. 'It's just behavioural,' Tina said. Her response to Drew, and patients like him, is not uncommon, and it is completely understandable.

To appreciate what is going on around us, we do not have to collect all the evidence and then analyse it. We are very adept at coming up with explanations. Rather than experiencing the world as a sequence of unconnected events, potential causes automatically pop into our minds. Dwelling on these fleeting explanations is mostly unnecessary. They usually float through without contradicting our predictions. One reason to pay more attention is when it is expected of us by virtue of our role. As mental health professionals we are supposed to be able to explain behaviour and use these explanations to make predictions and direct treatment. Making sense of complex data is crucial to what we do, but it is not something we are taught. We 'learn' it on the job.

I made my way from my office up to the ward to discuss the situation face to face with the nurses. Like other consultants, most of the administrative element of my job – updating patient notes, etc. – is done from my office, which is at the hospital, but separate to the inpatient ward. The main door to the ward opened on to a wide corridor leading to a lounge area from where two other corridors led to individual patient bedrooms. The nurses' office was placed at the centre, to allow staff clear lines of sight across the patients' communal area. It also allows patients to observe staff without obstruction, meaning that the arrival of their consultant would be an opportunity to demand clarity in the face of frustratingly vague promises. 'Why can't I go to the dining room for meals?' 'Are you going to give me leave?' ('Leave' is the term used to describe permitted time outside the secure area.) 'Why do I need to stay here?'

Convening the staff in the patients' quiet room (which was, on request, vacated by Jordan, a recent arrival from prison, who, deeply immersed in tormented introspection, left the room quickly), I needed to get a clear picture of what had happened so I could do a medical review. Was the rationale for detaining a patient, in this case Drew, in the seclusion room appropriate? (As with most hospital checklist-tasks, the original purpose becomes lost and the completion of the form becomes the objective.) Tina repeated the account she had relayed over the phone, and I then teased out a fuller explanation. *Why do we think he was asking for medication?* He is always drug-seeking, came the immediate reply. *Why now, though?* He was bored. He had been winding himself up all morning. It's easier to give him the medication, but we're trying to encourage him to use other methods to calm himself down. With her colleagues nodding supportively, Tina repeated her concern that Drew wasn't benefiting from being in hospital. 'What are we doing for him? He's not motivated to use the coping strategies. Is it time to send him back?' To prison, she meant.

As a consultant I am not able to be on the ward to witness the events that sometimes shape my clinical decisions, so I rely heavily on my nursing colleagues to report such incidents and give their insight into the motivations of the patients. Their intuition about a patient's state of mind is thus invaluable and, almost all of time, very accurate. On this occasion, though, I didn't agree with Tina's assessment of the situation; I didn't feel her version of the story was quite sound.

Storytelling is a crucial human trait. Early humans were not particularly strong or fast when compared with many of their animal competitors. Still they became the predominant species, and they were able to do so thanks to an exceptional ability to acquire skills and knowledge. Along with advanced cognitive faculties for problem-solving, humans' capacity for language enables us to share critical information remarkably quickly and efficiently – whether it was information about our own social group, or competitor groups, or the topography and flora and fauna of the surrounding landscape. Humans could transmit information without necessarily needing direct experience. Consequently it took less time to acquire survival information and storytelling became a pervasive method of sharing knowledge. Stories are more than a catalogue of facts or events, they also perform an explanatory function. Some serve to explain the present and the past; others help us to predict the future. Due to the survival benefits, a mental architecture that encourages a narrative structure evolved, and so it is no surprise that a readiness to tell stories and a desire to hear them are such universal human traits.

The story of the incident involving Drew started with triggers for his aggression. Then there was the incident itself and the finale was his confinement in seclusion. Critical to humans are assumptions about the minds of others. In this case, we were focusing exclusively on Drew's mind: he was bored, he is always desperate for a hit (the hit is no less because the drug is prescribed rather than bought on the street), he can't bear hearing 'no'. He is used to threatening and intimidating to get his way. He knows if he cuts himself, we have no choice but to give him the medication in order to calm him down. Then, when we do, we reinforce his behaviour; we make him worse. This story pointed to one outcome: Drew's return to prison.

Drew's every move on the ward was being closely observed, and not just any old observations, but ones by mental health professionals. It also corresponded to what we knew about his life more generally. He was a drug user whose desperation for drugs was reflected in his criminal record. Most of Drew's offences involved acquiring what didn't belong to him: shoplifting and burglaries. He was, in his vernacular, 'grafting' to pay for his habit. A closer look at his record also supported the impression of a readiness to use aggression to get what he wanted. Some of the offences were qualified by the term 'aggravated', which denoted the use of aggression in the course of the crime. Most powerfully, the story resonated with some of the things Drew had recently said. As he was being held down, he screamed out that he would 'get the fucking PRN anyway'.

Stories with variations on this theme are told across mental health services to explain self-directed violence. Psychiatrists, as well as nurses, base their stories on what they see. I used to do so. As a junior doctor in my first year of psychiatric training, I remember being called upon to tend to a patient's self-inflicted wound. Interrupting a busy list of tasks in preparation for the ward round the next day, I dutifully examined the wound and, once it was dressed, took the opportunity to try out my newly acquired psychiatric skills. I quizzed the patient about her motivation. She shared with me her overwhelming desire to die. I – somewhat dismissively – educated the patient on the apparent contradiction between this claim and my appraisal of the wounds, which I emphasised were superficial and not indicative of suicidal thoughts. I had effortlessly constructed a story that relied on an analysis of the observable data. Although I was training in psychiatry, I continued to adopt the stance of a physician; I looked at the evidence objectively and constructed my own narrative. I cannot recall now exactly what my feelings were – I probably wouldn't have had much idea at the time – but, now, with twenty-five years of experience behind me, I wonder whether my condescending intervention was in part driven by resentment at having my schedule interrupted. Or, maybe I needed to distract attention from my realisation at how ill equipped I was to understand what had occurred. Either way, at that time, I did not realise the potential effect of my cynical invalidation of the patient's personal disclosure.

As medics, psychiatrists can invest this genre of stories with extra credibility by adding a diagnostic subplot: Drew had been diagnosed with borderline personality disorder – a term used to describe a disorder of mood that affects how a person interacts with others, characteristic features of which include repeated suicidal behaviour, uncontrolled mood swings, relationship volatility and an impaired capacity to inhibit impulses. This diagnosis can be used to explain Drew's self-harm; it was, so the story went, due to borderline personality disorder that he could not control his impulse to use drugs. Combined with another key diagnostic marker (mood swings), his impulsivity also contributed to his tendency to overreact. As a central feature of borderline personality disorder, self-harm at times of crisis is to be expected.

It is worth taking a moment to consider how we have arrived at the diagnostic criteria of the manuals. Peering back through the history of psychiatry we might expect to see that over time there has been a process of refining diagnoses to match the underlying pathologies better. But the development of the 'borderline' concept illustrates a very different pattern – one that is common in psychiatry.

In 1930s America, mental disorders were viewed as either amenable to analysis (psychoneurotic) or not (psychotic). Adolph Stern, a Hungarian émigré who had trained under Freud, wrote about his experience of a middle – or border-line – group, in which individuals displayed symptoms of psychosis under stress, but who were able to become relatively functional again when the stress had lifted. The idea did not really catch on. 'Borderline' was lifted from relative obscurity three decades later by Otto Kernberg, an Austrian-born psychotherapist who had fled Nazi Germany and later settled in America. Kernberg co-opted the label to describe a particular set of defence mechanisms that would make the patient suitable for the type of psychotherapy he had devised. By the 1970s the psychiatric establishment was starting to tire of psychoanalysis. Classification based on nebulous notions such as defence mechanisms was too unreliable. Symptom lists were seen as the answer. A 'borderline' list was drawn up and studied, and tweaks to that original list have produced the current diagnostic criteria. The origin of a psychiatric diagnosis often follows this path. Changes in the use of the diagnostic term and modifications to the symptom list are not anchored to an identifiable underlying disorder or pathology. There is not a tangible thing common to all cases that causes the symptoms on the list.

Including a diagnosis of borderline personality disorder makes a story explaining behaviour sound more authoritative. But in reality there is a sleight of hand. The emotional vola-tility, self-mutilation, impulsivity and relationship intensity are the features we observe in Drew and that we use to make the diagnosis. Having made the diagnosis, we then, without anyone (including psychiatrists) noticing, use the diagnosis to explain the features. Borderline personality disorder is both defined by and the cause of the self-harm and emotional volatility.

Recognising that the same symptom can be caused by different diseases, physicians do not define disease by symptoms. It would be like saying that chest pain and shortness of breath were both the symptoms of a heart attack and the cause of it. Diseases are defined by pathology, the thing that causes the symptoms. Symptoms give us a clue but are not determinative. The underlying cause of a heart attack is a sudden occlusion of a blood vessel that leads to the death of a portion of the heart muscle. This pathology often causes symptoms that may vary between people. The chest pain and shortness of breath make the physician suspect a heart attack, but she then checks for the pathology of a heart attack with investigations such as an ECG and blood tests. Similarly, in psychiatry, symptoms such as emotional instability and self-harm make us suspect borderline personality disorder. Like the physician, we also seek to confirm our suspicions by undertaking tests, but the difference is that our tests do not identify the cause, they merely involve looking again at the symptoms. We are seduced into thinking these are diagnostic tests by the formal booklet of scoring rules or the impressive list of references that testify to their validity, but they are only valid insofar as they have been compared to other symptom checklists.

In another role, as visiting psychiatrist to a local prison, I had been seeing Drew before he came to hospital, meeting him every three or four weeks. The prison-based nurses had for some time been making the case that Drew's level of self-harm and aggression was more than could be managed in a prison. This was the same central message as the story told by Tina on behalf of the staff on the hospital ward: Drew would be better off somewhere else, not here anyway. When Drew attended my prison clinic, we were both drawn to think about another reality; it could be one brought about by the effects of a different type of medication, if only I was prepared to alter his prescription, he would plead. I resisted, sure that the effects of medication would be merely cosmetic. I could pharmacologically subdue his thoughts and emotions and therefore his behaviour, but medication would not change them. I had heard of a unit specialising in his type of problems that was due to be opened in another prison. Filling our meetings with talk of these elsewheres meant that we avoided the necessary, but much more difficult, task. Without developing some sort of shared understanding of his destructive actions, change in his behaviour (and our response) was unlikely. I knew that it would be hard for Drew to think about his own mind and the minds of others; this was a major cause of his problems, and the busy in-and-out clinic did not allow enough time to progress. We agreed that he needed a setting that was more therapeutic than the prison could offer.

I was aware that psychiatric hospitals – including ours – were not necessarily therapeutic in the required way; our admissions ward lurched from one aggressive crisis to another and in the lulls the air was tense with anticipation of the next incident. Was it realistic to expect the ward staff, when they were not grappling with the patients, to grapple with the complex and counter-intuitive explanations for the patients' behaviour? I even considered the possibility that admission to hospital may worsen Drew's problems. While many of our treatments can induce unwanted complications, in the round they should be beneficial. Yet some research shows that hospital admission for people susceptible to suicidal crises may increase the risk of suicide, but this sort of evidence does little to dilute the force of feelings to do something, or for that matter, anything, in cases like Drew's. Against my rational judgement I gave in to the pressure to admit Drew.

As I had promised Tina, I arranged to speak to Drew before leaving the ward. To open the door so that we could talk face to face, he would have to sit against the back wall with his legs crossed and his hands on his thighs. He laughed and swore at the suggestion. The alternative was to speak through the open hatch, but he showed us that there was no point by throwing a plastic cup towards the hatch while Tina was unlocking it. We agreed among ourselves that for the time being we should not push him any further to speak to us.

From my early days of working in forensic hospitals I developed a strong admiration for the ward-based nurses. The doctors, including myself, would breeze in for a brief meeting and then leave. The nurses were there for hours and hours. Tension on some wards simmered just beneath the surface. As often as not, it would dissipate without incident, but occasionally it would boil over and patients would become aggressive. It was not knowing what was going to occur, or when, that took its emotional toll on the nursing staff. But despite this pressured uncertainty, almost all the nurses I worked alongside were able to maintain a professional and compassionate approach.

However, the assumed motive for Drew's behaviour did shape my colleagues' response to it. Aggression that appeared obviously irrational did not shake the nurses' concern for the aggressor. If the patient seemed engrossed in their own psychotically simulated world, the staff would retain a sympathetic attitude despite the aggression. Discussions about how to manage the aggression would centre on how to understand the behaviour and how to help the patient. In contrast, violent conduct that was assumed to have a rational explanation would tend to provoke a different response.

Over the rest of that day, Drew became more receptive to attempts to speak to him. Conversations started off through the hatch, then with the door open. After a successful trial of time out on the ward, we all agreed that Drew no longer needed to return to the seclusion room. Everyone moved on and the TV incident was seen as another example of Drew not wanting to help himself.

The following week, I arranged to collect Drew from the ward. He had agreed to meet me somewhere neutral, a space that was not so coloured by recent experiences: a bland meeting room. Drew's demeanour exuded confident disinterest: he was an old hand at being interviewed. From his early teens, he had been schooled in how to bat off assertive police questioning. Unless he was withdrawing from opiates, he would relish the opportunity to spar with the interrogators. His probation officer was just an authority figure who wielded power over his future; I fell into the same camp. Through bitter experience, he had erected defences. Drew was prepared to be tripped up, and was watching out for being tricked into making a disclosure that would be turned against him, to keep him locked up for longer.

In turn, I knew that a friendly approach may arouse his suspicions more. I had to be patient. In the deliberately vaguest of terms, I asked how he was. For some, this would be enough to trigger an outpouring. Given what I represented to Drew, I was not surprised that my vague opener was met with an equally non-committal response. 'OK,' he replied curtly. Why would he give up his private world? What would I do with this information?

There was also a more technical problem. To answer such open-ended questions, Drew would have to turn his gaze inwards and make sense of what he saw. Difficulty doing this was part of the problem. I tested this hunch with other general enquiries. Were there any problems on the ward? Did he have any issues he wanted to raise? In the face of a 'nah' and a shrug, these questions also fell flat. A more targeted approach was called for. When I asked him to tell me what had happened, I sensed that he would be more willing, and probably more able, to explore a territory of concrete events. The workings of his own mind were, I suspected, too ambiguous for him to readily grasp. Aware of his life history, I also speculated that what he sometimes saw was too terrifying.

He pushed his sleeve up. Rather than multiple linear scars of surface cutting, Drew's forearm was a messy legacy of repeated deep mutilating incisions. He pointed at a line running about half the length of his forearm – his injury from the TV incident. The dark crimson highlights made it stand out as a more recent injury at which he appeared to have been picking.

'Tell me about earlier in the day,' I asked, staying in the domain of events.

'It was a shit day, everything was wrong.'

'Why was that particular day so shit?'

'I dunno, I just wake up like that.'

'Was it anything to do with the tribunal?'

Two days after the incident, he was due to have his detention reviewed by a tribunal, which involves one of our meeting rooms becoming a court for the afternoon. An independent panel scrutinises the grounds for the patient's detention, and as a representative of the 'detaining authority' I am required to make the case for detention.

'It was nothing to do with the tribunal,' he asserted, 'I don't know what it was.'

I had in my mind the account of events from the observers. From the perspective of the nurse in the office, he would have seen that she was busy giving out medication and could not speak to him. By putting up her hand with fingers splayed and mouthing five minutes, she made it clear that she would be with him as soon as she could, but – the nursing staff assumed – this was interpreted as a 'no' and Drew doesn't like hearing no. 'Unless we drop everything, that's how he reacts.' I wanted to check whether this explanation fitted with what was going on in Drew's mind.

'I didn't give a fuck about talking to my solicitor. I just wanted to talk to someone.'

'Why?'

'I was feeling shit, I've already told you that.'

I redirected our attention back to events. 'What happened?'

'I tapped on the window. I didn't know what I was going to say.' Showing me his pleading expression, he mimed popping a pill into his mouth.

Over the next hour and a half, I tried to prise more details from him. Very occasionally he would succinctly describe his feelings and intentions, though mostly his unfinished descriptions begged follow-up questions in order to be understood.

Eventually I was able to get a picture of the mind accompanying Drew's actions that day. From as soon as he woke up, he felt unsettled. The feeling was not one that he could easily put into words. He couldn't pinpoint a particular reason or trigger. This feeling intensified throughout the morning. The nursing staff's encouragement for him to come out for breakfast was met with a sullen snub. Unprompted, he told me that the nurses hadn't done anything to deserve this. Their presence at his door was an opportunity to release some of the building feelings, and he thought they would have been justified in shouting back at him; that they didn't added to his anguish. Together with the growing tension was an unbearable emotional void. He knew there were people around who were supposed to help him; he could hear them outside his room. In his mind they had bodies that took the form of people he knew, but these images were feelingless. He said that it felt as though he may as well have been on a desert island. He toyed with the possibility that going out of his room and seeing others in the flesh would bring their bodies to emotional life. He stopped himself because he knew in this state he was more likely to lose control, but he could only resist for so long.

As he made his way on to the ward, Drew had no idea what he was going to say or do. He felt out of his body, as if he was a bystander looking down on himself. Two patients and a nurse were sitting on the sofas and another patient was standing by the kitchen area. When they beckoned him over, the space around him seemed to close in. With pretended purpose, he walked past them towards the nursing office. He was still not sure what he was going to do. The tension coiled tighter. Through the window, he gestured for some medication. The nurse in the office raised her arm with her palm facing him and mouthed something. He did not know what any of this meant other than he had to turn around. It was as if everyone was now staring at him. He had to escape. He knew his room was no sanctuary from his mind. The nurse on the sofa shouted, 'What's up, lad?' From then there was a gap in his memory.

The sceptic may take Drew's claim of amnesia to be a ploy; a convenient way to avoid taking responsibility for his own destructive actions, but this didn't tie in with his willingness to accept that he was responsible, or his seeming frustration at not having his own memory for this incident. He could see some unmoving images, like photographic stills, of his stand-off and scuffle with the nurses, but in between these momentary flashes there was nothing.

Drew came round to find himself in the seclusion room. The pressure in his head seemed to have eased. He now had tangible emotions. Even though he didn't like the anger he felt, he would prefer it any day to the previous emptiness. His mind seemed to be back in his body and he was more connected to the physical space about him. Knowing that the seclusion room would contain his violence allowed him to express his anger without restraint. It felt good to boot the door as hard as he could and swear obscenities. He felt safe. Over the next few hours the anger lessened and he became more compliant.

When reading a novel, we conjure up an imaginary world that is separate from the real world around us. Someone passing the window may bring our mental gaze from the place we have created in our mind back to events in our immediate surroundings. Then, distracted from reading, we might decide to put the book down to go and make a hot drink and, because making a hot drink is something routine that we can do without needing to plan or monitor our actions, so our thoughts are liable to wander. We might replay an earlier conversation with someone, effectively stepping into the past, or we might plan out a discussion we will be having later that day, casting our focus forward to an anticipated future. When we go back to the novel, we will have no problem slipping back into the fictional world. Our mind can flick between the novel-induced landscape, our immediate surroundings, and our time-travelling self as easily as switching between television channels.

Subjectively these are distinct states of awareness. When immersed in the book's reality, our conscious awareness is largely detached from our surroundings and thoughts about our self. That we are able make the hot drink while cogitating about unrelated matters illustrates a capacity to separate different functions at the same time. Dissociation of functions can even extend to complex tasks: when driving, we can become absorbed in thoughts that have nothing to do with our actions in controlling the car or navigating our route. Faced with an unexpected hazard, we are able to bring ourselves back round to our immediate surroundings and take action to avoid danger.

The separation of aspects of awareness and function has obvious advantages. What would it be like not to have control of the switch between these different states of existence? One consequence could be having the sense of separateness from our environment and self of the sort that comes with reading a captivating book, only without there being a book or any other mental distraction. Or, when we surface from our distracted thoughts to focus our attention on what we are doing, we would find that we can't. As a result, we would not have a sense of ownership of our body's movements. They would feel automated.

Running through Drew's account of the period leading up to the TV incident were descriptions of dissociation, the pathological uncontrolled separateness of feelings and thoughts from each other and from external reality. He couldn't connect with his own emotions. His concepts of others were not underpinned by feelings – they seemed to be soulless avatars. He was unable to predict how he was going to feel from one minute to the next. A cloud of despair could unexpectedly descend over him. Sometimes it was in response to someone's passing glance or comment. At other times he could not find any reason. He could not put his finger on why he felt so uptight that morning. When particularly tense he would start to dissociate. The resulting unbearable disorientation from normality stoked up the tension further, worsening the dissociation and so on. He reached a point when he dissociated from his memory.

When I looked back with Drew at a whole series of such episodes, we agreed that the endings had one thing in common: there would be a physically dramatic act that demanded others act. We could also see that this was the juncture when his mind would reconnect with his body, with his environment and with people in that environment. The act was sometimes outwardly directed aggression. More often it was aimed back at his own body. Out of hospital, taking an overdose sometimes had the same effect. Mostly, he would cut himself. While cutting, Drew explained that there was a sensation like pain, but it didn't hurt; as he watched the blood ooze from the wound his mind re-entered his body. In the moments when his mind was spiralling out of his control, expressing his feelings verbally would have no effect. Gouging at his arm made it real, and when the staff grabbed him, the physicality of his interaction with them gave their bodies and their presence meaning to him.

Exploring Drew's mind had uncovered a very different explanation for his actions to the one that had been immediately assumed. Like the psychotic patient taking instructions from angry voices, Drew was battling against frenzied forces that were outside his control. Superficially his actions looked like a transparent attempt to manipulate the staff to immediately respond to his demands. Getting beneath the diagnosis and into his experiences revealed that he was at the mercy of the rampant dissociation of his mind.

When I presented the formulation at the next team meeting, it was not resisted. It helped us to explain other difficult interactions with Drew. We debated the reasons why he might be so prone to such catastrophic dissociation. Everyone accepted that it had something to do with his upbringing.

At the age of nine, Drew and his younger half-brother had been found alone in a house while his parents had gone out for the night. During the next two years of social services support, Drew's mother often complained that she could not manage the children. When Drew's stepfather left the family home, his mother asked for the children to be taken into care temporarily. She always put off their return and eventually adoption was considered. A family was found for Drew's half-brother, but it was not so easy for Drew, who had already been moved between several foster families. He was seen as inherently naughty, as a child who did not respond to discipline. He was then moved into a children's home. One home where he lived for two years in his early teens was later discovered to be the workplace of a group of serial sexual abusers.

Drew had made it clear in our meeting that he did not want to be asked questions about his childhood. Despite this, every so often he did briefly take our discussion back to his early life. I learned from him that his first memories of dissociation were when he was violated in the children's home. Back then, taking his mind out of his body made the experience less real and therefore less violating.

We discussed in our team meeting how dissociation had started as an adaptation to extreme threat and crushing fear. Since the threat was frequent, he found himself dissociating frequently. Eventually, he could not control what became a habitual response to threat. In parallel, the unpredictability of the abuse meant he adopted a permanent state of hypervigilance. If it meant that he sometimes saw threat when there was none, so be it.

In agreeing a more informed explanation for Drew's behaviour, the tenor of the team discussion changed. Whereas explaining his actions in terms of conscious manipulation had shut down interest in Drew's problems and activated disapproval of him, our desire to help him was now fired up. But two weeks later, at the next scheduled meeting to discuss Drew's care, I noticed some of the old assumptions had crept back in: he didn't want help, he was deliberately sabotaging his progress, he doesn't like hearing no.

I was not surprised. Observers of patients in acute psychotic crisis are reminded that the patient's mind is burdened by strange intrusions because of their bizarre behaviour. Patients with Drew's type of problem do not seem outwardly odd. It feels right to rely on assumptions that we use in everyday interactions. I would be much more liable to making those assumptions if I spent all day on the ward. To counteract them requires effort and concentration and maintaining this viewpoint becomes even more difficult when dealing with the day-to-day obstructive behaviour.

After a few months, I gave in to the pressure to look for an alternative placement. Drew joined me and the team in pinning our hopes on a new elsewhere. I suppressed the feelings that we were colluding with each other to put off the hard work required to help Drew change. I knew that the elsewhere we spoke of was not real – the perfect elsewhere for Drew did not exist.

That was many years ago now and I have not seen Drew since. But the relatively small circle in which forensic psychiatrists move provided occasional updates on his progress. His stints in the community were brief. In prison, he came to the attention of other psychiatrists and there were further attempts at treatment. A couple of these were short-lived and culminated in feedback to Drew that he was not sufficiently motivated to deal with his problems. Other attempts repeated the sequence of his admission under my care; each crisis chipped away at the therapeutic instincts of the team until they all joined Drew in peering out towards an idealised elsewhere and sent him on his way. We had built hospitals with the physical strength to contain his dangerous behaviour, but what we lacked was the psychological strength to keep working through the crises for long enough to make a difference.

3

Amit

THE PATIENT'S EXPRESSION combined serenity, condescension and a comic glint, which gave away that he was toying with the interviewer. Watching him made me feel uneasy.

A formal psychiatric examination involves deconstructing the way the patient presents him- or herself. How did he dress, hold himself, move, speak, communicate, gesture, emote, respond, think, perceive, focus and so on? But fixating only on what I see and hear (the 'mental state examination', to give it its official title) risks neglecting the more abstract and subjective aspects of the encounter. No less important is what was happening to me. What feelings are evoked? What impulses are provoked?

I take a moment to introspect. There was a flicker of irritation and a strong urge to take control. Without meaning to, I had adopted the interviewer's perspective. On this occasion I could relax. It was not my interview. I was studying a recording of someone else's attempt to engage an archetypal psychopath.

By their absence in this patient, I was reminded of the changing signals most of us continually issue from our face and body when we communicate with others. Even ignoring what is said, a meeting between two people is a complex coordinated dance. If we step out of the moment and self-consciously think about ourselves interacting, it can disrupt the flow.

Pausing and rewinding the recording confirmed that this patient was not playing by the ordinary rules of social reciprocity. His posture and facial expression were fixed. Whether he was talking or listening, his demeanour did not change. He seemed un-affected by the presence of another person. His head was inclined slightly downwards so that his gaze was that of a parent calmly chastising a child. Without doubt the interviewer was being con-summately dominated.

The level of precautions needed so that this assessment could take place safely reflected the patient's extraordinary offending profile. The interviewer had been instructed to maintain a safe distance from the strengthened glass that separated her from the prisoner. Her lack of experience of working in such conditions was obvious. To be fair to her, the circumstances of the meeting were highly unusual. This inexperienced interviewer had been sent to the most secure area in the forensic hospital to persuade a notoriously uncooperative patient to assist the authorities in their investigation of someone else's offences. His profile was legend-ary. He was a convicted serial killer who also had a gastronomic predilection for the flesh of his victims.

My unease at re-watching the footage was as much to do with the feeling that this was a cartoonish parody of psychopathy. For many, Anthony Hopkins's portrayal of Hannibal Lecter in *The Silence of the Lambs* is the benchmark of a psychopathic offender. It is true that there is often something peculiar about the way psychopaths interact. It is also the case that they usually contra-vene unspoken interactional rules. Some, but by no means all, can be very dangerous. Yet, cinematic versions almost invariably inflate one or two psychopathic traits to grotesque proportions. Infinitely more complex and intriguing than these caricatures are real-life psychopaths.

Corinne's agitation grew as she struggled to read the map. Lost in a sprawling woodland, they were late for their Saturday evening dinner engagement. For a second time, Jean-Claude stopped the car to look for a number to call ahead. He rummaged in the boot. There was no number, but he seemed excited to have stumbled on a gift he had been meaning to give to Corinne. In a moment of light relief, she joined him by the side of the road and gracefully waited for him to put the necklace on her. But then came a sudden stinging sensation on her face and neck that was followed by painful spasms that gripped her entire body. What had just happened? Jean-Claude's explanation at the time defied credibility. Corinne would soon learn that this incident was part of a much bigger and more preposterous series of events.

Corinne and Jean-Claude had become lovers before she left the village where Jean-Claude lived with his wife and children. She had heard about the illustrious circles Jean-Claude moved in and knew also of his reputation as a doctor and internationally renowned medical researcher at the World Health Organization. That night, Jean-Claude had invited Corinne to accompany him to dinner with Bernard Kouchner, the co-founder of Médecins Sans Frontières.

There was no obvious connection between this incident in the woods and the fire at Jean-Claude's house the following day, 300 miles to the south. Jean-Claude was rescued from the fire in a critical condition, and as he lay in his hospital bed, Luc, his friend since medical school, dreaded the moment when he would have to tell his friend that his wife and two young children had perished in the fire. But within days, Luc would be faced with a far greater test of his sanity because revelations from the investigation into the fire at Jean-Claude's house upended Luc's world.

Enquiries uncovered that Jean-Claude Romand was not known to Bernard Kouchner. The World Health Organization had no record of him. He was not even a doctor. Almost two decades before, this unassuming member of Luc's friendship group who sat with them in the medical school lectures had given up his right to be there after he did not show up for the second-year examinations. There had been an opportunity for Jean-Claude to re-sit his missed exams but, instead, he chose to tell a lie.

We have all told lies. Most of the time, though, we tend to tell the truth. Looking back at our evolutionary heritage, both hunting and gathering were far more productive when we shared information honestly with our in-group peers about sources of nourishment and threat. The prehistoric survival advantage of cooperation is the reason for our natural inclination towards honesty. But, to understand the functioning of the mind – and, critically for psychiatrists, deviations in the way the mind works – we need to consider the cause of, not just the reason for, our inclinations.

Reflecting on how we decide to act in a certain way gives us the impression that we chose a course of action on the basis of a rational appraisal of the options. This may be the case for some decisions, particularly if they are complex and there is enough time for deliberation, such as which make and model of new car to buy. But, if this were the only way to decide how to act, we would quickly become so overwhelmed by the number of decisions to take that we would grind to inaction. Should we keep scrolling through our social media account or get out of bed? Should we answer the call from an unknown number or ignore it? Should we empty the bins now or later? We can keep going because most of what we do is the result of processing that is incessantly running in the background. The potential outcomes of our actions are predicted and those predictions influence whether to act, and if so, which type of action to choose. All this can happen without needing conscious analysis. Our automated processors have some default settings that influence a general preference for certain types of actions. These default settings encourage cooperation with others we identify as being in the same group as us.

The usual settings discourage lying as the automatic action of choice. But, nevertheless, people do lie.

Some lies may be considered justified. Parents aren't usually condemned for peddling falsehoods about a jolly bearded benefactor delivering Christmas gifts to all the world's households at the same time. Then there are those less well-intentioned, but still relatively trivial, lies to cover our minor misdemeanours. We may falsely claim the local shop had closed early instead of admitting that we forgot to stop on the way home to buy milk, for example. Other types of duplicity may be viewed more seriously. Take, for example, the spouse who repeatedly explains his unfaithful absences in terms of unexpected work commitments. In his own mind, he may engage in a type of cognitive chicanery known as minimisation. Addressing his conscience, he explains, 'It's just a physical thing – it doesn't mean anything.' For good measure, he adds, 'It won't hurt her if she doesn't find out.' This downplaying of the negative consequences of his behaviour lessens his personal discomfort. Whether it is an occasional 'white lie' or more frequent dishonesty, the essential point is that expenditure of effort is required to override the natural inclination to tell the truth. Lying takes more energy than being honest, and so the majority of people only lie occasionally and when it is deemed necessary. But there are rare exceptions. A very small number of people do not possess a baseline preference for truthfulness. And the faulty calibration of processing that facilitates abnormal levels of dishonesty may, in some cases, extend to urges to act in a more dramatically immoral way.

Hovering with his friends outside the examination halls, Jean-Claude Romand shared their pre-exam jitters; at least, he showed the signs of doing so. In the melee when the doors opened, they did not notice that he slipped away rather than entering with them. He went on to establish himself – in the eyes of his family and friends – as a successful doctor. His wife and neighbours had no cause to question that his morning commute was across the French/Swiss border to his office at the World Health Organization headquarters in Geneva. If followed, he would sometimes be seen to enter the 1960s complex. Passing through the public areas, he would sweep up some free pamphlets with the WHO logo, which he would leave around the house to support the charade.

For eighteen years Romand seemed to pass off his counterfeit life to those around him with ease. But his downfall came with the unravelling of the scam that had allowed him to fund the lifestyle of a wealthy doctor. In order to give the impression that he was earning a good salary, Romand, in the role of a benevolent son, had offered to use his connections to deliver a better return on his parents' savings. Instead, he transferred the money directly into his own bank account to withdraw when he needed it. When his parents' savings began to run out, he extended his 'benevolence' to his in-laws, and then to his lover Corinne. But when Corinne asked Romand to return some of her 900,000-franc-investment, a request that threatened to reveal his many mistruths, Jean-Claude was forced to change roles.

In the hours before he picked up Corinne for their dinner date, Jean-Claude had bludgeoned his wife to death and shot his children through the head as they lay in bed. Driving the fifty miles to his parents' address, he shot them and their dog before travelling to Paris to remove the last piece of incriminating evidence. He used pepper spray and a cattle prod to subdue Corinne so that she was easier to strangle. But he had not expected the strength with which she fought back. Having failed to kill her, Romand begged Corinne to excuse this outburst as a reaction to his recently diagnosed cancer – another fabrication – and he returned to the family home, where, unperturbed by the slaughtered bodies of his wife and children, he calmly staged a suicide attempt. He splashed petrol over the corpses and around the house and, after swallowing some tablets well past their sell-by date, he started a fire. By the time Romand regained consciousness in hospital, the evidence stacked against him was overwhelming. With hindsight it is inevitable that his first response would be to deny having a hand in it. Lying came naturally to him.

In *The Mask of Sanity*, first published in 1941, the American psychiatrist Hervey Cleckley presented rich case studies that typified a group of patients he had spent decades studying. He concluded:

> [He, the psychopath] shows a remarkable disregard for truth and is to be trusted no more in his accounts of the past than in his promises for the future or his statement of present intentions. He gives the impression that he is incapable of ever attaining realistic comprehension of an attitude in other people which causes them to value truth and cherish truthfulness in themselves.

The thing that distinguished these people from other patients was the absence of outward signs of insanity. Dishonesty is one hallmark of the Cleckley psychopath, but even if this characteristic is present to the level in Romand, it would not in itself be sufficient to diagnose psychopathy.

In common with Daniel M'Naghten, part of the world Jean-Claude Romand inhabited was fabricated. The difference was Romand could distinguish between fabrication and reality. In M'Naghten's world, the victimisation he perceived was as real to him as all other aspects of his life. Even if confronted with objective evidence to the contrary, he would have continued to hold these beliefs. This is how we define a delusion: a fixed belief that is both based on incorrect inferences and held in the face of strong opposing evidence. Romand, on the other hand, knowingly created the falsehood. Although lying was for him effortless, to maintain his complex deception, he had to simultaneously hold in his mind both fact and fantasy. Whereas M'Naghten would reject the perspective of others, Romand needed to look at the world he had created from their vantage point. He had to anticipate and cover up contradictions that might blow his cover. It became obvious to those interrogating M'Naghten that he was insane. Even before he assassinated Edward Drummond, there were signs of mental breakdown. In contrast, neither Romand's family or friends, nor the investigating police officers, had reason to suspect mental illness.

As a forensic psychiatrist, I am tasked with not only explaining the nature of overt mental derangement (such as that displayed by M'Naghten), but also exploring beneath facades of sanity for less obvious abnormal mental activities. But before embarking on my search for the processes that explain violent behaviour, I need to be sure that I am clear about the nature of the particular processes. Cruelty is one of the most striking features of many fictional psychopaths. It is also essential in my assessments of real violent offenders that I do not miss signs of cruel tendencies. But to understand how cruelty may be part of an explanation for a violent act, it needs unpicking. Setting out to wilfully cause pain or suffering is one definition of cruel behaviour; another is behaving without any concern for the pain or suffering. The dictionary definition of cruelty does not require a distinction to be made between whether causing the suffering was the intention or whether it was a consequence about which the actor felt indifferent. Subjectively, there is a very clear distinction. Being actively motivated to cause suffering is a sign of an unusual drive that is additional to the usual human make-up. A more passive indifference to the suffering caused by our actions indicates a failure of an expected human response. The melodramatic incarnations of psychopathy that appear on our screen conflate these two elements of cruelty. They give the impression that psychopathy and sadism are one and the same thing. My clinical experience tells me otherwise.

The walk along a three-storey high wall brought me to the prison reception; a 1980s extension to the Victorian brick perimeter overseen by CCTV. I noticed myself taking a deep breath in preparation for the series of security checks. My impatience used to clash with the more casual and civilised pace adopted by prison staff, but I have learned that huffing and puffing does not speed the process up. Once inside the reception, I stood in front of the reinforced screen waiting to be dealt with. Through the toughened glass, I could not hear what was being said, but the officer did not seem in a hurry to finish what looked like a jokey exchange with a colleague. As he neared the window, he reached out to his left to activate the intercom. Leaning down towards the small circular grille in the wall covering the microphone, I introduced myself. At the same time, I slapped my photograph identification against the glass for him to inspect. He pushed the drawer beneath the screen in my direction to indicate that I should drop it in. He then pulled the drawer back and scooped out the badge, which he placed face-up next to a clipboard. Occasionally flicking his gaze back to the badge, he ran his finger down a list of names, turned to the next sheet and did the same.

'You're not on the list.' If that were true, there would be no way to get into the prison that day. Trying to find another free half-day in my diary to come back and complete my report within the agreed deadline would be almost impossible.

'Surname's Nathan,' I explained. He looked down again. Marking the list with a highlighter pen and asking whether I had electrical devices were confirmation that I had now passed this first check. I pushed my phone and car keys through a tray beneath the screen. In exchange, he passed a key for the locker where he had stored my belongings. Moving on to higher-tech checks, he stared at his computer and asked whether I had been before. 'Yes, but not for some time,' I replied.

My first entry into prisons twenty years ago was a much more casual affair. It seems hard to believe now, but I would drive up to the gatehouse and on the nod of the patrolling officer the gates would open, allowing me to enter the prison without even alighting from my car. I became a regular visitor to HMP Liverpool. Prisons on this scale are a relatively recent phenomenon. Before the late 1700s British criminals were mostly dealt with by shaming rituals (such as being placed in the stocks), corporal punishment (such as flogging) or capital punishment (execution). Incarceration was generally reserved for those awaiting trial or payment of their debts. The imperial expansion into the New World provided a novel solution to deal with convicts. Transportation to the colonies in the Americas continued until the start of the American Revolution in the 1760s, and in due course there was an Antipodean alternative, though the option of transportation began to fall out of favour. Against this backdrop and given the changing sensibilities against capital punishment, the purpose of prisons shifted from temporarily housing offenders to becoming the punishment itself. From the mid-1800s, the Victorian mastery of grand building projects, which produced the rampant growth of mental asylums, also delivered the required prisons. Victorian prisons, with modern adaptations to enhance security, are the most common type of prison I visit.

The officer instructed me to step back to a black strip on the floor. I knew the drill. I looked up for the webcam that would take my picture. Back at the counter, I placed my index finger on the scanner. It took several tries before it could recognise a print pattern (I am told that my dermal ridges lie flat, making them difficult to scan). In the queue I held a plastic tray into which I had deposited my folder, pens, belt, shoes and jacket. After placing the tray on the conveyor belt, I automatically went through my own pre-search prep – patting my shirt breast pocket and checking for stray items in my trouser pockets. I threw a ragged tissue in the bin beside the metal detector archway that I then walked through. As I stepped up onto a raised wooden platform, a female officer wearing purple disposable gloves mumbled some sounds. Her question repeated hundreds of times day in, day out had lost any meaning to her. Although it was difficult to make out distinct words, I knew from experience that she was asking whether I had any objection to being searched. I didn't. Once fully dressed again, I went to stand with the group of 'official' visitors. A glass panel slid open, we shuffled through and filed along a corridor to another waiting area where once again our names were checked on a list and then matched with our fingerprints. We were about to be taken deep into the prison, to the area for category A prisoners.

Since 1967 all prisoners in England and Wales have been assigned a security category. The introduction of this system was a response to the case of George Blake in the mid-1960s who, like Jean-Claude, had assumed a false identity. In the post-Second World War stand-off between the superpowers, George Blake, a British secret service agent, had been uncovered as a double agent whose loyalty lay with the Soviet Union. Blake had made a career out of lying, though to him there was a reasoned justification – a deeply held belief about the virtues of communism.

Appearing in court number 1 at the Old Bailey on 3 May 1961, Lord Justice Parker had pronounced to Blake, 'your case is one of the worst that can be envisaged in times of peace'. Parker went on to impose a longer finite prison sentence than had ever been passed before, provoking audible gasps by onlookers. It was later claimed that the forty-two years of the sentence represented the lives lost due to the defendant's treacherous activities.

Just over five years after he was sentenced, a routine evening roll call in Wormwood Scrubs revealed that George Blake was missing. It transpired that he was able to squeeze through a landing window. It was then a step onto a roof built – conveniently for George Blake – just under the window and a clamber down a drainpipe to the ground. From there was a short unbroken dash to the prison wall where a rope ladder was waiting for him. The security agencies envisaged a well-resourced plot by his former Soviet employers. In fact, his accomplices were an amateurish band of former inmates, two of whom were peace campaigners hostile to the sentence meted out to Blake, and the third an erratic rogue with ill-formed romantic ideals. Once over the wall, Blake was whisked to a local address where he laid low nursing a broken hand sustained in the 22-foot drop to freedom. Hidden in a makeshift secret space in a camper van, he was driven by one of the conspirators across Europe. Once in East Germany he made himself known to officials and then was spirited away to Russia where he continued to live until his death in 2020.

The embarrassing failure of British prisons to hold on to one of their most notorious prisoners was all the greater when seen against the backdrop of two earlier headline-grabbing escapes. In 1964, Charles Wilson, a member of the gang who carried out the most lucrative robbery in British criminal history until then – the Great Train Robbery – was sprung from Winson Green Prison in Birmingham. The following year, Ronald Biggs, also a member of the gang, managed to break out of London's Wandsworth Prison. The Home Secretary at the time, Roy Jenkins, attempted to deflect political criticism by announcing an inquiry and the resulting Mountbatten Report recommended improving perimeter security and assigning every prisoner to one of four security categories, a system that has endured to this day. The lowest category, D, is applied to prisoners who are not deemed to pose a risk to the public and so can be held in prisons without walls. The other categories indicate the need for secure conditions; more for category B than C prisoners. Category A is reserved for those prisoners whose escape would be highly dangerous to the public or the police or to the security of the state.

Having finally reached the 'Cat A' area I was assigned a room – with its table, which was fixed to the floor, the only separation between me and the prisoner. After a few minutes, my patient, Amit, appeared at the door wearing a grey tracksuit and an orange tabard. Almost immediately I noticed a clash between this attire, which marked his identity as an inmate, and his air of friendly confidence. Once seated, his impeccable posture was a contrast to the nonchalant slouch I often encounter. Before I could begin my routine introductory speech, he said that he had been so looking forward to our meeting – which is unusual to hear under the circumstances. There were no signs of the apprehension that I usually must manage before the formal assessment can begin. But Amit's cheerful countenance belied the reason we were meeting. He had been charged with a double murder.

If there is some question about the balance of the mind of a defendant charged with a criminal offence, the lawyers have the option to commission a psychiatric assessment. No one was suggesting Amit was mentally ill, but his solicitors thought something was amiss. In advance of the assessment, a large package had been delivered to my office. The 'prosecution bundle' includes first-hand accounts of incriminating events gathered by the police. I pored over these witness statements. Much of the content is not especially useful to me. Still, I go through each page line by line, searching for any insights into the defendant's state of mind. One police officer recounted how she retrieved a recording from a shop CCTV. Another, with IT expertise, explained how he undertook analyses of Amit's computer and iPad. Of more relevance were the accounts given by the two officers who first attended the scene of the crime. A work colleague of Amit's step-sister, Prya, had explained in her call to the police that she was probably overreacting, but she thought she should notify someone about Prya's unexplained absence from the offices of the corporate law firm where they both worked. Once they had gained entry into the house where Prya lived with her mother, Laxmi, the officers found a bloating body lying face-down on the floor of the living room. Their suspicions that the cause of his step-sister's death was stab wounds to the back were subsequently confirmed by the post-mortem examination. They could not see evidence of disturbance elsewhere in the room; however, a sweep of the house found a second unidentified female body, at a similar stage of decomposition, on the landing upstairs. It turned out to be Laxmi. She had sustained two knife injuries, but the cause of death was determined to be suffocation.

What stood out from witnesses who knew Amit was that when they first heard he had been arrested, they found it hard to believe he was involved. He was forty-three and they had never known him to be violent. Some, but not all, commented that they could not recall him ever losing his temper. This was worthy of note, as a 'positive negative'; a positive finding of the absence of something that in a homicide case is usually expected. Many acquaintances felt the need to comment on how they found Amit as a person. Each passing comment was too brief to put any weight on, but collating and comparing the descriptions of aloofness, superiority, condescension and pomposity pointed to a pattern. The police were particularly interested to hear from the witnesses about the way he flaunted the trappings of his presumed wealth. At this early stage in the investigation, most witnesses did not know that of Amit's many business ventures all eventually failed and his extravagance was funded by money he had extorted from his mother, or that much of what he had told them was fantasy. The police were drawing together evidence of dishonesty of Jean-Claude Romand proportions.

Within the prosecution bundle is also a printout from the Police National Computer of any previous offences – there were none – and transcripts of the recorded police interviews with the accused. In the first interview, Amit vehemently refuted all allegations about his involvement in the death of his mother and stepsister. He presented himself as the grieving son lamenting that if he hadn't left to go back to London so soon, he would have been able to prevent this tragedy. He maintained the same line in the second interview. Listening to the officers' questions, he must have started to appreciate the strength of the case against him. I thought this was likely to explain the wholesale change of story in the third transcript. He accepted his involvement but regretted that he could not assist in explaining his behaviour. He told the officers that he had blacked out.

From a folder he had been allowed to bring into the interview, Amit fished out several sheets of paper. 'I made some notes,' he explained. He told me he thought it would help my assessment. Presenting them under my nose with his outstretched hand, he did not seem to be in any doubt that I would accept them. I took the papers, but without looking at them I placed them on the table. At the same time, I took a breath to begin my routine introductory briefing.

Prior to starting the psychiatric examination, there are some preliminary formalities. The subject of the assessment needs to understand what they are letting themselves in for. This is not a private medical consultation. They must understand that the entirety of the discussion will appear in a report that is shared with the defence, prosecution and court. I advise them to assume that everything we discuss will be shared through my report. Just as I was about to start the explanation, Amit cut in. 'Professor Lambert, you probably know him, he was my father's friend. They played tennis together.'

At that interruption, I became aware of my own slight irritation. I had ignored his handwritten notes, but now there was this other distraction to deal with. The strict scheduling of prison visits meant that I had limited time to complete this assessment. Delays could hinder my ability to make sense of the patient and their offence. It was the urge that accompanied my irritation on this occasion that revealed to me that it may not just be an issue of the available time. I knew Professor Lambert, but I felt impelled to deny that I did. For a split second, I speculated whether the urge was because I was sensing a hierarchical manoeuvre.

Hierarchy is built into relationships. It may not always be obvious, but one person is usually in a position of relative advantage over the other. The advantage can be trivial and only held momentarily. It may repeatedly shift between two people over time. Sometimes, there is a greater and more enduring imbalance. In certain settings it is institutionalised. By necessity, police and prisoner officers are invested with powers that create an officially sanctioned inequality.

Under pressure of time and with limited information, decisions about the best course of action tend to rely on broad categorisations. On meeting someone new, a readily available and crude categorical distinction is between in and out groups; us and them. In our hunter-gathering past, being able to rapidly make a distinction between our own group or a hostile competing group could mean the difference between life and death. While the general survival benefits are not so obvious in our present lives, our immediate judgements about others continue to be coloured by this dichotomy. It is safer for my interviewees residing at Her Majesty's pleasure to assume I am in the 'them' category until they have good reason to conclude otherwise. In this category, I join police, prison and probation officers; essentially a group that from the inmate's position has unwarranted and potentially harmful dominance over them. By association, and until the contrary is proven, I come to represent a source of threat.

In my assessments, I usually strive to reduce this sense of authority. It is not just to lessen the discomfort I feel when faced with signs of someone else's vulnerability. Attempting to flatten the perceived hierarchy is a practical necessity. The prisoner is unlikely to share their life history with someone who they sense to be a potential source of harm. Also, insights into the patient's emotional world will be obscured by the defensive and reticent stance they adopt in the presence of the assumed threat.

The difference with Amit was that there were no signs of such vulnerability and his manner conveyed that from the outset I was in his 'us' category. My interactional antennae were twitching. Perhaps it was coincidence that Amit mentioned a colleague whose status in the world of British forensic psychiatry would by any standard exceed mine. I needed to be careful about casual assumptions. If there was meaning to his interruption, maybe it was nothing to do with status. Was it merely his way of forging a connection? Alternatively, was it more an indication of my own oversensitivity to hierarchical cues?

Whatever the reason for my urge, I did not act on it. I confirmed that I knew Professor Lambert. Paying attention to an urge and contemplating possible reasons for it often offers clues about the unstated priorities of my patients (and for that matter my own), but acting on them can be unhelpful. If Amit was using a self-promoting tactic, then reacting against it would have meant I was engaging in a status competition. A narcissistic stand-off is not helpful to start a psychiatric assessment.

I readied myself for the response to my confirmation that I knew Professor Lambert. It was not conclusive, but I saw some support for my initial speculation. Without any prompting, Amit launched into a tribute to the eminence of the great psychiatrist with whom his father had a close bond. I politely interjected and explained that we needed to press on with the assessment, but maybe if there was anything else he wanted to mention we could discuss it at the end, if there was time. He agreed and added he thought it a very good suggestion.

I then delivered the consent and confidentiality briefing. As is standard in my explanation, I prepared him for the need at some point to discuss the offences. Finishing off the explanation, I started scribbling a sentence to confirm that this introductory step had been undertaken. Before I had completed my note, a repetitive gasping and squeaking sound caused me to lift my gaze. As Amit unscrewed his eyes, I could see tears running down his face. He was sobbing. I paused and placed my pen down. I offered an apology in case it was something I had said.

'No, don't worry . . .' It was not me, he said. It was just that mentioning the offences reminded him that his mother never got to hear the fantastic news.

I was confused. 'What news?' Whatever it was, he was the cause of her not getting to hear the news, I thought. He had killed her.

Needing no encouragement, he explained that he had approached an old school friend for a position in a company selling and leasing super-yachts. It was months since the conversation, so it came as a surprise to be told that the board wanted to meet with him. He told me that he was saddened that his mother could not share his joy. The letter had come two days before his mother died and he had not got around to telling her. I did not notice the point at which he recovered his composure; the tears had gone as quickly as they arrived.

In the act of shedding light on the facts, he had caused me to have even more doubt that he experienced the world as most of us do.

It's impossible to make complete sense immediately of all the information gathered at the time of an assessment. Looking out for interactional idiosyncrasies and monitoring my fleeting reactions, while at the same time gathering and recording the biographical data, makes it difficult to notice all the connecting threads. But that evening, sitting at my desk at home, a clearer picture emerged. Reading through the dictated account of the assessment on one monitor, I was able to pull out each note-worthy comment and reaction (in myself as well as him) on a second. Status did turn out to be recurring theme. Whether Amit moved in such prestigious circles wasn't the issue; of more interest to me was the way he introduced me to the people in his world. It could be his family, friends, partners or even passing acquaint-ances, but what stood out from his descriptions was who they were connected to, how lavish their house was, or how wealthy they were. To him, the identity of others seemed to be shaped by their social rank. It was as if his relationships were built on the status of, rather than feelings for, the other person.

Amit sobbed again a few times during the assessment. His tears tended to coincide with discussions about the index offences – a term we use to describe the most recent offence. Becoming upset in this type of assessment is not particularly remarkable, but it was his explanation for the tears that struck me as odd: he was in each instance reacting to the effect on him rather than mourning the loss itself. It was also notable that there seemed to be no build-up to the displays of emotion and that there was an equally sudden resumption of composure. On one occasion Amit became angry. I was taken aback at the time, but it was not outside the character that I came to see. A definite picture was taking shape. I stretched to the shelf behind me to reach for one of my diagnostic manuals.

Hervey Cleckley's contribution to understanding psychop-athy was recognised in his lifetime, but his continued legacy was assured when his description of psychopathy came to the atten-tion of Canadian psychologist Robert Hare. Hare recognised that to properly identify and research psychopathy, a reliable measure was needed. By tweaking, testing and revising Cleckley's description, Hare produced a list of criteria with clear scoring rules. The resulting Psychopathy Checklist–revised, usually shortened to PCL-R, has become the most widely used test of psychopathy in forensic settings.

My PCL-R manual is not particularly well-thumbed. In its purer form, psychopathy is actually quite rare, even among offenders. I laid open the manual at the beginning of the item descriptor chapter. Amit was certainly charming; but I wanted to be sure there was enough to satisfy Hare's rating rules for 'superficial charm'. On balance, I thought there was. There was probably also enough evidence in favour of 'grandiose sense of self-worth'. Having read the complete evidential set of papers, there was no question that the criteria for 'pathological lying' and 'manipulative' were fully met. Amit's displays of emotion when talking about the offence hinted at remorse, but paying attention to his words indicated it was not regret for the consequences on others, but on himself. Alongside this, his failure at any point in our meetings to express any sorrow for the impact of his actions on others was enough to endorse the 'lack of remorse' item. The speed with which he shifted in and out of states of distress was strong evidence of 'shallow affect'. The picture was of a psychopathic way of experiencing emotions and relationships.

How does identifying signs of psychopathy help me? It tells me something about the risk of violence recurring. The PCL-R score is one of the strongest predictors of offenders committing violence in the future. I certainly cannot know for certain whether Amit is at higher risk of future violence than non-psychopathic offenders, but I can say that more offenders with the same PCL-R score as Amit go on to commit another act of violence in comparison to a group with a score below a predetermined threshold. Knowing that Amit meets the core criteria for psychopathy might tell me something general about a group of offenders similar to Amit, but it does not help me answer my main question: why did this man kill his mother and stepsister?

More informed accounts of psychopathy in the clinical literature refer to an impairment of emotions. Emotional responses to moral transgressions, such as guilt, are said to be lacking. We are also told about a deficit in the formation of social emotions, such as shame and compassion. In my assessment of Amit, I saw evidence of such deficits. The way he constructed his explanations for his upset about the offence revealed it was regret not feeling-based guilt. I found further supportive evidence when, towards the end of our first meeting, I took a more direct approach to assessing feelings.

'When you look back at what's happened, what do you feel?' I asked casually. A low-key approach to this enquiry was essential. I had been his faithful audience for almost two hours and he now seemed at ease; I wanted to elicit unprepared responses.

In common with many offenders to whom I have posed this question, Amit answered that he felt terrible. This non-specific answer sets the scene for my next question. In an off-the-cuff way and with slight deference, I asked him if he would mind telling me why he felt terrible. 'Well, there's so many lost opportunities,' he mused. Suppressing any signs of incredulity, I nodded to encourage him to continue. Nostalgically, he reminisced about how his life was just turning a corner to success – the murders and his subsequent imprisonment had derailed this.

I was now ready to try to provoke a more strategic explanation. 'Can you think of other reasons you might feel terrible?' The words are carefully chosen. I emphasised 'think' and deliberately asked for 'reasons'. I wanted him to engage higher order conscious reasoning. The use of 'might' gives licence to respond with why he *should* feel that way; not only with why he *did* feel that way.

In that instance his posture stiffened. As if preparing for a speech, he straightened his back and pushed his chest forward. He was reverting to the formal, but still good-humoured, demeanour I saw when we first met. 'Of course, two people have lost their lives,' he began. 'Loss of life is such a terrible thing. How can you ever get over that?' Even when trying to convey remorse, Amit used the impersonal third person, rather than owning the sentiment with the use of 'I' or 'me'. The change in his demeanour as he relayed this response led me to think that it was taking effort. He was reasoning, but there was no sense of a visceral accompaniment to his words.

Without a doubt, I usually find evidence of a shortage of certain emotions in offenders who fit Robert Hare's description of psychopathy. Consistent with the research, the problem appears to be a specific limitation in social emotion formation. Does this help in my quest to understand the origins of the violent behaviour? A limited capacity to experience social emotions is often presented as the root of the psychopathic disturbance and so maybe I need look no further. Even when I apply my reading of this scientific literature to the offenders I assess, I am still left with an incomplete explanation for their violence.

I am not suggesting social emotions are irrelevant to behaviour. Compassion, for example, encourages us to act to alleviate suffering. Guilt may motivate us to seek to readdress the effects of our transgressive acts. But these complex emotional states are not the critical influence on our moment-by-moment decisions to act in one way or another. In fact, the social emotions are the manifestations of something else that I am interested in.

Despite their presence in our everyday existence, the phenomena that have the decisive influence on which actions we choose and which we do not are not widely recognised. They are called integral affects and occur when we are faced with an immediate decision. There is a flash in our mind in reaction to a change in our body. This feeling usually passes unnoticed. If it does come to our attention, it may be experienced as a flip of the stomach or a heaviness inside. While there are many different sorts of emotion each with its own characteristic quality, these integral affects are less well defined and more fleeting. They are crude feelings that provide an immediate guide to the way we behave.

Learning to monitor feelings is part of a technique that has been shown to improve our mental and physical well-being. Mindfulness entails paying attention to immediate experience. As well as the contribution from external stimuli, our experience is made up of an internally generated state. From within appears a stream of thoughts and feelings that the mindfulness practitioner learns to notice as a detached observer.

If identifying these ephemeral feelings in ourselves is not easy, it is even more difficult to identify them in someone else. Nevertheless, when interacting we are perpetually reacting to signs of how others feel. It is a process that will run without needing our conscious attention. If a listener responds with signs of sorrow to sad news, then our attention is not activated. If, on the other hand, they show an unexpected response, we sit up and notice. Even those occasional mismatches between a person's outward display and their underlying feelings may not go unmissed. We are sometimes able to spot the initial incongruous facial expression that is momentarily held before the real feeling is disguised by the adoption of a socially appropriate expression.

On meeting Amit for a second time, I sensed in him a slight edge of excitement. He was eager to tell me that he could now remember the offence. Where previously there was an amnesic gap at the central point in the story, a fully formed memory had appeared. My hunch was that this was a strategic change of tack rather than a recovered memory; it seemed more than coincidental that I had already filed a preliminary report to his solicitors. In that report, I had explained that the amnesia made it difficult to comment on whether the criteria for a defence of diminished responsibility were met. The blackout for the period in which the offence occurred prevented me from quizzing him about his state of mind at that time. Making assumptions about the mind on the basis of behaviour alone is unreliable. Before my first report, did he think that amnesia would give an impression of a disordered mind? If so, did he now realise that, if anything, it compromised the achievement of his goal of securing a defence of diminished responsibility? Although I was interested in his reasoning for the change, I did not ask. The assessment is as much about resisting impulses to ask the obvious questions as it is asking the right questions. As well as data gathering, I was interested in what he said unprompted, the words he chose and the signs of feelings he displayed.

The mental act of preparing to deceive others can make us feel uncomfortable. This discomfort is partly due to an anticipation of the potential social consequences of lying: being shown to be a liar. The ability to establish strong cooperative relationships has been critical to the success of the human species and giving the impression of being untrustworthy can be socially disastrous. The discomfort in the moment when we get ready to lie occurs almost instantaneously. It is a reflexive process that does not require us to carry out an explicit analysis of the situation. We do not need to read the situation; we are feeling it. Also, without the need for deliberation, we are by default motivated to dispel the sense of discomfort. Inhibiting the impulse to tell a lie would be one way. If we go ahead and lie, we are then inclined to employ tactics to reduce the impression of untrustworthiness. This is the point at which we engage effortful strategic thinking.

The way Amit departed from the expected response was in part a failure to volunteer an explanation for the change of story.

Without a misstep, he went from enthusing that he now had a memory straight into talking about the detail of what he could remember. At no point did I see any overt demonstration of a change in how he felt. I suspected he had not experienced the reflexive unpleasant feelings; hence no signs to show and no discomfort to allay. Without offering any challenge to this unusual sudden recovery of memory, I allowed him to give his account of the offence.

He had, he told me, been desperately depressed about a failed financial investment. He would be mocked by his new London friends, his reputation would be in tatters and he did not know how he could go back. Feeling suicidal, he ended up in the bathroom with a knife hovering over his wrist, at which point his stepsister came charging in to stop him and 'somehow' she was stabbed. He had then gone into a strange trance, which he explained must have been triggered by the incident with his sister. In this trance, he stabbed his mother.

This account was light on detail and in some significant respects it was not supported by the evidence. When probed around the inconsistencies, his answers were woolly and, rather than provide clarity, they added to my scepticism.

I then covered the remaining routine assessment questions that I did not have time to ask in our first meeting. With ten or so minutes left of this second meeting, I returned to the issue of the recovered memory. I had postponed the question, because what I planned to ask risked arousing a negative reaction. It was not the reaction in itself that would be the problem, but the effect of it on Amit's willingness to continue to talk openly to me. I told him that I just didn't understand how he could now remember what he had forgotten.

When confronted with evidence of dishonesty, most offenders show some signs of a change in the way they are feeling. I look out for an alteration in the tone of their voice. Their facial expression may briefly give away their discomfort, before a more fully formed emotion appears. It may be embarrassment. More often it takes the form of irritation. Occasionally, there is outright aggressiveness. In the initial moment, as they have to accommodate to the negative emotions, they are prone to becoming slightly less coherent and sometimes stumble around for words. In contrast, Amit held his cheery smile and without any hesitation said that he was as surprised as me.

Cleckley proposed that the disturbance in psychopaths was the inability to grasp emotionally the feelings that are usually implicit in our thoughts and experiences. When account is taken of the role of emotions and feelings in how we interact, Amti's preoccupation with status is more understandable.

Status concern is not abnormal. Sometimes the signs are overt; the make of our car or the logo on our clothes. Even those who claim to reject materialism still cherish other status indicators. It may be their position at work, their qualifications, their sporting prowess, their knowledge of cultural references, their green credentials. While most of us attempt to disguise our desire for prestige, Amit is, at least in this respect, much more candid. We tend to be inhibited about boasting by our sense of the listener's reaction. We do not need to spend mental time working out that we will appear boastful. There is an instantaneous emotional response that usually restrains the urge to show off. Sometimes we override this response. We may be spurred on to do so by an explicit challenge to our status – such as a patronising comment from a junior colleague. But more often, if we do make a status-related comment, it is casually slipped into the conversation. Amit appeared to suffer an impairment of the emotional mechanism that normally moderates arrogance and consequently was more transparent.

Psychopaths are often caricatured as emotionless automatons. Amit did not lack emotions, he just had a different pattern of emotional responding. He didn't possess the sense of discomfort that should have flashed into his mind when anticipating certain feelings in others. Having spent time with Amit, I could see what caused witnesses to describe him as aloof. While he was able to express himself articulately and confidently when on script, in more intimate situations he fell out of step with the rhythm of the social dance.

Amit's excessive dishonesty can also be explained by his failure to experience the adverse feelings that should accompany an urge to say or do something that would damage his reputation. As a result, he did not possess a default inclination towards honesty.

Deficits of emotions and feelings are present in different forms and degrees but there is not a formula that would fit my patients. Amit showed signs of a profound deficit. Even when he experienced a transgressive urge as extreme as killing family members for material rewards, no inhibitory emotional response was provoked. He did not, however, conform to the fictional stereotype. He was not driven by a desire to harm and his goal was not inflicting suffering on others. He was not a cackling evil genius or a budding sadistic serial killer. It was merely that he didn't care about the suffering of others. More accurately, he didn't *feel* the suffering of others.

Whatever the seriousness of Amit's disturbed mental processing, the defence team calculated that relying on a diagnosis of psychopathy would doom a diminished responsibility defence to failure. Hoping for a reduced tariff, he entered a guilty plea to the charges of murder and was sentenced to life imprisonment.

4

Joe

JOE HAD RECENTLY been transferred from another prison, and was referred to me for an assessment. After his arrival, his medication was stopped by the prison GP, who had been led to believe that he may not be taking it. Equivalence – or parity – of health care for prisoners has been consistently touted by leaders of prison health services. I doubt that the first response for a patient not in prison with questionable compliance would be to summarily axe their prescription. Be that as it may, I was often asked to see if a recent arrival needed the medication prescribed by psychiatrists either before they came to prison or when they were in other prisons. The benefit of the doubt seemed to often fall away from the imprisoned patient; certainly in comparison to patients without a known forensic history. In Joe's case, I had to accept that there were some questions about the rationale for starting an ADHD medication

Opening my email, I read the letter from the psychiatrist who had made Joe's diagnosis. On first reading, it covered the main diagnostic criteria. The psychiatrist had been told by Joe that he had been a disruptive and disobedient child, which the letter advised was very typical of children with ADHD. His school attendance was poor and when he did attend his behaviour was so unruly that he was eventually excluded and allocated to a specialist school for problem children. Again, this is a common pattern with ADHD. By his mid-teens, Joe was heading along the recognised trajectory from ADHD to childhood behaviour problems and on to more established criminal activities. The letter listed a continued history of defiance, resistance to instructions, distractibility, and disruptiveness, which I could agree were manifestations of the attention–deficit component of the diagnosis. The other component – hyperactivity – was less obvious now, but I accepted the psychiatrist's explanation in the letter that this is a recognised pattern. The studies demonstrating the persistence of ADHD into adulthood also showed that it applied more to the inattention symptoms than the hyperactivity ones. I did not have an issue with the features of ADHD that the psychiatrist had found; the problem was that I could not tell whether she had found only what she was already looking for.

My task was to assess Joe and advise the prison doctor about whether or not to restart the medication. As doctors, we are (quite rightly) obliged to be sure that there is a good reason for a patient to be prescribed medication. Prescribing in prison brings added complications. The value of drugs, including prescribed ones, is inflated in prison and they can become a tradeable commodity and trading in prisons can be dangerous. Payments of debts are enforced by intimidation, which if necessary is backed up with actual violence. Prisoners are made very vulnerable by being indebted to their drug suppliers. The leakage of medication prescribed to prisoners into this illicit market is impossible to stop completely. Nonetheless, some steps can be taken to reduce it. Making sure there is a sound basis for the prescription is one such step.

While there are disagreements about how effective psychiatric medications are, many have been shown to have a positive effect on mental health symptoms that is unlikely to be due to chance variation. Drugs for ADHD, like Ritalin or Concerta, are no different to many other psychiatric drugs in that there can be serious side effects. Also, as is common in psychiatry, the exact physiological mechanism by which the drug treats the condition is unclear. A chemical known to stimulate the central nervous system would not be an obvious choice for the treatment of people who already appear overstimulated. Given this counter-intuitive effect, it is unsurprising that its discovery was serendipitous.

The history of our understanding of ADHD begins with Heinrich Hoffmann, a German doctor who moved from general practice into psychiatry. Hoffmann was persuaded to publish anonymously a series of illustrated stories that he had written as a Christmas present for his three-year-old son. Held to be an early forerunner of the comic book, *Funny stories and whimsical pictures with 15 beautifully coloured panels for children aged 3–6* appeared in print in 1845. The individual tales, told in rhyming verses, each centred on a child character with unusual habits. Kaspar steadfastly refuses to eat his soup and over the next few days he perishes and dies. Fascinated with matches, Pauline accidentally sets fire to herself with fatal consequences. Struwwelpeter, or Shaggy Peter – the title used for later editions of the book – failed to look after himself and became so unattractive that even the author could not bear to look at him. The cautionary stories show how by their misguided actions the children became the authors of their own misfortune. The popularity of Hoffmann's book has endured through generations of German children. It has also had much wider appeal. Among the many translations was an English one by Mark Twain, which went unpublished until a quarter of a century after his death.

Relative to the standards of the time, Hoffmann held a more enlightened and humane attitude towards mental disorder. After intensively lobbying the press and politicians, he was able to establish an innovative mental hospital in Frankfurt. Alongside his successful medical career, he pursued an abiding passion for writing and illustration, which he put to practical use. In his autobiography, he told of drawing pictures and telling stories to calm his child patients into allowing him to examine them. Commentators have interpreted Hoffmann's brief portraits as early depictions of childhood behaviour problems that now form the basis of established diagnoses. Kaspar, who refused to eat, is said to have had an eating disorder. Pauline was a pyromaniac. Hoffmann himself wrote that 'these stories are not invented from scratch, one way or the other these stories grew up in a fertile soil'.

The name of another of his characters was later adopted as a German alternative for a diagnosis that was not introduced until over a century later. Unable to follow his father's instructions to sit still at the dining table, Zappel-Philipp, or Fidgety Phil, wriggled and giggled and swung back on his chair.

> See the naughty, restless child
> Growing still more rude and wild,
> Till his chair falls over quite.
> Philip screams with all his might,
> Catches at the cloth, but then
> That makes matters worse again.
> Down upon the ground they fall,
> Glasses, bread, knives, forks, and all.

In the German vernacular, Zappel-Philipp syndrome is used as a term for hyperactivity disorders. Doctors before and after Hoffmann had noticed that some children stood out as being unduly restless, distractible and inattentive. In the medical literature, these problems were clustered under various diagnostic headings such as defects of moral control, hyperkinetic disorders of infancy, and minimal brain damage. It wasn't until 1980 that the official diagnosis of attention deficit disorder, or ADD, appeared in the third edition of the American Psychiatric Association's Diagnostic and Statistical Manual of Mental Disorders. With the fourth edition came the diagnostic term that is used today, attention deficit hyperactivity disorder, shortened to ADHD.

In the course of my clinical career, I have seen the notion of ADHD evolve from a disorder of childhood to one that can persist into adulthood. It also became of interest to forensic psychiatrists because it was found to be more prevalent among offenders. As with all psychiatric diagnoses that are associated with an increased likelihood of offending, most people who develop ADHD don't go on to offend. The increased risk is at the level of groups not individuals, which means that although most children with ADHD don't grow up into antisocial adults, a greater proportion do than is the case for children without ADHD.

By the 1930s Dr Charles Bradley was working in a Rhode Island hospital and investigating brain abnormalities in children. The brain-imaging technique he employed was commonly used before the more sophisticated scanning machines that we now take for granted. X-ray imaging, which had been routinely used since the beginning of the twentieth century, relies on the fact that different tissues absorb different amounts of this form of electromagnetic radiation. Tissues that are particularly absorbent, such as bone, prevent most of the X-rays passing through to the film. The fewer X-rays reaching the film, the whiter it appears. As a consequence, bone is represented in white and the lungs, which allow many more X-rays through, appear black. Pathology is identified by looking for unexpected areas of contrast. A fracture produces a bone/non-bone contrast where there should not be one. Plain X-rays are more limited for identifiyng brain lesions because the contrast between different shades of grey is more difficult to spot.

At the end of the second decade of the twentieth century, a procedure to enhance contrast in the central nervous system had been introduced. Covering the brain and spinal cord is a narrow layer of space that links with a system of cavities in the brain. This network of spaces and cavities is filled with a fluid, the cerebro-spinal fluid, or CSF. Removing the CSF and filling the space with air produces greater contrast with the tissue of the nervous system. It is then easier to identify alterations in the normal structure of the brain. Although Dr Bradley saw the benefits of this technique, he was also well aware of its major limitation. Afterwards patients were left with a fierce headache. Dr Bradley hypothesised that if the headache was a result of CSF loss, then accelerating its production after taking the X-ray pictures should ease the severity and limit the duration of this after-effect. He used Benzedrine, a powerful amphetamine-based drug, to boost CSF production. The results did not support his hypothesis. The headaches were no less. But there appeared to be a remarkable improvement in some of the children's behaviour and academic performance. Despite publishing his findings at the time, the immediate impact on practice was limited. It wasn't until the mid-1950s that psychiatrists started using a related drug – also allied to amphetamine – on children with hyperactivity.

Joe had been prescribed a variant of this amphetamine. On the day I visited him, he was on the wing that was last on our list for medical appointments. As I waited for my next patient, I watched as an officer opened the door to the waiting room and called his name. One of the prisoners turned to look over his shoulder and shouted to the officer, 'Hang on, boss!'

Joe's aura was much bigger than the space taken up by his wiry body, which was about five feet ten. He was standing with his outstretched right arm leaning against the wall and his right foot resting on a low bench. Before the officer's interruption, he had seemed to be engrossed in a discussion with two other prisoners. He turned back to them briefly, as if he needed to finish something. As he moved to walk away, they loudly exchanged farewells and laughs. Joe then sauntered with no urgency over to the door grinning patronisingly at the officer. If any of the other prisoners looked up, it was the briefest of movement and no eye contact was made with any of the group of three. The hierarchy in the room was obvious.

Across many animal species, groups of individuals coalesce according to identifiable structures. Having a structure means that a group will achieve more than the sum of the potential achievements of the individual members. Hierarchical structures, which are ubiquitous, are one way that allows resources to be allocated. The individuals at the apex of the hierarchy benefit from greater access to factors that facilitate survival, or the survival of one's genes, such as access to resources and mates. In any case, there is an overall benefit to the group that comes from the coordinated actions, no matter how low down you are in the pecking order.

Social rank can be communicated without a word being uttered. It is obvious from observing interactions between a group of non-human primates, such as chimpanzees and gorillas. High-ranking members of the group puff out their chests, extend their arms outward, and adopt open stances. The submissive individuals tend to avoid direct eye-to-eye contact with the dominants. Failure to avert gaze increases the risk of inviting attack. Non-contact communication of respective positions in the group hierarchy is much less costly for all. Social psychology studies have demonstrated that the non-verbal displays of social rank in humans may be more subtle, but they are no less prevalent. Body positioning and posture, gaze orientation, arm and hand gestures, and vocalisations are all used as part of attempts to seize power within a group. Some people can achieve dominance over others by using threats and intimidation to create an atmosphere of fear and forced deference. This is not the only way to become a leader. Responding empathically, helping others, and sharing valuable knowledge produces what has been called a prestigious leader, as opposed to the fear-inducing dominant leader.

Observing Joe and his fellow inmates, it was clear that dominance strategies were at play. These dynamics are well recognised in prison and there is a focus on the dominant leaders. Even so, narrowing attention down to certain individuals ignores the broader setting in which these micro-interactions take place.

What makes the prison environment promote dominance over prestige dynamics? Not only does one group (made up of prison guards) have rights and privileges that the other group (made up of prisoners) does not have, but the prison guards are also given the means to control the prisoners. One of the most famous experiments in the history of psychological research was presented as evidence that the role people are assigned can have dramatic effects on their behaviour. Philip Zimbardo randomly allocated a group of students to one of two roles, that of either a prisoner or a guard. He then watched a scenario unfold that was so nightmarish that the experiment had to be stopped prematurely. Those assigned to the guard roles began showing brutal and sadistic behaviour towards the students in prisoner roles, who responded by becoming more submissive. Despite the column inches that have been devoted to the Stanford Prison Experiment in both the academic and popular press, subsequent analysis of the study design and attempts to replicate it have cast serious doubt over the validity of the original conclusions of the study. One research group subsequently ran parallel studies in which rules taken from actual prisons were compared with more liberal regimes. The hostility between prisoners and guards that emerged in the study mimicking a standard prison was not seen in the comparison studies, which adopted different regimes. The nature of the interactions was not just a feature of the role assigned, it also depended on the type of regime in which the interactions took place. Is the way that status is acquired in prison a result of the presence of some people with bullying tendencies? Or is it that certain traits are selected by the social environment of prisons that tend to authorise dominance interactions?

On the way down the corridor to the interview, Joe asked, 'What's this about, boss? Am I getting shipped out?' Unaware that he was about to see a psychiatrist, he suspected that this was the routine medical assessment prior to transfer to another prison. I told him he was not being moved and I was seeing him to review his medication. 'Yeah, about time,' he replied. 'Dr Richards, you know him, don't you, he said it's official, I'm hyperactive. When I told me ma you stopped me meds, she was bouncing. She's been on to my solicitors. Are you going to put me back on it?' We were now in the interview room and pulling our seats up to a small unsteady table.

I explained that the meeting would stretch over two assessments and I would not be able to say anything about diagnosis or medication until the whole assessment was complete. First, I wanted to get a broad overview. How old was he? What was his sentence? What was the offence? When was he due for release? Joe told me that he was twenty-nine and he was serving an eight-year prison sentence for manslaughter. He could be considered for release in eighteen months. The offence Joe was serving time for involved an encounter between two groups of youths that had quickly escalated. It was the availability of a weapon that turned a brawl into a homicide.

Knife crime is a particular concern in the UK. The decline in the UK's homicide rate from the early years of this century went into reversal in 2015, and use of bladed weapons has been held up as a major cause of the recent increase in violent deaths. The social issues that fuel this kind of crime are complex, but though this feels like a very contemporary problem, youth violence, gang violence and knife crime have always been present in society. For evidence of that, one might look to one of William Shakespeare's most famous tragedies: *Romeo and Juliet*.

Although a theatrical rendition of Act 3, Scene 1 of this play may seem a far cry from current day episodes of street violence, to me the similarities are obvious. On a swelteringly hot day, Benvolio and Mercutio, two young men from the Montague family, are aimlessly wandering the streets of Shakespeare's Verona. Mindful of the hair-trigger temper of Mercutio, and the fact there is a good chance they will come across their rivals, the Capulets, Benvolio wants to head back home. The feud between these two groups has been long-running, much to the frustration of the residents of the area. Locals without allegiance to one group or the other have even previously intervened physically to stop the violence, but this has done nothing to dim the factional tension being played out across their neighbourhood, a fact that is established in the opening scene of the play:

Gregory [a Capulet]:	I will frown as I pass by, and let them take it as they list.
Sampson [a Capulet]:	Nay, as they dare. I will bite my thumb at them; which is a disgrace to them, if they bear it.

Enter ABRAHAM and BALTHASAR [Montagues]

Abraham:	Do you bite your thumb at us, sir?
Sampson:	I do bite my thumb, sir.
Abraham:	Do you bite your thumb at us, sir?
Sampson [Aside to Gregory]:	Is the law of our side, if I say ay?
Gregory:	No.
Sampson:	No, sir, I do not bite my thumb at you, sir, but I bite my thumb, sir.

Benvolio's fears are realised when a small number of Capulet men come their way, and almost immediately the fiery-tempered member of the duo locks horns with the cocky leader of the other group:

Tybalt:	Gentlemen, good den: a word with one of you.
Mercutio:	And but one word with one of us? Couple it with something; make it a word and a blow.
Tybalt:	You shall find me apt enough to that, sir, an you will give me occasion.

The tense stand-off is not helped when Romeo arrives. Rather than joining the fray, Romeo, who is disinclined to fight because he has struck up a romantic attachment to Juliet, tries to de-escalate the situation, and tells Tybalt that he feels love for the Capulet name, which sounds to Mercutio like a betrayal, 'O calm, dishonourable, vile submission!' Their argument suddenly becomes more dangerous by the appearance of a blade. During a brief and frantic scuffle, Mercutio is stabbed and dies at the scene.

This episode shows how passing encounters between groups of young adult male rivals have the potential to erupt into aggression, and then to become even more dangerous if there is a weapon to hand. The presence of onlookers can fan the flames of aggression since the loss of face is so immediate. Benvolio's advice that 'for now, these hot days, is the mad blood stirring', is in fact supported by research. Higher ambient temperatures have been found to be associated with increased levels of aggression. Recorded more than four centuries ago, Shakespeare is describing a type of clash that was not uncommon in Elizabethan England. When Shakespeare wrote *Romeo and Juliet* the rate of homicide was still over ten times that during the middle of the twentieth century. Homicide rates continued to fall, until, from the early 1960s, the direction of the curve changed and violence rates headed upwards. Even so, it is worth noting that even at its peak the homicide rate in England and Wales of 1.8 per 100,000 people in 2003 – a year that included 173 victims of Dr Harold Shipman – was at least a twentieth of the peak of the European average in the Middle Ages. And yet, reading Shakespeare's depiction of gang violence resonates with the kinds of stories I hear from young male patients all the time.

From everything I had read about Joe in his medical records, I was sure that there would be enough 'yes' responses to reach the threshold for a diagnosis, but I would be left no more satisfied that he had ADHD than I had been after reading the other doctor's assessment letter. I wanted to understand him, not just to identify symptoms. I warned Joe that the assessment may not be what he was expecting. It was, I continued, going to involve what may seem like a general discussion about many aspects of his life. Fortunately, although Joe was eager to restart the medication, he also enjoyed talking. In his own words, he had 'the gift of the gab'.

I began by asking him about important people in his life and the parts they had played. When he told me about his close relatives, I sketched out a family tree to check that I had got it right. His mother was the most important person to him. 'She has always been there for me.' She had visited only a few days before. 'She's had a hard life. It's made her tough.' He did not have strong feelings either way for his father. His parents had never formally separated, but his father was not much of a presence, having fallen into drug addiction when Joe was about eight years old, and thereafter was often away in prison. The prison sentences were short – mostly for shoplifting to fund his habit. In the days or weeks after release, he would sometimes turn up at the house, but then he would disappear as the pull of a supply of drugs was something he could not resist. Joe got used to not thinking about him. His mother did not remarry or, as far as Joe knew, form another serious relationship; Joe said to me that he would not allow it.

While still in junior school, the absence of his father left a patri-archal mantle that Joe thought he should take on. Even before he could clearly articulate why, he felt that he should protect his mother from other men. He recalled that they were put off because of his behaviour. He would 'chase them out'. He spoke also in terms of defending the family's reputation. His father's heroin addiction became the butt of cruel jibes about him and his family, but Joe's readiness to resort to aggression soon dissuaded children from teasing him about this or about anything at all. It seemed to have the opposite effect on one adult in the neigh-bourhood. Probably spurred on by seeing Joe's overreaction, this man seemed to take pleasure in winding him up. If he saw Joe in passing, he would call out that he was the son of a 'smackhead'. The power of heroin over an addict's life meant that they risked losing everything, even their own self-respect. Joe's *raison d'être* was respect. Interestingly the man who taunted Joe came from a family that Joe considered to be a rival clan to his own.

Family was an important part of Joe's life. He had two sisters and, even though one was eighteen months his senior, he thought it his duty to look out for them when he was still a child. Now, they both had their own children, all four of whom worshipped him. His mother was one of five children and most of his aunties, uncles and their children lived in the same part of the same city; some were in the same prison where I was meeting him.

The discussion moved on to his experience of school. In his own way he stamped his authority on his peers there. A physically bigger boy joined the school when Joe was ten. He brought with him a reputation that threatened Joe's hard-earned position. In this final year of the primary school, Joe was dominant not just in his year, but over all the boys in the school. It did not matter that the new boy was bigger and may have been stronger; Joe could not contemplate backing down and he was prepared to go further than most. It remained the case, even as an adult, that if he was facing someone who could physically overpower him, he would pick up any available object to use as a makeshift weapon. The new challenger in primary school learned of Joe's unrestraint when he limped away from the inevitable confrontation with a stab wound from a sharp pencil that Joe had thrust into his thigh. A point was emphatically made not just to this rival, but also to anyone who was considering trying to topple him.

I wondered how Joe would explain the path his life had taken and so asked him. Without hesitation, he started by talking about the area where he was brought up. I had already noticed during our discussion that if he had reason to specifically mention the district, he marked the name with pride. He gave the impression that it was part of his developing identity. For all his fondness for his home area, he often described it as rough and poor. To him, the area was as distinct from other areas of equal deprivation in the city as it was from the more affluent areas. But the better-off parts of the city did not seem to interest him. The other deprived areas were the territories of his rivals. It was as if, much like bearing the name Montague or Capulet, being born on the other side of an arbitrary dividing line was enough to make someone an enemy.

In 1970 a paper described a University of Bristol experiment in which a group of forty-eight teenage boys from a local school were shown paintings by the two abstract artists Wassily Kandinsky and Paul Klee. Without knowing the identity of the artists, they were asked to express a preference between a series of six pairs of paintings by two 'foreign painters'. Afterwards they were taken to one side and each boy was told who they had preferred.

In fact, although the groups were labelled as Klee and Kandinsky, the boys were randomly assigned to each group; it was nothing to do with their preference. They were informed that, as a reward for taking part, money was to be given out among the boys and they had a say in how this money would be distributed. Separated from each other in individual booths, the boys were given a booklet to mark how much money would go to other boys. The only means of identification of the others was whether they were labelled as being in the Klee or Kandinsky group.

After collecting up the booklets and collating the marks, the results showed that the boys systematically gave more money to those who were in the group with the same name as them. It was particularly interesting that they seemed prepared to give less to their own group if it meant that they could maximise the difference between the two groups in favour of their own. The researchers had set out to minimise the actual difference between the groups. In making their decisions, the boys could not have been thinking about previous connections with their peers because they did not know who was in which group. There was no reason to believe that these groups would have a shared future. Simply identifying oneself as part of a group appeared to activate psychological processes that cause us to want our group to be better than another group.

The findings of this study, which have been replicated hundreds of times, were the foundation of what became known as the social identity theory. This theory showed that our sense of who we are is not just a matter of our personal and idiosyncratic traits: our identity is also defined through the groups we feel part of, such as being male, European, of Indian descent, a doctor, a psychiatrist and a supporter of Liverpool Football Club. The psychological processes leading us to assume membership of certain groups include a tendency to immediately see differences between us and members of the 'opposing' groups.

Unlike the Klee or Kandinsky groups, the people in the community that Joe spent time with did have a shared history and a sense of a shared future, which strengthened their bonds over and above being part of a group with a geographical label. Some of what Joe told me illustrated that this label as an in-group marker still had its own power. If he learned that someone who had previously been a stranger to him was from the same area, he described developing an immediate willingness to include them. While not as clearly defined as the one Shakespeare demarcated between the Capulets and the Montagues, family allegiances were also a factor in assignment to Joe's in- and out-groups. Joe's group of mates included members of some families and excluded members of other families. The bad blood sometimes stretched back to past generations. Joe spoke about a collective memory of a spate of tit-for-tat violence between his family and another local family in his parents' generation.

The more I talked to Joe, the more I sensed that he was able to make connections between his life circumstances and his lifestyle. This did not mean he saw himself as a victim of those circumstances. 'Everything I did was my own choice,' he told me. What then influenced his choices to commit crime? 'We saw older lads with the nice things, the clothes, the girls, some had cars. We looked up to the older lads.' I asked how he knew about the route to their success. 'On the park, you'd hear them talking. They'd get us to do some running for them and chuck us a tenner.' While still in primary school, Joe was playing his part in this criminal economy. It was an apprenticeship for a career pathway limited by a lack of more conventional opportunities, and one that even when he was young Joe recognised. 'Where I grew up, you had to be a football player, or win the lottery . . . or be a drug dealer . . . the easiest is to be a drug dealer.'

Although the outcome of extensive research has demonstrated the influence of broad social conditions on criminal behaviour, these conditions alone are not sufficient to turn someone into a criminal. Joe knew that many of his childhood peers from the same area had not ended up where he had or even got close to it. Those that did, he explained, often also came from a household where the mother was trying single-handedly to bring up her children. To him it was enough that she had lovingly nurtured him and his three sisters through their younger years and continued to maintain a home where they always felt safe and welcome to return. He thought that he was probably in a minority by virtue of being so independent of parental rules by early adolescence. There seemed to be an unspoken agreement with his mother that suited them both: she did not have him under her feet and he was able to do what he wanted.

By the time he was eleven and moving to the senior school, Joe was part of a group of youngsters that would wander the streets of their area. To others they looked like a gang, loitering in certain locations or moving in packs. They had an unofficial uniform of branded sportswear. The use of hoods, caps and scarves made individual identification difficult. For some members of the group, including Joe, the intimidating impression was deserved. Yet to Joe they were just a group of mates. There was a fluidity to the membership and no clear hierarchy. I asked about the members of the group now. Because of their common fate, he knew more about those that continued getting into trouble. On reflection, he could see that he was probably part of a minority who went on to become involved in serious offences. He could think of some he knew who had recently 'settled down'. Given that he did not know about the remainder, he assumed that they had also largely left their delinquent days behind them.

Psychiatrists identified a paradoxical pattern of criminality well before they had an explanation for it. It may not be surprising to find that almost all antisocial adults begin behaving antisocially as children. But most antisocial children do not grow up into anti-social adults. So, what happens to some antisocial children that doesn't happen to the majority? Because early studies of antisocial behaviour took place either in child clinics or adult prisons, the critical intervening period of development was neglected. This is the very period when antisocial behaviour reaches its peak.

In the 1990s a new approach in the study of antisocial behav-iour became popular. Rather than taking snapshots of young people at different ages, researchers began tracking the same peo-ple through time. The gold-standard design involved identifying newborns who were representative of the general population and then following them up as they aged. Among academics in the burgeoning field of developmental psychopathology, a city on the South Island of New Zealand acquired an iconic status. The Dunedin Study was set up to investigate child health and development by identifying a birth cohort and assessing them again when they were three years old. The cohort, which is still being followed up, is now made up of people in their late forties.

Professor Terrie Moffitt, an American psychologist who joined the Dunedin Study team, was interested in studying delinquency. She proposed a developmental taxonomy for offenders that hundreds of subsequent studies have verified. Research into delinquency has shown that the proportion of adolescents who have committed some sort of antisocial behav-iour is so common that it should not be viewed as abnormal. It is not a coincidence that adolescence is the period in which we are most likely to violate social norms and the rights of others: Moffitt highlighted the lag between biological maturation in early teenage years and social independence in late teenage years – essentially, the body reaches maturity before the brain does. While stuck in this maturity gap, adolescents become impatient for the privileges of adulthood and some cross boundaries of wider social norms to get them.

By illuminating brain functioning, neurobiological studies have given us a better idea of how the minds of adolescents make them more inclined to transgress into socially proscribed activities. From early teenage years, novel and exiting stimuli become particularly attractive. The resulting desire to seek out new sensations peaks in mid-adolescence and then declines into adulthood.

There are good reasons for the adolescent spike in sensation-seeking. While early psychological development is promoted by the tight bond between the child and their caregivers, long-term success requires individuals to eventually achieve autonomy. Rather than falling off a precipice of care, the drawn-out period of relatively safe experimentation allows learning of new skills for future independence. This explains why Joe's friendship group was at its largest when he was fourteen or fifteen years old. There was a surplus of youngsters wanting to feel the excitement of breaking the rules.

Although large numbers of teenagers behave antisocially the overwhelming majority do not graduate into persistent criminals. Most possess the personal characteristics, and have sufficiently good family support, to emerge from adolescence not only more able to survive independently but to do so in a pro-social way. Moffitt labelled the type of antisocial behaviour shown by the majority of teenagers as adolescence-limited. But hidden within the large group of adolescent offenders is a tiny minority whose behaviour does not improve in adulthood (this minority were labelled the 'life-course-persistent offenders'). When the researchers looked back at the assessments of these individuals as young children, even then they were different.

Grouping humans by certain characteristics can be helpful to understand behaviour. But whether the group is defined by diagnostic criteria or behaviour patterns over time, we need to guard against assuming that the members of each group are alike in all respects. Just like patients with the same diagnosis can be different, so individuals on the life-course-persistent pathway of offending vary considerably.

Joe fitted the life-course-persistent offending pattern. As well as the stabbing incident at school, he admitted he was a 'little bastard' at home and his notoriety for shoplifting was acquired while still young. But despite being at the more extreme end of the spectrum of antisocial behaviour, Joe did not find himself isolated or excluded. He was socialised into a group, but it was a group who also seemed to have antisocial inclinations.

I had put off asking specific ADHD questions. Narrow questions about this or that behaviour or symptom tend to elicit yes or no answers. When examples of the behaviour or symptom are sought to back up a 'yes' response, the patient may be more motivated to come up with ones that support their original response, even if they aren't particularly representative of their everyday behaviour. And, even if the examples are representative, they are just descriptions suspended from the wider explanatory context. I give more weight to characteristic features that I appear to stumble upon. In reality, I am steering the interview towards topics that may throw up such features, but the information gathered is more valuable to my assessment if the patient experiences the dialogue as conversational rather than as a series of rapid-fire questions.

The first part of our meeting had thrown up behaviour patterns that were potential clues for an ADHD diagnosis. In class Joe was easily bored and often disruptive. His first impulse was to react against instructions issued by his teachers. He didn't acknowledge the deadlines they set, never mind manage to meet them. If he did complete his homework, which was rare, he more often than not forgot to take it in. Being out and about was always his preference. Running through the activities he was drawn to, there was definitely a theme of behaviours that are associated with ADHD.

Risk-taking is the term used, but Joe didn't appreciate the risk. That was why he was able to go further than his friends. When playing 'chicken', he could outwait most others before the last-minute dash across the path of the oncoming car or train. Not being deterred by the more fragile branches in a tree meant he could climb higher than his peers. 'They thought I was a psycho,' he said. Partly it was the absence of fear but there was also an emotional pull: 'The pure adrenaline of it, you can't beat it.'

Being attracted to the experience of danger is not abnormal. Some people even pay for it. Examples of this so-called benign masochism include eating hot chillies, watching horror films, skiing off-piste and rock climbing. Whether it involves simulated danger or taking calculated risks, these types of activities allow for comparatively safe testing of our abilities and responses. We are then better prepared to tackle a real threat should it arise. But Joe's risk/safety gauge was more askew than most; the risks he was taking were just that: risks.

Combining Joe's unflinching response to threat with an unwavering commitment to defend his reputation made aggression almost inevitable. He said: 'You never show your fear . . . I'd never back down . . . I'd rather get knocked out . . . I've got no fear.' Unsurprisingly, there were previous violent offences on Joe's record, but the record did not reflect the extent of his past violence. He and his rival combatants subscribed to a code according to which it was shameful to involve the police.

The offence for which he was now serving his longest prison sentence only really stood out from his previous violent behaviour on account of the outcome. One of the participants in this violent encounter died. 'Me and me mate were walking through the park. There was a group of lads. I recognised one of them.

I knew there was going to be trouble.' At this, Joe exaggerated a nonchalant shrug to show me he was unconcerned by this prospect. 'There were more of them. Four against two. Two on two no problem, but we kept our heads down and kept going. We weren't looking for trouble, but if someone brings it to us . . .'

As Joe explained, Rich, his friend, 'flashed his blade'. Joe acted out lifting the edge of his shirt. He was showing me that Rich had a knife in the waistband of his trousers. If they had seen it, the group of four was not put off. They began following Joe and Rich, who decided to stand their ground. Rich went to take out his knife just before they came to blows. It was knocked from his hand almost straight away. Joe told me that while he was holding off two of them, he could tell Rich was being overpowered. He took a chance to pick up the knife. The biggest of the four turned towards Joe and asked, 'What the fuck are you going to do with that?' Joe said that the man ignored his warning to stand back. 'I just flicked it out to keep him away. He walked onto it. It went straight through his heart.'

Wrapping up the discussion, I asked Joe how he came to have the previous ADHD assessment. He had heard about Dr Roberts's clinic from a couple of prisoners on his wing. His mother had told him that she had seen similarities between him and a case she had read about in a magazine. When he mentioned the assessment clinic in the prison, she kept on at him about getting an assessment. She even asked his solicitors to write to the prison doctor.

The conventional view of ADHD is that it is a behavioural disorder caused by an as yet undefined brain dysfunction. According to this view, the assessing psychiatrist's role is to determine whether the patient has this dysfunction. To do this, the psychiatrist searches for symptoms from a predefined list, which are said to be the diagnostic criteria.

But there is a problem: how do we know that we have the correct diagnostic criteria? We can't check them against the brain dysfunction because we don't know what it is. The researchers trying to find it start by looking at the patients who have the diagnosis. This means they start by identifying a group of people who have in common a list on which some of their experiences appear. It does not matter if they have no experiences in common or if they also have other experiences that appear on completely different diagnostic lists; the fact that there are a certain number of experiences that feature on the ADHD list is enough to credit them with the ADHD brain dysfunction. By grouping such a mix of people together it should not come as a shock to the researchers that a specific ADHD brain dysfunction has proved elusive.

Even a casual glance at scientific papers about the origins of ADHD shows a consensus among experts that when all the studies are looked at a single neurochemical or neuronal pathways pattern linked to the diagnosis has not been found. I am not questioning that there is a relationship between the functioning of our brains and our experience of the environment or our response to it. My point is that this type of medical model is flawed on two levels. Firstly, it gives the impression that psychiatric diagnoses are equivalent to physical ones. Secondly, it feeds a faith in unifying biological explanations for our experiences.

Whatever experiences Joe had during his life, he may always have been at the higher end of a scale of impulsiveness and risk-taking. Does that mean his experience of his father being absent and his response to that absence is irrelevant to who he is and how he behaves now? Likewise, should we immediately reject the possibility of lasting effects on the way he experiences, and responds to, how adults and peers behaved towards him and his impulsive risk-taking?

The weakness in the purely physical account of mental phenomena – the one that locates our behavioural differences in the mechanics of the brain – is on show in the most unlikely place. Academic papers about human behaviour written by neurobiologists are littered with terms that are not in themselves physical things. These important studies examine the physical structure and function of parts of the brain such as the prefrontal lobes butting up against our forehead, or the amygdalae buried away deep inside our heads. But to make their findings relevant to human behaviour, scientists have to talk about phenomena of the mind such as emotions, cognition, perceptions, memories and attention. Even if it becomes possible to identify the unique patterns of my brain function that correspond to all the different types of emotional experiences I have, it is still not possible to fully understand the emotions I experience. Some would argue that our experiences are epiphenomena – by-products of biology that have no role in themselves in how we behave. Whether that is true or not, for the time being it does not seem possible, even for those who reject the real-world validity of the mind, to be able to understand the brain without reference to it.

I was in a dilemma. There was a case, albeit not a completely clear-cut one, to consider medication, but I was not sure whether Joe had ever complied with it. He could describe neither the benefits, apart from in the vaguest of terms, nor any side effects. His being desperate to receive a prescription if he had not been taking it led me to suspect that he was trading the tablets. This medication is known as a stimulant, a class of drugs that also contains cocaine and illicit amphetamines. They can induce a euphoric 'high'. The likelihood was that, even if I persuaded the prison doctor to restart the prescription, Joe would continue to trade the tablets.

I thought that adopting a different frame of understanding would lead to a different conclusion. Joe had not railed against the system, he had adapted to it very well. He had the skills to maintain a high rank within his social groups, particularly in prison where the system depended on dominance dynamics more than prestige. There was limited opportunity to access a currency of any value, but when it arose he took it. In that environment he judged there was more to be gained from selling the medication than ingesting it.

Rather than declining to offer Joe the medication again, my view was that extra effort was needed if he was to receive help. At a weekly meeting of the prison health-care team, I presented a plan for Joe to take the medication. He would have to wait until the other patients on the wing had received their medication, then he could be closely supervised while he swallowed the tablet. I accepted the challenge from two nurses in the meeting that if he really wanted to he could hold the medication in his mouth and later spit it out to sell on. The eventual consensus was that it would not be worth his while going through this process every day. Having persuaded the prison staff, I still did not know whether Joe would agree to it. To my surprise he did, if only, I wondered, perhaps to keep his mother happy.

In my clinic over the next few months I monitored Joe's response while gradually increasing the dose. If he told me there was a dramatic improvement then there could be two explanations: one was that he was genuinely benefiting from it, the other was that he was able to get round the monitoring regime and continued to sell the tablets. What he actually said persuaded me that he was probably taking it. It was also the type of feedback that is more common than either the ADHD promoters or naysayers would lead us to believe.

'I think it's helping, but I'm not sure,' he said. I pushed him for something more specific. 'You said it may help my concentration. Maybe I'm not all over the place as much.' He was certainly not singing its praises. Neither was he rejecting positive effects out of hand. I asked what his mother thought. 'She's set on me staying on it.' Was this because she had seen a difference? 'Not that, but she's always thought I needed it and told me it will take time to work. I think she thinks it will stop me coming back to prison. It breaks her heart.' What did Joe think? 'Why would it stop me coming back? I'm not planning to.' With a slight smile, he added, 'But I never do!'

We continued in this vein. For each of the possible signs of improvement, he said there might have been a change. I did not feel he was trying hard to convince me. It was himself that he appeared to want to convince, but he was struggling. At the end of this review, I was left undecided, but I was helped in my decision by Joe, who decided that he didn't really like taking medication, particularly if he wasn't sure if it was working.

Whatever the diagnosis and whoever is doing the prescribing, over the years I have seen different responses. Some patients unequivocally benefit from the medication. Some see absolutely no change, but have been introduced to a whole load of new problems courtesy of the medication's side effects. Between these extremes there is a large group like Joe. If there is a change, it is not dramatic and it is difficult to tell whether it is due to the medication or natural fluctuations in behaviour patterns.

Our understanding of psychiatric conditions comes largely from research studies that are so selective that their subjects don't look like patients in real-world clinics – certainly not like most of the patients I see in prison clinics. The diagnostic approach does not account for the possibilities that there are multiple psychological routes to the same behaviour or symptom, or that the same underlying brain dysfunction may produce vastly different behaviours and symptoms.

I would never know how much of Joe's impulsivity was being driven by an immutable biological defect. Accepting that he was born with a tendency towards risk-taking does not preclude the possibility that he was more likely to express this tendency in dangerous and antisocial ways because of the circumstances of his life. Could the absence of a dependable and positive adult male influence have had wider effects? He had described a pressure to take what he saw as an adult male role well before it should have been expected of him. Assuming that there was no one else that had his back, he could not risk the consequences for him or his family of backing down. Needing to become, as he believed he did, a leader at such a young age – at an age before he had learned sufficient skills and acquired sufficient knowledge to use prestige tactics – meant that a dominant style became embedded early. Such a style was bound to pit him against authority whether imposed by teachers or other servants of the state. The greater freedom given to him meant that there were fewer limits to experimenting with independence. It also came with more opportunities to learn about an achievable way to succeed against the disadvantageous odds given to him by the accident of where he was born. The successful roles were modelled to him by older boys who had on show the trappings of their criminal activity. As someone who was more prepared to take risks, he turned out to be an enthusiastic pupil.

As the pre-eminent way of understanding mental health problems, many diagnoses give succour to the idea that there are defined conditions, each caused by a specific brain dysfunction, each of which in turn has its own specific cure. Joe was no more the product of his biology than he was a victim of his circumstances. There had been a continuous two-way interaction between him and his environment. As he changed over time, he reacted to his environment differently and the way it responded to him changed. He would continue to evolve.

5

Alex

O N MY WAY to give evidence in court, I often talk to myself. This is my preparatory ritual that allows me to transpose my concept-based ideas into meaningful sentences arranged in a sensible sequence. Within the privacy of my car, exaggerating the affectations of an imagined barrister, I ask Dr Nathan for a summary of his opinion. Resuming my own identity, I tell the imaginary jury about my main conclusions. The next step is the critical part of the preparation. I adopt the character of a cross-examining barrister to test the potential flaws in my opinion.

What made this spring Friday morning unusual was that I was en route to court without knowing why and was thus completely unprepared. The outcome of the trial at hand was probably going to hang on a fairly narrow psychiatric issue, and unless I knew what that was, I could not subject my evidence to the usual scrutiny.

Three days earlier, among the unmanageable torrent of emails dropping into my inbox, the heading of one – R v Stephens – had caught my attention. A criminal case. Criminal charges are prosecuted by the Crown, denoted by 'R' for Regina.

I read in the body of the email from my secretary that she had taken a call from a police constable. There was a court hearing that day and they urgently needed to know when I would be available to attend a trial later in the week. There were no more details. Cryptically, the officer had said that a new barrister for the defence had taken over. Could I call the officer back? I could not place the name 'Stephens'.

If my attendance at a criminal court is required it is often to offer psychiatric advice about the sentence. To reach the point of sentencing, the defendant has either pleaded guilty, or been found guilty at the conclusion of the trial. Offenders in need of psychiatric treatment in hospital can be sentenced to an order mandating that treatment as an alternative to incarceration in prison. A minority of offenders due to be sentenced to hospital treatment may pose such a high risk of harm to others that additional safeguards need to be imposed. In this case, the judge is able to apply special restrictions limiting the power of the doctor in the hospital to make decisions independently. Before adding such restrictions, the judge must hear in person from a psychiatrist.

Requests to give evidence during the trial itself are less common. Murder trials are rarer occurrences, but there is a greater chance of being called to give evidence. A lot more is at stake. A conviction for murder automatically leads to a life sentence. The definition of insanity agreed following M'Naghten's trial sets the bar too high for most mentally ill offenders. Diminished responsibility, a defence only available to a charge of murder, has wider applicability, though it is not a full defence and so it does not lead to acquittal. If a defendant's responsibility is deemed to be diminished, then the conviction is manslaughter rather than murder. Sentencing for manslaughter leaves sentencing discretion with the judge. It does not rule out the possibility of a life sentence, but it is not inevitable, and depending on the case the judge could impose a sentence of hospital admission, a finite sentence or even a community order. Diminished responsibility relies on evidence about the defendant's state of mind at the time of the incident and thus calls for a psychiatric assessment.

The introduction of this defence to English law in 1957 was in response to the growing queasiness about the sentence that was mandatory for murder: the death penalty. A 25-year-old Welshman was one such convict. In the early months of 1950, Timothy Evans was held in Pentonville Prison awaiting the hangman's noose. Dr Coates, the principal medical officer at the prison, administered tests that led him to pronounce that Evans had a mental age of ten and a half years. In the November of the previous year, Timothy Evans had walked into a police station in Merthyr Tydfil and told the bemused officers that he had disposed of his wife's body. He volunteered to make a statement, but as he couldn't read or write, the officers would have to transcribe what he said. According to this statement, about three weeks earlier Evans's wife, Beryl, had threatened to take steps to abort the pregnancy of their second child; a course of action that at the time was both illegal and dangerous.

The following day, during his shift as a van driver, Evans was sitting in a transport cafe when another customer sat close by asked him why he looked out of sorts. On hearing about Evans's domestic problems, this unnamed traveller left the cafe briefly and returned with a brown paper parcel. A small bottle therein contained a preparation that the man advised Evans to give to his wife. The man said this would do the job, which Evans understood to be a reference to abortion. That evening Beryl found the bottle and demanded to know what it was. Evans told her, but also cautioned her against taking it. He returned home after the next day's work to find the house in darkness and Beryl unresponsive in bed. He explained in his statement how, in the dark hours of the night, he took her lifeless body down the stairs and pushed her into the drain outside the house. Shortly thereafter, he left London to return to his hometown in the Welsh valleys. He seemed evasive on the question of the whereabouts of his baby daughter, and in quick succession gave contradictory accounts before settling on the claim that he had left her with a neighbour.

Evans matched the profile of a domestic abuser. He was known to have a short temper and to be a heavy drinker. From the statements later obtained by the police it was learned that Evans had jealously slapped his wife and then made a scene at her workplace leading to her dismissal. Rows between the couple in which Evans threatened Beryl had been witnessed. A wider question about his trustworthiness was suggested by the reputation he had in his family for lying. A stolen briefcase and newspaper cuttings about another murder were found in his flat.

Within minutes of receiving Evans's confession, a Welsh police officer telephoned his London colleagues. They dispatched officers to the house of the alleged crime. Although the gentrification of Notting Hill in the late twentieth century has made the postcode exclusive, in the 1940s the squalid streets were typified by the multi-occupancy tenancies where the Evans family had lived. In those first few hours of the investigation, a shadow of doubt was cast over Evans's testimony when the officers attending the scene found that, in order to access the drain, it took three officers working in unison to lift the heavy cover. Evans could not have done this alone. And, crucially, no body was found in the drain.

After receiving this update, the Welsh police questioned Evans again. Under pressure from the officer, he changed his story. In a second statement, he accused the male occupant of the ground-floor flat of having a hand in his wife's death. He removed the transport cafe encounter from this statement and replaced it with an allegation that his neighbour had botched the abortion of his wife's pregnancy. He claimed that he did not know where her body was because the neighbour had offered to remove it.

Two days after he had turned himself in, Evans was conveyed under guard to London. Earlier that day, the police had found the bodies of Beryl and her daughter wrapped up and hidden in an outbuilding behind the house where the Evanses lived. On learning of this discovery, the police recorded that Evans then admitted to the killing by strangulation of both his wife and daughter. At his trial, the defence restated Evans's claim in his second statement that his neighbour was responsible, but they failed to convince the jury and, on 13 January 1950, Evans was found guilty of murder at the Old Bailey. A panel of three medical luminaries examined Evans to see if there was any reason he should not be executed. Despite the evidence of intellectual impairment presented to the panel, they did not find any medical reason why the death sentence should not be carried out and so, on 9 March 1950 at Pentonville Prison, Timothy Evans was executed by hanging.

This case could have been elevated to a cause célèbre for abolishing the death penalty on account of Evans's patent mental vulnerability. But its notoriety rested on a far more rudimentary problem: Evans was not guilty.

Beresford Brown was a Jamaican jazz musician who, along with compatriots, travelled to London following an invitation by the British government for people to come to fill the severe labour shortages in the aftermath of the Second World War. In search of cheap accommodation many of the immigrants gravitated to Notting Hill and Brown moved into the house where, three years earlier, Beryl Evans had been murdered. Within days of moving in, Brown was fixing a bracket to the kitchen wall when, pulling at some wallpaper, he found a concealed door of a cupboard. Peering in, he saw the naked back of a human body. He immediately called the police, who made the grisly discovery of three female bodies stuffed into the space. A further search of the property revealed another female body under the floorboards of the front room and the remains of two other women buried in the garden.

Until his disappearance four days before, the occupant of the flat where the bodies were found was one John Christie, the man identified in Timothy Evans's second statement as being Evans's neighbour. On 31 March 1953, a dishevelled John Christie was apprehended on the embankment of the Thames. He eventually admitted to killing all the women whose bodies were found at 10 Rillington Place. He also admitted responsibility for the death of Beryl Evans.

James Chuter Ede, the Home Secretary, who approved the execution of Timothy Evans, came to believe his decision had been wrong and committed himself to the cause of abolishing the death penalty. Although the repeated efforts to pass a law for abolition were unsuccessful during the 1950s, out of the debate came the compromise that was the Homicide Act 1957. The English lawmakers looked to Scottish law, where the concept of diminished responsibility had had a tradition stretching back to the 1830s. Once the Homicide Act 1957 was enacted, the defence of diminished responsibility became available to English and Welsh defendants. The success of the defence rested on a finding that the defendant's responsibility was substantially impaired because of an abnormality of the mind. The death penalty remained a possibility until 1965 when it was finally abolished as a punishment for murder.

At the point of signing off my report, the familiarity I have with the offender's life story feels strong; as if it will endure. More often than not, it quickly fades because there is no reason to rehearse the details. The point of completing the report is usually the last time I am knowingly connected to that individual. But still, I was unsurprised that the name Stephens did not trigger a memory of an individual or an offence. I ran through recent assessments in homicide cases. The last murder report I could recall was for a case in which a man had been stabbed a few streets away from a nightclub. To the door staff he had been a recurrent but low-level nuisance for much of the night. Many of the revellers into whom he stumbled felt that there was more deliberate intent to his random unsteadiness than was warranted. Some asked the staff to deal with him before they did; others directly confronted him. His drunkenness did nothing to dampen his barbed wit. With a few words he was able to put down his challengers, but to most it was clear that he was no real threat. As he delivered the punchline, he was stepping away, dropping his shoulders and showing his palms, signalling submission. Why would one of the club-goers have left prematurely, darted home for a kitchen knife and come back to stab a man who had been described as a drunken but harmless fool?

Once I began reconstructing the offence in my mind, I felt surer that Alex Stephens and the nightclub attacker were one and the same. My memory of defendants in criminal cases tends to be built around the offence. Having not heard anything in the three months since sending off my report, I had assumed that the matter had been concluded. I remembered that there were some minor differences of opinion between me and the other psychiatrist, but we were as one on the central issue of whether we supported a defence of diminished responsibility. There was no abnormality of mental functioning, we agreed. Without this, there is no defence, and so I had assumed that the accused was likely to have entered a guilty plea, thereby removing the need for a trial.

I called the police officer, who launched straight into a desperate plea for my availability to attend court that week. I wanted to ask why it was so last-minute, but I sensed from his insistent tone that we would not be able to discuss matters until we had resolved the issue of my availability. He would have known that this was an unreasonably last-minute request; court attendance is usually fixed well in advance. I told him that I could be available at the Crown Court in the morning, as long as my evidence was dealt with early. He was audibly relieved.

I asked him for more details on the case. He did not say as much, but it became clear as we spoke that he had only been on the margins of the prosecution team's discussion. He had picked up that a new defence barrister would bring a change of tactic. But he was as much in the dark as me about the crucial detail: what the new tactic was. Were they even presenting a diminished responsibility defence? I wondered. The prosecution solicitor who set the original questions for me to answer in my report mentioned in passing that, as well as diminished responsibility, they would also need to prepare for a 'loss of control' defence.

Loss of control as a defence is a relatively new addition to English law. Although it first appeared in 2009, it is a reshaped version of the previous defence of provocation that was introduced alongside diminished responsibility in the 1957 Homicide Act. The success of the loss of control defence depends on persuading the jury that the defendant experienced an impairment of self-restraint due to 'a fear of serious violence or being seriously wronged'. Just like diminished responsibility, loss of control is known as a partial defence since it does not lead to acquittal.

Arriving at court that Friday feeling disconcertingly underprepared, I passed through the security check and reported to reception, from where I was taken to meet a Mr Roper and

Ms Rickett, the junior barrister. I recognised Mr Roper, but I couldn't recall us ever working on the same case. Mr Roper told me that he had read many of my reports, and gave an update on Alex's trial. The issue was diminished responsibility after all. Mr Roper explained that, although the odds of success were slim, the new defence barrister had concluded that it should at least be presented for the jury to consider. Before getting underway in court, Mr Roper needed to check that his understanding of my evidence was correct. He offered his summary and I deferentially corrected him on some minor points. Then he and Ms Rickett made their way to the court for the start of the day's proceedings and I was left alone in the room.

Twenty minutes passed before a court usher appeared and I was escorted to the court. As I entered the grandly proportioned room, absorbed in silently rehearsing my assessment, I suddenly felt the weight of expectation behind the eyes trained on me from all directions. I had to quickly get my bearings. The 'twelve good people and true' of the jury were in two tiered rows in a boxed-off area against the opposite wall. The judge was sat at ninety degrees on a raised platform to my left and at right angles to the jury. Facing him behind the first of three lines of extended desks stretching across the well of the court were the barristers. I looked in the direction where I knew the witness box should be: located directly opposite the jury.

Once in position in the witness box, I noticed that I was an uncomfortable distance from my report and the seat was set too high for me to fit my legs under the table. While I fumbled for the lever to lower the seat, the judge directed Mr Roper to begin his examination. In the customary way, Mr Roper asked me to confirm my full name and role. My seat dropped as far as it would go. I introduced myself and I listed my NHS and academic positions. My knees would still not squeeze under the table. Mr Roper then followed convention with his introductory questions, which invited only brief responses.

'How long did you interview Stephens for?'

'Approximately four hours over two separate interviews,' I replied.

'Have you studied the witness statements?'

'Yes.'

'Have you read the transcript of the emergency services call?'

'Yes.'

'Have you read the defendant's offending record?'

'Yes.'

'You did not see the defendant's medical records?'

'No.'

'But you have seen a summary of them in Dr Lawton's report?'

'Yes, that's correct.'

This routine start to my evidence assures the jury that I am not just basing my opinion on what the defendant tells me. Expecting that the next phase of questioning would require my undivided attention, I gave up my efforts to adjust the seat. I dragged the microphone towards me, but to be heard I still had to lean forward awkwardly.

Mr Roper took me through my evidence. He would sometimes ask me to confirm his paraphrasing of a part of my report. At other times he would ask what the defendant had said in response to this question or that, expecting me to read short verbatim extracts from my report. It seems to me that this approach is preferred over me just reading out large tracts from my report to the jury, because that would be dull and overly technical. It also allows the barrister to be in control of the structure and delivery of the narrative. This was how my opinion that Stephens had suffered from alcohol use disorder was presented. With encouragement from Mr Roper

I explained that alcohol use disorder is the diagnostic term for a condition more generally known as alcoholism or alcohol dependence, and with further prompting I highlighted the key features that set alcohol use disorder apart from excessive but non-pathological drinking.

Mr Roper moved on to the issue of memory loss. 'You are aware that the defendant claims not to remember what happened at the material time? Is that what he told you?'

I agreed that this was the case.

'You have set out in your report the possible explanations for the memory loss which he claims?'

I agreed again.

'Would you explain to the court what those possible explanations are?'

I prepared to condense an hour's seminar into a handful of sentences.

'There is always a possibility that the perpetrator of a seriously violent offence falsely claims amnesia as they may perceive that there is some advantage to them doing so. This is feigned amnesia ...' In fact, it makes the job of assessing whether there is psychiatric support for a diminished responsibility defence more difficult, since the main access to the person's mental state at the time of the offence – their memory – is blank.

'... The second scenario that I think should be considered in a case such as this is that the loss of memory is due to alcohol. An alcohol blackout is a loss of memory that can occur in some people who have drunk excessive quantities of alcohol. Individuals who have a history of excessive drinking over a prolonged period may be more susceptible to alcohol blackouts. As well as feigned amnesia and alcohol-related amnesia, we know that a person who commits an act of serious violence may experience amnesia for psychological reasons such as the effects of emotional over-arousal on memory formation. The fourth explanation that I would usually consider is whether there was an acute mental illness and that in such a state a patient sometimes has phases of amnesia.'

Mr Roper thanked me and enquired which explanation I would favour.

'I have not found any evidence that he was mentally ill around this time, so I feel confident in excluding that. I find it difficult to distinguish which of the other three explanations is more likely. I cannot say for definite that the amnesia is feigned, but equally I cannot rule it out. The defendant has spoken about previous blackouts when drunk, so this is a possibility. If the amnesia was genuine, equally there may have been non-pathological psychological processes at play in addition to the effects of intoxication.'

'Would you mind explaining what you mean by non-pathological?' asked Mr Roper.

'I am using the term to distinguish a state of mind that might be unusual but not of clinical significance, from one that is clinically significant. By clinically significant, I mean a state of mind that occurs in a psychiatric illness. My assessment has not uncovered evidence of such a mental state.'

'To summarise for the benefit of the jury, am I correct in understanding that you think there was a mental illness that we would understand to be alcohol dependence, but you don't think there was an abnormality of mental functioning?'

I hesitated. 'Well, just to be clear, alcohol dependence is not conventionally considered to be a mental illness. It is listed in the diagnostic manuals, such as DSM-5*, and therefore falls under the broad category of mental disorder, but the term mental illness tends to be reserved for diagnoses such as clinical depression or schizophrenia and is not generally used for alcohol dependence. But either way, there is no evidence of abnormality of mental functioning.'

* The fifth edition of Diagnostic and Statistical Manual of Mental Disorders.

'You will know that an abnormality of mental functioning is necessary for diminished responsibility?'

'Yes, it is a requirement for this defence.'

'And there was no abnormality of mental functioning?'

'No, in my opinion there was not.'

'Thank you, Dr Nathan, please stay there.'

Mr Roper sat down and tipped his head to his right in the direction of Mr Haslett, the defence barrister, who got to his feet.

'We need to be careful, don't we, Dr Nathan? The question of diminished responsibility is for the jury and we should not usurp their role.'

Saying 'we' rather than 'you' was a positive sign. He didn't seem to be personalising the matter by choosing to present me as the outlier. It was too early to say whether this congenial approach would continue. Was he lulling me into a relaxed state in order to trip me up?

I agreed completely with his substantive point. Diminished responsibility is a legal, not a medical term. Its constituents, such as 'recognised medical condition' and 'abnormality of mental functioning', sound medical, but it is worth remembering that they are terms that do not appear in our texts about the psychiatric examination of the patient or in our diagnostic manuals. They are terms from a document that is drawn up by parliamentary draftsmen who articulate the consensus from a dialogue between politicians, civil servants and legal and medical experts. The concepts are not tested by medical research or refined by psychiatric review. A defendant dissatisfied with the outcome of the case can try to come up with a credible challenge to the way the law has been applied in his case. He can then ask a higher court to adjudicate on whether his challenge has merit or not. In this way the appeal courts provide clarification on how the legislation should be interpreted. Critically though, the arbiters of the definition of diminished responsibility are lawyers, not doctors.

Without hesitation, I concurred with Mr Haslett's statement that ultimately it was for the jury to decide on whether Stephens's responsibility was diminished.

'You are a psychiatrist?' asked Mr Haslett.

I agreed, wondering where this was heading.

'What does that mean?' he continued. I had never been asked this in court. I remained vigilant: he must have been building up to something.

'Psychiatry is a medical speciality in which we are concerned with an individual's mental health.'

He proceeded to present a series of truisms I could not disagree with. I affirmed my agreement after each.

'So you are firstly, if I might use the term, a proper doctor, and then you specialised in psychiatry?' 'You are heavily dependent on what the patient tells you?' 'Aside from scanning the brain to see if there is a degenerative condition, you cannot look into the mind in the way a surgeon can look at an X-ray of a broken leg?'

I explained that we do take into account other information. We observe the comportment of the patient. We compare what they say to what others have said about them. We study their medical notes if they are available. This additional information helps define an outline, but I reaffirmed my agreement with the point that we have to rely more than other doctors on the words of the patient to identify pathology, or what we call psychopathology.

The general thrust of the point for the jury to take away seemed to be that they should retain a certain level of independence of mind. To question the assumption that my role as an expert, with however many years of experience and a long list of letters trailing my name, means that my evidence should not be accepted unreservedly.

I agree wholeheartedly with this point, not just as it applies to my expert role, but as it does to my everyday practice. Our medical training encourages a belief that, in the way there is a broken leg for the surgeon to find, psychiatrists are in the business of finding discrete pathological entities. We are hampered, so the theory goes, by not having objective tests. This is true, but there is a more fundamental issue. The evidence for a discrete pathology hiding underneath each of the diagnostic labels is almost non-existent. Our labels are more the accidental product of history – adherence to notions developed in the nineteenth century and the first part of the twentieth century – than the result of empirical research. I am reminded of the call by the political forecaster Nate Silver, in his book *The Signal and the Noise*, for a constant questioning attitude to reach the most likely approximation of reality. He contrasts this probabilistic approach with that of the ideologue who stubbornly holds on to simple rules to make sense of data even if those rules don't stand up to empirical scrutiny.

Mr Haslett then began building the next pillar of his case. 'You have confirmed your opinion that the defendant was suffering from alcohol use disorder.' I thought he probably chose the official term rather than a colloquialism such as alcoholism as it emphasised the medical status of the problem. 'It has been termed a condition of denial. Would you agree?'

I didn't know whether I agreed or not. I was aware of the tactic where the expert is guided down a path so that each step did not seem unreasonable, only to realise too late that the end point was an unacceptable distance from any opinion they would hold. One might assume that experience would have given me the skills to rebut these tactics, but in fact experience had taught me not to get too caught up in tactics and has given me the confidence to go with the flow.

'I have not heard it described in that way, but I can see a point behind using a phrase like this.'

'The person afflicted with this condition is in denial?'

'Yes, denial of the problem is often present.'

'You have mentioned in your report the defendant's problem with temper control. You may know that the members of the jury have heard about this in the evidence presented to this court. It may be suggested that he is also in denial about the temper problems.' His intonation, if not his syntax, invited a response.

I now had an inkling of the intended destination of this line of questioning. First, invest the tendency to deny with a medical flavour by linking it with a diagnosed condition – the alcohol use disorder – and then once the tendency is medicalised, suggest that it may also be behind the temper outbursts. Then present the offence as one more manifestation – albeit a tragic one – of the temper control problem. Finally, conclude that the denial of his problem meant he was less aware of his actions and therefore less responsible.

'I would agree that individuals who are prone to aggression often minimise their own contribution to the aggression and sometimes to such an extent that they claim not to have been aggressive. I would stress that this process occurs irrespective of alcohol problems.'

He did not pursue this any further. As long as I didn't reject it out of hand, maybe Mr Haslett thought it was enough that he had been able to sow a seed in the minds of the jury members. I thought he was using our exchange to make certain statements that when taken in the round would support a diminished defence.

'You were mostly in agreement with Dr Lawton, but there was one point where your opinions diverged. That was on the matter of whether the defendant's drinking was voluntary or involuntary.'

'Yes, that's correct.'

'Dr Lawton thought his actions may have been involuntary and you did not agree. Would you accept that it is not a straightforward issue?'

Without a doubt, I thought. The problem is wider than I would have the latitude in the witness box to explain. The question of the voluntariness of an act in criminal proceedings extends much further than whether an alcoholic's first drink of the day was voluntary or not. The notion of criminal responsibility assumes that the criminal act was undertaken voluntarily, which in turn relies on the notion of free will. The academic jury is still out on whether there is such a thing as free will. In an oft-quoted 1980s study, Benjamin Libet identified activity in the parts of the brain controlling movement before the participants in the study experienced the urge to carry out the movement. This so-called 'readiness potential' in the brain has been taken as evidence that 'free will' is generated retrospectively to give the illusion of control. The results of subsequent and more fine-grained studies have shown that it is not so simple. For example, not being aware of the initial urge does not mean that there is an inability to resist the urge. Nevertheless, an agreed brain process that could explain decision-making completely suspended from the influence of events and other experiences is yet to be discovered. If we cannot agree that free will in this sense exists, then this is not just a problem for the psychiatric expert – it would require a complete revision of the way justice is administered in response to criminal behaviour.

Accepting as I do, the social legitimacy – if not the neuroscientific legitimacy – of the criminal justice system means that I rely on what I consider to be the scientifically informed next-best-thing to free will. Rather than trying to fathom whether a decision was voluntary or not, we can explore the processes by which our decisions are influenced. While we are aware of some of these processes, others are not readily accessible to conscious reflection.

Take for example, a supermarket aisle discussion between a couple about whether to buy a bottle of red wine for their Sunday evening meal. The conversation triggers agreeable images – opening the bottle, holding the glass, and consuming its contents. The precise form of the images may differ, but the state of pleasurable anticipation is shared. When one of the pair introduces the reminder that they both have an early start for work the following morning, it is initially downplayed by the other, but eventually they settle on the decision that the bottle should remain on the shelf. The couple could later relay quite clearly how they came to make their decision.

Now consider the recently abstinent alcoholic who is shopping for his meals. Despite his resolve to maintain his sobriety before entering the shop, he leaves with a bottle of cider in his groceries. He could describe his actions, but he is unlikely to be able to accurately describe the influential mental processes that led to his decision to buy the cider.

Researchers have a range of techniques to reveal biases that affect our decisions even if we do not recognise those biases. One fairly straightforward technique, called the Stroop task, involves asking participants to look at a list in which different words are displayed in different colours. The task is not to read the word, but to correctly identify the colour. The time to complete the task and the number of errors is increased if the list includes words that tap into something especially important to the reader. This interfering effect of personally salient words is based on the tendency for our attention to be drawn to stimuli that for us are associated with a state of heightened emotion.

Without realising it, we are momentarily distracted from the task of identifying the colour. Heavy drinkers are slower to name the colour of words on the Stroop task where the words' meaning is linked to alcohol. This provides support for the idea that alcohol-related stimuli inadvertently capture the attention of problem drinkers.

Other tests have been developed that can demonstrate the effects of these unintended biases. Using eye-tracking devices, researchers can study in real time how we allocate attention to various objects in our environment. In another test the speed with which subjects press a button to categorise words into one of two groups is used as an indicator of the strength of associations between concepts. The results of such studies indicate that on average people with an alcohol use disorder unwittingly attend and respond to what is around them in biased ways so as to increase the likelihood that they will consume alcohol. They may have an awareness of the decision to have the drink, but they are unlikely to be aware of the strong mental undercurrents flowing in the direction of that decision.

All of us are influenced by a combination of both hidden (or implicit) processes and those that we can recognise (explicit)–termed the dual processing model. The difference is that the problem drinker has to use more explicit effort to resist the combined effects of implicit forces pointing in the direction of continued drinking.

I agreed with Mr Haslett that whether an action is voluntary or involuntary is not straightforward.

'Is it something that is difficult to assess?' he continued.

Even if I were to explain that we could use the dual processing model as a proxy to examine voluntariness, there is a further difficulty. The techniques used to detect implicit processes can identify average differences between a group of people with alcohol problems and a group without such problems. They are not sensitive enough to confidently identify an individual's specific biases. Again, I agreed with his assertion, expecting at some stage that he would turn my evidence to his favour.

'If it was accepted that his drinking was involuntary and alcohol was the major factor in the incident, then by extension his actions were involuntary?'

Before I had conceived exactly why, I could sense that the logic of this proposition was flawed. I paused to structure my thoughts. I played for a moment more to prepare my answer. 'Can I clarify my opinion on the relationship between the defendant's alcohol use disorder and the alleged offence?'

Oral testimony by an expert requires the ability to snappily summarise complex issues without undermining the evidence base that supports the claimed expertise. I have previously tried to set my responses to this type of question within the context of the evidence on implicit and explicit processes only to be given short shrift by the lawyers.

'In alcohol use disorder, one feature is a craving for alcohol. If this craving is not resisted, then intoxication is likely to result. Intoxication is likely, in my opinion, to have played a part in the defendant's actions at the material time. Alcohol in itself does not lead to aggression. It can increase the likelihood of aggressive urges being acted upon, through processes such as disinhibition.'

'So, Dr Nathan, the disinhibition is due to the alcohol use disorder.'

'No, sorry, to be clear, the disinhibition is a result of the alcohol. It is not a diagnostic feature of alcohol use disorder. Disinhibition can result from alcohol whether or not the person has alcohol use disorder.'

'Thank you, Dr Nathan, we will be hearing Dr Lawton's evidence later.'

Mr Haslett was now seated and Mr Roper was on his feet again. The prosecution can clarify points that have arisen in cross-examination but not introduce new lines of enquiry. 'Dr Nathan, I would like to clarify, if I may, the points raised in the last exchange. Alcoholism . . .' – he had ditched the diagnostic term – 'increases the chance of drinking, but it is the drinking, not the alcoholism, that leads to disinhibition?' I confirmed this was a fair summary.

On my way out of the court building, I mused over how the two positions being offered to the jury differed in terms of the immediacy and inevitability of the connection between the alcohol use disorder and the violent act. The defence tried to truncate the causal chain and emphasise involuntariness. The prosecution countered with a longer and less inevitable causal chain. But neither of the narratives was able to explain why Alex committed this homicidally violent act when he did. Being drunk in the nightclub was not unusual for him and did not make him unusual among his fellow clubbers. He was probably not the only one in the nightclub that night who had a problem with alcohol. The rules for diminished responsibility often constrain the criminal justice process to only a small slice of the explanation for a violent incident. If an explanatory factor is unconnected to a diagnosable condition, even if it is critically important in explaining the violent act, then it would be unlikely to feature in the picture presented to the jury. This in turn has a bearing on the public's perception of the causes of violence, since trials are a major source of publicly available information about individual acts of violence.

Those of us interested in understanding violence mustn't ignore the important role of alcohol. Drinking to excess undoubtedly raises the chances of violence for some. Under the influence of alcohol, Alex's attention narrowed so that he devoted disproportionate attention to perceived immediate threats. The inhibiting effect of the more distant potential threat of the legal consequences of his actions was diluted by the intoxication. Alcohol induces psychological short-sightedness, a state known as alcohol myopia.

Once alcohol myopia has been factored into the explanation, we still do not have a reason for the violent act. What provoked Alex's reaction? Even if he misread the signs, why did he react so ferociously? I was unlikely to arrive at a satisfactory answer by asking Alex to answer these questions; my caution about using such a direct approach is to do with more than the possibility of deliberate dishonesty. On the occasions when I can test the story told by my patients against independent sources, my experience is that most are more honest than their criminal history would lead many to believe. I have to accept, though, that some are dishonest. The difficulty is that picking out the less reliable minority from the majority is not easy, and so I can't just accept their responses to leading questions. I also need to acknowledge the default cynicism the criminal justice system applies to the defendant's evidence. By extension, I need to expect stiff cross-examination if I base my opinion unquestioningly just on what the defendant tells me.

Unintended dishonesty is much more of a problem. Alex, and other defendants facing criminal charges, do not differ from the rest of us in an exercise of persuasive self-deception. Explaining our own behaviour to ourselves is something we do all the time, without thinking. In fact, we don't need to think; reasons for our actions jump into our mind effortlessly. For example, research has found that the reasons we give for the way we vote are more likely to reflect rationalisation for our political decisions than to be the cause of them. Our experience is that we act as a consequence of the reason, but it is often not so straightforward. When asked to give a reason for an action, we are likely to come up with one that was composed after the decision and that serves the purpose of justifying the act. The experience that reason leads to action gives us the impression that we are in control; that we possess what psychiatrists call a sense of agency.

I thought back to my first meeting with Alex and how I'd approached questioning him about the murderous attack. I started with an invitation to tell me about what had happened. It was deliberately vague. I listened for how his story began. Alex was not unusual in responding to a 'what' question with a 'why' answer, and in line with how we commonly explain our actions to ourselves, his most immediately accessible explanation started with the action of another person – or to be more specific, it was the intention of another person.

'He threatened me,' Alex said. Familiar with all the statements gathered by the police, I knew that none of the witnesses saw anything close to an overt threat; not to Alex, nor for that matter to anyone else. I would go on to point out the contradictions to him, but not yet: it risked stoking up emotions that experience tells me could be channelled into defending his stock explanation even more vigorously. Too strong a connection with our emotions disrupts our ability to reflect, but I needed to be careful not to completely remove feelings from the room. Emotional disconnection produces an account that is without real meaning. An assessment interview is more than just data gathering. Like a therapeutic session, the relationship needs to be carefully managed. My goal was to tease apart what Alex saw from what he thought this meant. I moved the focus of attention back in time looking for a less emotive point.

'Can I take you back a bit? What were you doing when you first got to the club?'

He told me his memory was sketchy, but he was having a laugh with his mates. I asked what he was doing when he first saw the victim. He couldn't be sure. It may have been when he went to the toilet.

'When did you next see him?' I asked.

'I don't know, I wasn't interested in that fucking pervert.' He was hunched forwards looking at the ground and leaning his forearms on his thighs. He apologised for swearing. I noticed his fingertips blanched with the force he was clasping his hands together.

By this time, I was halfway through my second meeting with Alex. Throughout our time together, he had shyly avoided eye contact. I do not think he would have been able to talk so frankly about his life if he had to look me in the eyes. His awkward self-consciousness had been constantly palpable.

Listening to his description of previous violence, it was clear that there was always an identifiable event that ignited his temper. If someone insulted him, he experienced an all-consuming fury. It became clear though that the fury did not always lead to violence, but what he could not bear was being made to look stupid. The bigger the audience, the more face there was to be lost.

Alex was seven years old when his father gave up on his alcoholic mother and left. Now the oldest male in the house, Alex took the brunt of his mother's cruelty, but he preferred this to his younger sister being the target. He became immune to the physical pain of the beatings, but the hurt caused by her derision never lessened. Despite his athleticism, at his core he felt weak and unmanly. Being accepted into a peer group through school sports teams did not diminish his sense of being an outsider. He did not seek out fights, but when they occurred he noticed a brief sense of power as he dominated his rival. Over time, he could see that his friends were wary of what to them was an unpredictable temper. Even within his friendship group he became an outsider.

'Did he say anything to you in the toilet?' I asked.

Alex said that the victim had propositioned him. He did not react then, and instead he rejoined his friends. Later – he was not sure how long – he noticed the victim again. He seemed to be hanging around Alex's group. He had a memory of the victim pointing at his crotch. At the time Alex was sure that his friends could hear what the victim had said to him, but by the time of my meeting with him he accepted their statements that they had not seen or overheard any interaction between the two of them. But it was what he believed at the time that was important: the victim had made a mocking quip about the size of his genitals. The effect on Alex was amplified beyond his control by his belief that others had witnessed it and from that moment the memories he had were dominated by an image of being humiliated. It replayed as if on a recurring loop. The only relief was when he visualised seeking revenge. He remembered leaving the club because his night had been ruined. He told me that he had not thought about coming back but, whatever his intention, he returned armed with a knife and lay in wait for the victim to leave the club.

Violent offending is often taken as evidence of a lack of concern about others. Alex's problem was the opposite. His already fragile sense of self was shattered by a disabling oversensitivity to the imagined minds of others. In the interaction with the victim he had experienced a threat; not to his physical self but to his core being. While this might seem like an exaggeration, and the insult itself trivial and certainly not warranting a violent response, Alex's subjective experience of being humiliated was something that is difficult to appreciate by just looking at the facts. For him, the impulse to respond with violence had become almost habitual. Giving in to the impulse brought some immediate relief, but that was followed later by self-loathing. There was a destructive feedback loop that had parallels with his dependence on alcohol. Alcohol-induced myopia made drinking appear more attractive because the anticipated benefits appeared magnified while he lost sight of the later and almost inevitable problems of his drunkenness. Similarly, in an emotionally charged state of humiliation, Alex was drawn to the most effective way to immediately reverse the dynamic – physical retaliation – despite the lasting harm to others and himself.

After the trial – in which Alex was found guilty of murder – I agreed to offer him appointments in my prison clinic. In the first appointment, Alex described how he had felt some relief once he had learned about his sentence. Up to the point of sentencing there was uncertainty, and even though a lesser sentence remained a possibility until the jury delivered its verdict, he preferred the certainty that came after sentencing; the certainty of a life sentence.

Alex's no-show for the second appointment was not unusual. He could have decided that he no longer needed to see me. There might have been a better offer of attending the prison gym. There may not have been enough officers to escort him to the health-care department, where I ran my clinic. By the end of the morning, when I had finished seeing the other prisoners and typing up my clinic notes, I asked a nurse whether she could check with the wing if Alex wanted another appointment with me. She made some calls and learned that he would not need to be seen again because he had been 'ghosted out', transferred to another prison as a response to a serious incident. The nurse was told by the wing officers that Alex had attempted to slash an officer's face. He had made a weapon, as is often done, by melting the blade from a disposable razor into a toothbrush handle. He had waited for a particular officer to come to his cell and flicked the blade out towards the officer's face. He missed but left the officer with a gaping wound to his arm. The reason was not completely clear, but I thought the rumoured explanation was credible. The day before the attack, this officer had mocked Alex in front of other prisoners.

6

Michelle

THERE IS ALWAYS a purpose to violence. At a basic level it is a type of interaction to achieve an objective. The objective is sometimes obvious, such as the mugger who is intent on taking the victim's phone, or the sexual offender who uses violence to overpower the object of his deviant urges. Forensic psychiatrists use the term 'instrumental' to describe this type of premeditated violence, which is enacted for a predetermined reason. By contrast, 'reactive' violence is hot-headed. Typically, the reactive aggressor lashes out in a fit of temper aroused by, for example, being made fun of. It is an impulsive reaction to a frustration of one sort or another. The violence is propelled by quick-fire automatic mental processes.

Whether the violence is reactive or instrumental, the in-the-moment goal is to favourably adjust the perpetrator's feelings. Seb wanted to bring to an end the all-consuming and delusional fear that his mother's life was in danger. Alex needed to reverse the intolerable feelings of being humiliated. But the potential gain of using violence to reach a preferred state of mind comes at a cost. Violence is generally counterproductive because the violent act usually brings the connection with others to an abrupt end. Although in some scenarios the connection does not end. In cases of domestic abuse, violence dominates the relationship.

Tireless campaigner Jack Ashley MP is credited with first using the term 'domestic violence' to describe aggression within spousal relationships. In a speech given to the British Parliament on 16 July 1973, Ashley reflected on the social stigma that victims of domestic violence experience:

> I want to draw the attention of the House to a subject cocooned in prejudice and buried in fear – the problem of wives who are victims of domestic violence. Thousands of men in this country are subjecting their wives to physical brutality. Some are psychopaths, some are alcoholics, and some are sadists. All of them must be stopped from indulging in gratuitous violence. If necessary, they must be given psychiatric treatment, but the first priority must be to protect their wives. Yet many women allege that they are refused protection by the police and neglected by the social services. The general experience of these women is that no one wants to know.

Today, despite increased awareness in the decades since that speech, domestic violence continues to be a huge problem. A 2018 United Nations study found the share of female deaths from partner or family-related homicide was on the increase. This study concluded that, because the majority of female victims of homicide worldwide are killed by partners or family, the most dangerous place for women is the home.

As a forensic psychiatrist, I am usually called on by the criminal court to assess the perpetrator of violence. But in a very different court setting, it is the victim who is more likely to be the subject of legal scrutiny and, as a consequence, who may be referred to me for an assessment.

Michelle was unable to prioritise her children's needs over her own. That was the conclusion of the social worker's report. The effect of the report – the children being taken away – was devastating for Michelle. Where once there had been an incessant demand for her attention, there was now an aching silence. Being in the house was almost unbearable. Whether it was a doll's arm spilling from the over-filled toy box in the sitting room, or the Disney towels in the bathroom, avoiding reminders of her loss was impossible. Being out of the house was no easier. She could not face the world. Or the thought of being judged by acquaintances who would notice her children's absence and know her to be a failed mother. She was left feeling ashamed and heartbroken.

Waiting in my car outside the solicitor's office, I jumped from one highlighted part of the social work report to the next. Michelle's children were living with adults she had never met. Of course, she had been given several chances before they were taken into foster care: stop drinking and stop taking her husband back, she was advised. But it was not as easy as that, she had pleaded. There was help available, the social worker countered. They had directed her to an alcohol support service and to a domestic violence course, but Michelle did not turn up. These – and by extension her children – were not her priority, the social workers concluded.

The very first entry in the social work report noted the birth of Michelle twenty-four years earlier. Next were some lines about referrals to the local authority when Michelle was a young child. Michelle's teachers at primary school had tried to find out why she seemed so tired and, from reading between the lines of the six-year-old's attempts to explain, the teachers realised that Michelle was being caught in the crossfire of her parents' violent late-night arguments. A social worker visited the family home to investigate, but no reason was found for continued social service input and the file was closed.

Then there was a sixteen-year gap up to two years ago when social services received a referral from the police. After taking a call from neighbours who had overheard adults screaming and a child bawling, the police had sent officers to an address, which turned out to be the home of the now-adult Michelle, her husband and their children. The officers were welcomed into the property by Michelle's husband, who confirmed that there had been 'a domestic'. The children were now settled in bed, he said, and Michelle was in the kitchen. An officer, who went through to see her, could tell she had been crying. He also noticed her slurring her words and smelling strongly of alcohol. When asked to explain the developing bruise around her left eye, Michelle said that she had accidentally walked into the edge of the door.

This police visit set in motion a series of events involving the social services. The police strongly suspected Michelle was being beaten by her husband and that she had an alcohol problem. She did not completely reject either allegation. Her argument was that the problems were being unfairly overblown. She could not see why they had any bearing on her ability as a mother so long as the children were being looked after. She accepted that the children may have heard the arguments, but in her view they were too young to know what was going on. Her daughter was just two and her son was four.

Michelle believed from that point on she was being set up to fail. Having her every move analysed placed the family under unbearable pressure. If they just left her alone, she protested, everything would be OK. The social workers, on the other hand, could not ignore the potential risk to the children. They did not doubt her love for them, and they could not question her ability to attend to their practical needs, but the risk came from what the children were likely to be witnessing.

When asked to recall their earliest memory, some people describe an event in their first two years of life. The event may have occurred, but is unlikely that they have a memory of it; at least not in the way we usually understand the idea of memory. In its everyday use, memory means a recollection of a specific episode. The activation of this so-called episodic memory does not simply entail retrieving a record of the event. By using a process of mental time travel, we return ourselves to that situation; we conjure up the scene as if we are in it. The cerebral components for episodic memory are not fully in place until at least the age of three, and so, if infants do not have the ability to recall episodes from infancy, did Michelle have a point, at least for her youngest child?

Running alongside our episodic memory is a system that stores experience in the form of emotions. This is usually a behind-the-scenes form of memory that we don't notice. The emotional memory system developed further back in our ancient ancestry and it also comes online earlier in each of our lives, possibly even while we are still in our mother's womb. These memories are not recalled in the traditional sense; we do not consciously retrieve them. Day to day they are activated without us noticing in the form of expectations, expectations about how others will behave or more specifically what their intentions are.

A particular psychiatric condition illustrates the potential power of this way of remembering: survivors of a life-threatening trauma can be left with serious psychological scars to memory systems. At the core of the condition known as post-traumatic stress disorder is an unwanted tendency to remember. In a flash the patient can be blind-sided by the feelings of being back in the moment of the trauma. Their experience would be of a paralysing sense of an imminent calamity; to a bystander it may seem as though they have suddenly entered a trance. These flashbacks are caused by bursts of overactivity in the emotional memory system.

Overhearing the occasional argument between adults does not cause an infant lasting damage, but regularly being in the midst of uncontrolled parental aggression is a different matter. The infant does not need to understand the meaning of the spoken words to sense the potential danger. Changes in the facial expression, body language and vocalisation pattern of the aggressor place the youngster on notice that an attack may be imminent. The response of the other adult party – whether that is to fearfully submit or to angrily rebut the attack – confirms this is a very perilous situation, and the emotional impact on the child is amplified by the aggressor and victim being the very people they look to for protection. Living in such an environment leaves its mark on the child's emotional memory. They learn to expect anger and aggression. Some children come to assume a state of perpetual readiness for danger and appear hypervigilant and overanxious, others become immune to signs of threat and disconnect from their own emotions. With repeated trauma at home, these adjustments become ingrained so that they influence the child's behaviour in other situations, even if they are not threatening. Being in a state of high-threat alert is not conducive to making friends or learning, and a child disconnected from emotions can appear indifferent, unconcerned and even callous.

In the solicitor's office and waiting for Michelle's arrival, I reread the letter of instruction. The questions for me to address were fairly standard: Was there a mental disorder? If so, what was the nature of this disorder and the diagnosis? What treatment would I recommend for any diagnosed condition? Was there any risk to others, and in particular to the children, arising from the condition? Did the condition affect her ability to parent? What was her insight into the social workers' concerns? What was her capacity to address those concerns?

Michelle was now about ten minutes late. I was on a tight schedule and couldn't extend the appointment without a knock-on effect for the rest of the day's commitments, so I gave it another five minutes before checking with the receptionist. She made a quick call and said that the solicitor would come down to speak to me. Out of earshot of others in the foyer, the solicitor said that Michelle had definitely been told about the appointment. When she was last in the office, the solicitor watched her enter it on her phone diary. As a final reminder yesterday, the solicitor's secretary had called Michelle. She promised she would turn up. This morning, they had called once more, but now their calls were going to voicemail. Sensing the solicitor was building up to apologise for wasting my time, I interrupted. 'Don't worry,' I said, 'it often happens.'

As I packed away my notes, I thought Michelle's non-attendance would be taken as further evidence of how she was not prioritising the needs of her children. If her children were her priority, she would have attended this appointment, so the argument would go. The court would look on disapprovingly. I did not expect to hear any more about Michelle.

It turned out that six weeks later I was back in the same office waiting once more for Michelle. The family court judge had agreed that she should be offered another appointment, but on the condition that she was made to understand it was her last chance. She was late again, but at least she made it this time. I didn't mention the previous missed appointment and neither did she.

Michelle sat upright with her hands in her lap. She did not take her coat off. There were no pleasantries. Her posture was tense. Maybe she was anxious, or angry; I couldn't tell yet. I wondered what I represented to her. I am often seen by parents sent for an assessment as an extension of a self-serving system that has nothing better to do than interfere in the lives of others or, even worse, that has to meet child removal targets. (There are no such targets.) Sometimes the patient arrives assuming that I will decide whether or not their children will return to them. In cases of domestic violence, I should also remain mindful that I may represent another incarnation of arbitrary male authority.

Michelle sat impassively through my explanation of the purpose of the assessment. I offered some reassurances to the usual concerns. I am not acting on behalf of one side or the other; I am independent. I do not decide the fate of her children; that is for the court. In assessing her mental health, it is my role to think about ways she can be helped. Her posture did not soften. Her expression did not alter. I asked if she understood what I had explained and she said yes. I asked if she had any questions and she said no. There was an unsettling awkwardness to this initial exchange.

An assessment that begins like this tends to go one of two ways. Occasionally, the patient is able to hold on to this defensive position well into the meeting. In attempting to avoid giving anything away, she would risk preventing me arriving at a more meaningful explanation than the one presented by the social workers to the court. To reach a sound formulation, I am dependent on the patient allowing me some access to their inner world.

To maintain forced aloofness in an interaction is unnatural. If and when I start to assume the identity of someone who is genuinely interested in understanding their predicament and comes to their own conclusions, I am likely to represent less of a threat, and the energy required to maintain an emotional distance no longer seems so necessary. Sometimes the patient realises that I am the best way they can introduce their perspective, which they feel has been drowned out.

Obtaining an account of recent biographical details tends to be a safe place to start. Where was she living at the moment?

How long had she been there? Was she in work? Answering such questions does not require self-reflection. With this approach, Michelle's defences seemed to yield slightly. Her answers were brief, but there was now a responsiveness in her facial expression. I moved on to general questions about her mental health. From my introductory speech before starting the assessment, she would have known that I had seen her medical records.

I had in mind a letter from a local hospital emergency department. Twelve months before, Michelle had been taken there by ambulance. Her husband had returned home early to find her slumped on the bathroom floor. There was a quarter-filled bottle of wine within her reach. To him it looked as if she had sat down against the bath and drunk herself into a stupor. He could not rouse her and so called an ambulance. Before the paramedics arrived, he found two empty packets of paracetamol in the bin. Blood tests taken after her arrival at hospital confirmed that she had taken an overdose. Two days later, she was deemed medically fit and, according to policy, she was referred to the hospital mental health team.

I had studied the letter from the psychiatric nurse dispatched to assess her. Michelle told the nurse that she felt fine to go home. She seemed ashamed about the overdose and stressed she would not do anything so silly again. The nurse felt that Michelle's appearance did not match her words. She looked glum and her mind seemed elsewhere. She did not refuse to take part in the assessment, but the discussion seemed to skim the surface of her life and experiences. They were interrupted by the arrival of Michelle's husband on the ward. He asked for a private moment with Michelle. The psychiatric nurse said that she would come back in about an hour; she had some paperwork to deal with. When she returned, Michelle had gone. The ward nurses had assumed the mental health assessment had been completed and did not object to Michelle's request to leave.

She had not been seen by any other mental health specialists, but dispersed through the medical notes were brief entries by general practitioners she had consulted for depression and anxiety. Three different types of antidepressant medication had been tried with mixed success.

I asked Michelle in the most general way whether she had suffered any issues with her mental health. 'Not for at least a year,' she responded. She divulged a history of mental health problems while emphasising that they were no longer an issue. As I made a note of her answer, I said, 'So you've not had any difficulties with your mental health for at least twelve months,' and paused. Overtly registering that the problems were a thing of the past should, I hoped, make it easier for her to talk about them.

When I asked her, she gave an account of sorts. 'I took some tablets. It was silly. It was something and nothing, but that's ages ago . . . It's not really relevant to this.' We both knew by 'took some tablets' she was referring to the overdose. I think she hoped that this would be the end of the discussion about the overdose, but I needed to know more.

'I don't want to dwell on it too much . . .' – from her downward gaze and restless fumbling with her handbag strap, her discomfort was clear – '. . . but before we move on . . .' – holding out the prospect of soon not talking about the overdose may encourage her to get it over and done with – '. . . can you help me understand why you took the overdose?'

'There was a lot of pressure at the time. The kids were young. I wanted to start studying but couldn't. Pete was working all the hours that God sends. I felt like I was drowning under the pressure. It got to me. I had this constant feeling . . . nerves . . . like something awful was going to happen, but I didn't know what.' Over-egging situational factors and downplaying our dispositional traits to explain our negative behaviour is a common tendency. By contrast, we are generally less charitable in the attributions we make for the behaviour of others. We are more likely to blame them for their misfortunes than accept the role of external factors.

Michelle may have had other reasons to present the overdose as an atypical reaction to an unusual set of circumstances. Parents fighting for the return of their children can be scared that showing inherent vulnerability will be used against them. By describing a past difficult period as an exceptional blip, they can distance their present selves from it. She should hear that I was not dismissing the role of the stressful circumstances before I moved on to explore what her reaction to those events told me about her. 'OK, so just to make sure I've understood the things that caused stress at the time; there was managing young children, not being able to start studying and your husband working a lot. Is that correct?' She nodded and then I asked, 'Why do you think when you were under all that pressure, that you took an overdose?'

'I wanted it all to stop. I felt stuck . . . I don't think it was to end it all . . . I wanted to not have to wake up . . .'

'What was it you wanted to stop?'

'Just how I felt . . . The dread.'

Mental health clinicians assessing someone who has taken an overdose are expected to work out the patient's intention just before or as they took the tablets. The task we are set is to determine whether or not they intended to end their life. There is even a scale available that generates a score of suicidal intention. We can be fooled by the need to determine someone's suicidal intention into thinking that if only we could freeze the recalled mental frame in the moment before they took the overdose then we would be able to see a clear intention. Subjective experience is not like that. The word intention refers to the aim of an act as anticipated by the actor. Patients who reach a point when they are prepared to inflict harm on themselves rarely have a crystal-clear objective. Rather, they are more typically lost in a jumble of half-thoughts and baffling feelings. A specific and fixed intention is the exception, but we still press most patients to try to tell us what it was.

The absence of a definite intention is not the same as the absence of a reason. The reason could be found in Michelle's choice of words. She had described being unable to escape the feeling of dread. She was experiencing a state we call entrapment.

To understand this frame of mind we should look to our natural response to signs of threat. Preparing to attack or to run away from threat was an essential reflex in Homo sapiens' early savannah-roaming history. At any moment, there was a real possibility of a life-threatening attack from predators or humans in competition for food, territory or mates. This state of threat-preparedness can be experienced in different ways depending on the response. Preparing to confront the source of the threat is experienced as anger. Preparing to escape it produces a subjective state of anxiety. Either way, these feelings pass once the threat has been neutralised or avoided. This fight or flight response has persisted despite the dramatic transformation in our habitat and lifestyle. Present-day dangers are rarely immediately life-threatening. Nonetheless, we can be subject to an existential threat.

Michelle's sense was that she was drowning, the weight of her existence pulling her under. Her brain had done what it was designed to do when presented with a threat and produced feelings of nervousness and dread. The problem was that this was not a time-limited threat, which our fight-or-flight response has been designed for. There was no escape. Without any prospect of the threat resolving, Michelle remained trapped in a defensive state of high emotional arousal. This soon becomes too much to bear and the emotion needs to be expressed in some way. For some people, including Michelle, turning the negative emotion inwards becomes the only available option. Professor Mark Williams of the University of Oxford coined the phrase 'cry of pain' to capture the expressive function of suicidal behaviour.

I reminded Michelle that she had mentioned being unable to pursue her desire to study. I wanted to know why, but I did not ask directly. 'Can you tell me more about that time?'

'I don't think I made the most of my education. I didn't get any qualifications to speak of, but I know I'm not stupid . . . Pete was not' – she hesitated as if thinking how best to phrase it – 'too happy. He had seen the email from the college.' The email was a response to her enquiry about an adult learning course in child psychology.

I was starting to wonder whether it may have been more than just not being able to see escape routes. Were her routes being blocked? 'Had you spoken about college before?'

'Not really. I might've said something once, but he made it clear it was not a good idea. He had a point. It was not the time to be thinking about myself. I was being selfish.'

'Had he given other reasons why he didn't want you to start studying?'

'He was always worried about other men. I sort of get it, he's had a tough life, but I did everything he asked. I always told him where I was going and who I'd be with. It wasn't much of a life.'

'It sounds really difficult . . . When he saw the email, what happened?'

'He went ballistic,' she blurted out, before adding in a more considered way, 'let's just say he wasn't too happy.'

I felt this was a point when I could ask about the allegations of domestic violence. I needed to be careful not to assume there had been violence, but if there had been, the timing and wording of the questions could be crucial. A mistimed or carelessly worded question could provoke a denial. Then the opportunity could be lost. Even if there had been a possibility that she would speak about domestic violence, it would have become even more remote after an initial denial.

I was mindful of how she had spoken about Pete. She seemed inclined to downplay his unreasonable behaviour. She was reversing the usual direction of attribution bias – convincing herself Pete was understandably reacting to difficult circumstances whereas she was a flawed person. Whether I am interviewing a victim or perpetrator, depersonalising the question often makes it easier for them to start talking more openly about violence.

'Did it become physical?' I asked, purposely using 'it' instead of 'he' and 'physical' instead of 'aggressive' or 'violent'.

'He was so annoyed he lashed out and caught me on the chin.'

'Gosh . . . Had that sort of thing happened before?'

'I can't say it hadn't . . . It was usually fine, but if he'd had a difficult day, I was treading on eggshells.'

'Did you ever have to get treatment for injuries?'

'Yes, I broke my arm. He pushed me really hard and I fell back over the armrest of the sofa into the fireplace. I told them at the hospital it was an accident.'

Michelle had now crossed a line. To say as much as she had about Pete's aggression, she needed to stifle her reflexive rationalisations. Then she became freer to continue. With little prompting, she was now able to reveal the extent of his controlling, coercive and abusive behaviour. As if by habit, her account was still peppered with excuses for him. The difference now was that these verbalisations no longer seemed to inhibit her commentary about how Pete treated her. She also appeared less reserved talking about how she coped.

Michelle's feelings were not necessarily better when she was drunk, they were just different. She was not so overcome by fear. Being able to stand up to a verbal onslaught gave her a moment of respect, which was worth it even when followed by more vicious aggression. She admitted, with what I felt was authentic regret, that the children would definitely have heard the ferocious rows and they were often in the room when Pete was violent. She recalled one time when he hit and kicked her while she was holding their youngest child. He was first physically violent when she was pregnant, but emotional abuse went even further back. Michelle had now confirmed the social workers' suspicions: she had stayed with this man despite the potential for harm to her children. However misguided her decisions were, she was able to make them for herself. Her children were not.

The legal process, by talking about priorities and choices, invokes the rational cost-benefit model of decision-making. According to this model, we first weigh up the pros and cons of the alternative choices. Then we pick the option we think best suits us. In his bestselling book *Thinking, Fast and Slow*, the Nobel laureate Daniel Kahneman offers an accessible and scientifically informed exposé of the limitations of the cost-benefit model of decision-making. He demonstrates that this model fails to recognise systematic biases. These biases are the automatic products of mental operations constantly running behind the scenes and as such are not immediately obvious to us. Given that Kahneman made his point by using examples of highly circumscribed judgements, such as predicting the risk of dying in a tornado, it should come as no surprise that the cost-benefit model is found even more seriously wanting as a framework that guides tangled relationship and parenting decisions. The fundamental mistake is to see an individual's existence as the result of a series of opportunities for rational choices and decisions. No one's life is like that.

It is worth taking a moment to consider why, against the tide of research findings, the rational cost-benefit model remains so compelling, even to the intellectually rigorous counsellors at law. Chief among the reasons is that what we see is constrained by the tools with which we look. Although our minds are much more than the product of the rationalising part of our brain, this is the part we use to search for understanding. It is not only that the subterranean mental landscape is obscured from sight – the tools at hand for introspection are designed to see a virtual reality; one that is retrospectively composed after a decision has been made.

How then should we make sense of why the mother continues her relationship with the abusive partner? As with so many other societal problems, health professionals (with their dialect of symptoms and syndromes) have taken ownership of domestic abuse. Specialists who became interested in the damaging effects of domestic abuse in the 1970s identified a cyclical pattern from the initial stage of growing tension leading to the battering stage, which was then followed by a phase of contrition. The phrase 'battered woman syndrome' was coined to describe the psychological effect of repeated exposure to this cycle of abuse. Its proponents drew on the similarities with post-traumatic stress disorder, a formal medical diagnosis. Battered woman syndrome was introduced to a wider audience, including the criminal justice system, by expert evidence in those rare cases when the victim becomes the aggressor. Articulating the problem in syndromal and diagnostic terms added medical prestige to the calls for courts to give clemency to women who had killed their violent husbands. However, this was not always welcomed by the women or their supporters.

In July 1991 Sara Thornton, while detained in Bullwood Hall Prison, started to refuse food. Her hunger strike was motivated by her first-hand experience of the gender bias in the criminal justice system's response to domestic abuse. She had just heard about the trial of a man who had killed his alcoholic wife. Releasing the man from custody to serve a community sentence, the judge expressed sympathy for the defendant and commented that his wife 'would have tried the patience of a saint'. Two days earlier, Sara's appeal against a murder conviction for killing her alcoholic and violent husband had been dismissed. She remained detained in prison to serve the remainder of a life sentence.

Sara Thornton met the man who would become her husband in May 1987 when she was thirty-two years old. Malcolm was not like her previous partners, who had not met the standards she believed her father expected. Her father's approval seemed unobtainable, but she continued to seek it. Malcolm was an intelligent bon viveur with whom she felt an immediate rapport. Outwardly, Malcolm was her father's type.

Malcolm liked alcohol, but so did Sara. By the time she began to appreciate he had a drink problem she was committed to the relationship and to helping him. Two months after they met there was an incident that, with the wisdom of hindsight, was the first sign of a more serious problem. Two work colleagues who had escorted a drunken Malcolm home one night watched as he was met by Sara at the front door. Sara's young daughter also looked on as Malcolm punched her with such force that she was lifted into the air and thrown into a hedge. One of his colleagues intervened and there was a violent struggle. The police were called but they dismissed the incident as 'only a domestic'. Despite this violent attack, Sara held on to the belief she could rescue Malcolm from his demons. She did not want to return to her previous drifting loneliness and to feel the weight of her father's disapproval. Malcolm's persuasiveness also encouraged optimism about the future. Knowing how the relationship turned out, Malcolm's apologies, remorse and vows to stop his unreasonable behaviour may be seen as predatory tactics to lock his vulnerable victim into the relationship. To Sara at the time, they were reasons to hold fast in her resolve to make the relationship work. Malcolm did go on to accept help and he managed a period of abstinence. This phase was the exception. The overall direction of his life's trajectory was downwards, and he dragged Sara with him. She was bound into a relationship with an alcoholic who was prone to attack her. In their final argument, Sara stabbed Malcolm once and he died.

Sara's lawyers considered whether there was evidence to support a defence of provocation. It would come down to whether this legal defence had been designed with the likes of Sara Thornton in mind.

In its modern form, provocation can be traced all the way back to the court's analysis of a violent confrontation in the Tower of London. On 7 June 1706, William Cope took a group of officers and gentlemen out for dinner in a local tavern. They ate and drank heartily before most of the group left. The remaining men accepted Cope's invitation to return to the guardroom at the Tower, where he ordered more bottles of wine. Their revelry was interrupted by news of a woman who had arrived in a coach and asked for Cope. One of the party, John Mawgridge, accompanied Cope to meet the visitor and then all three of them returned to the guardroom. The atmosphere soured when Mawgridge was rude to the guest. Following a sharp exchange between them, Mawgridge threatened the woman. Cope intervened in her defence, which inflamed Mawgridge's anger even more. He demanded that they fight to settle the matter, but Cope said it was not the time or the place and he advised his adversary to leave. As he made for the door, Mawgridge grabbed a full wine bottle and threw it towards Cope, who responded in kind with another bottle. Mawgridge then drew his sword. Another member of the party tried to come between the two men, but Mawgridge thrust his weapon into Cope's chest. Cope died almost instantly.

The jury sitting at the Old Bailey a month later agreed the facts of the case. They had more difficulty deciding whether Mawgridge should be found guilty of murder or manslaughter. It was a life or death matter for the defendant because a murder conviction automatically led to execution while the sentence for manslaughter was left to the discretion of the judge. The jury issued a special verdict, which in effect passed on this difficult decision to senior judges. The outcome of their deliberations would endure in legal history because the judges did not confine themselves to just Mawgridge's fate. The author of the ruling and the Chief Justice of England, Sir John Holt, pronounced, 'I shall consider what is such a provocation as will make the act of killing to be but manslaughter only.' This was an era when a display of male anger was justified if the man's honour had been impugned. Holt pronounced that a hot-blooded reaction would stand up as a defence to a charge of murder if it was provoked by the victim behaving aggressively.

When they turned their minds to the case before them, they held that Cope throwing a bottle was not sufficient provocation because he was only reacting to Mawgridge's initial use of physical aggression. Applying this logic, the judges found that under the law Mawgridge's actions constituted wilful murder. In an interesting footnote to this historic legal case, Mawgridge's automatic death sentence could not be immediately enacted. Two months after his initial trial, he escaped from Marshalsea

Prison and fled abroad. Since he was still at large when the chief justice delivered his verdict, Mawgridge was deemed an outlaw. Eventually he was apprehended and returned to London. In Newgate Prison he repented to the chaplain and prayed for God's mercy before being taken to Tyburn, then a village outside London, now close to the site of Marble Arch. There, on 28 April 1708, he was executed for the murder of William Cope.

The case of Mawgridge established the principle that for a defence of provocation, the killing must have occurred in the hot-blooded moment. Just under two and a half centuries later, in 1949, the Court of Appeal restated this requirement in its judgment that provocation is an act that causes the accused to experience a sudden and temporary loss of control. It was this requirement that put provocation outside the reach of Sara Thornton's legal team.

Sara's case was not unusual. The effects of domestic abuse on the victim accumulate over an extended period, rather than just occurring in the moment of the aggression. There was one domestic scenario that Sir John Holt's eighteenth-century legal judgment considered sufficient to be a provocation, but it most definitely was of no use to Sara. Justice Holt described a man coming across his wife engaged in an adulterous liaison. It was established in the eyes of the law that if the man reacted with homicidal violence, he could turn to provocation as a defence against a charge of murder 'for jealousy is the rage of a man, and adultery is the highest invasion of property'. Reflecting the social mores of the day, he went on to state that 'a man cannot receive a higher provocation'.

Despite the passing of almost three hundred years, a gender bias in the law of provocation had persisted. Worldwide the victim of a domestic homicide is more than four times likely to be female. A man who killed in a state of jealous rage could expect that the sudden discovery of his wife's infidelity would be accepted by the court as a provocation that reduced his culpability. If a woman who had been repeatedly beaten by her husband eventually resorted to aggression, she would find it difficult to persuade the court that her husband's actions amounted to provocation. The difference in physical strength and readiness to use aggression means that, when women do very occasionally turn the tables, they are less able to react in the moment. By its legal definition, provocation was unavailable to many women even where there was an accepted link between the offence and their previous victimisation.

The only defence realistically available to Sara at the time was diminished responsibility. If successful, it would have the same effect of reducing the charge from murder to manslaughter. But, the use of the defence for women in Sara's situation caused unrest among their supporters. Whereas provocation indicated that there had been an understandable reaction to extreme circumstances, diminished responsibility located the explanation squarely, but not fairly, in an abnormality of the woman's mind. With no other option, Sara somewhat reluctantly accepted the advice of her solicitors. The two psychiatrists instructed by her solicitors both found evidence in support of diminished responsibility.

In line with my experience of many trials where diminished responsibility is a factor, the prosecution contested this defence not only with their own psychiatric evidence – the Crown's psychiatrist did not believe that Sara's condition was so serious that her responsibility was substantially impaired – but they also sought to paint a picture of the defendant as a calculating killer. They called a witness who shortly before the incident had heard Sara saying that she was going to kill Malcolm. Snippets of evidence were presented that raised a question about whether Sara was motivated by financial gain, even though the reality (not presented to the jury) was that there would be no such gain.

Sara's call to the emergency services after she stabbed Malcolm was played. The matter-of-fact way she explained 'I've just killed my husband' and her calm and playful behaviour when the police and ambulance crew arrived did not conform to the expectations of a mentally unstable victim of domestic abuse. It has been suggested that there was a more misogynistic attack on her reputation. In her excellent book, *Sara Thornton: The Story of a Woman Who Killed*, the barrister Jennifer Nadel showed how Sara was also on trial for not conforming to society's expectations of a good woman.

The jury retired at 10.30 a.m. When more than six hours later they had not returned, the judge called them back and explained that if they could not reach a unanimous verdict, he would accept a majority one. They retired again, but by the end of the day they still could not agree and so they were taken to a hotel. The jury spent the next morning deliberating until eventually they reached a majority decision. They decided Sara was guilty of murder and she was sentenced to life imprisonment.

In July 1991, Sara appealed against her conviction. Her legal team sought to persuade the Court of Appeal that the defence of provocation should be available to her. The judges were not persuaded, and she was returned to prison to continue her life sentence. Another four years passed before she was allowed to present new psychiatric evidence about her mental condition and the effect of Malcolm's abuse on the state of her mind. This time the judges accepted that sufficient doubt had been cast on the original verdict and so they ordered a retrial. In May 1996 the jury at Oxford Crown Court concluded she was guilty of manslaughter and not murder. The judge decided that the time in prison she had already served was a sufficient sentence and she was released. After the verdict, she said, 'I am too tired to feel a sense of victory and there has been too much pain and, at the end of the day, Malcolm died.'

Sara Thornton's case was one of three domestic abuse cases in the 1990s that found the defence of provocation wanting. Kiranjit Ahluwalia had endured ten years of her husband's physical and sexual aggression by the time she put a stop to the abuse. He had been aggressive again, but on this occasion she set fire to him and he later died of his injuries. The trial judge impressed on the jury that in the eyes of the law provocation is an act that causes the accused a sudden and temporary loss of control. The problem for Kiranjit was that she did not take matters into her own hands until her husband had fallen asleep. The jury convicted her of murder.

Emma Humphreys was a seventeen-year-old who was in an abusive relationship with a 33-year-old man. One night she sat upstairs holding two knives that she had used to cut herself. As she heard her partner approaching, experience had taught her to expect rape, a beating or both. He mocked her about her self-inflicted injuries, and she turned the knife on him. Applying the law as it was then, the judge directed the jury that they should disregard the psychiatric evidence about her mental vulnerability. She was found guilty of murder.

Eventually it was recognised that the law was in a mess, and in 2010 provocation as a legal defence in English and Welsh law was once and for all abolished. It was replaced by the defence of 'loss of control'. This defence became available to women who had been repeatedly victimised by their partner, even if the final loss of control was not an immediate reaction to a provoking act. It allowed fear of violence, not just a provoking act, to qualify as a trigger for the loss of control.

The concept of battered woman syndrome may have lent medical legitimacy to the argument for a revision of the law regarding battered women who kill. Despite this, it is not particularly useful when it comes to answering the questions posed by the court in a case such as Michelle's. As with many mental health diagnoses, battered woman syndrome describes but does not explain it. This syndromal label serves as a flag to others that Michelle's psychological state is recognised among victims of domestic abuse, but in itself it does not explain how the particular relationship between Michelle and Pete led to the issues now before the family court. The clinical label may point in the general direction of therapy, but it does not inform potential solutions in this one case. Identifying processes within the mind – or ones that occur between two minds – is in my experience always more fruitful.

In experiments that to modern-day sensibilities appear cruel, a group of American researchers in the 1960s were examining the behaviour of dogs that had earlier been conditioned to associate a sound with an electric shock. The hypothesis was that having learned this association, the dogs would be quicker to learn that they could escape a shock in the floor of one part of a box by jumping a low barrier into the other part of the box. There was an unexpected problem. Instead of jumping across the barrier to escape the shock, the dogs often just stayed where they were and waited for the shock to pass. American psychologist Martin Seligman set about trying to understand this phenomenon. At the time, learning was thought to involve classical conditioning of the sort demonstrated by Pavlov, who trained a dog to salivate at the sound of a bell by repeatedly pairing the bell with food. Seligman recognised a greater role for mental processes and came up with the theory of learned helplessness, which suggested the dogs learned that they had no control over what happened to them. This theory was adopted by researchers studying abused women. Where battered woman syndrome describes the effects of abuse (which may occur in any intimate partner relationship), learned helplessness is an attempt to explain the mind of an abused woman. Here was a mental process that was said to underpin behaviour. As a concept learned helplessness is not without its problems. It reduces domestic violence to simple learning algorithms. It could not account for what Michelle told me about how she felt.

Michelle said she could not stop loving Pete. Even now that her detachment from the relationship allowed her to see his previous cruelty more clearly, she still felt love. Taken at face value, her comments could further damn her in the eyes of the social workers and court. According to the competing priority model, the feelings she had prioritised – her own for Pete – still lingered. She tried to reassure me that those feelings would not cause her to break the promise she had made that she would not take him back. She accepted that the risk to the children was too great but the difficulty was how much to rely on this promise. It may have been honestly made, but she had gone back on it before.

Like most parents I assess for the family court, Michelle was not able to keep up the guarded reticence she began the meeting with. Some, like Michelle, go on to a third phase of openly trying to make sense of the contradictory choices they have made. Scattered between Michelle's answers were spontaneous reflections about how her choices did not make sense. 'I don't get it.' 'Why would a mother put her children through that?' 'It seems crazy, even to me.' 'I wish I understood it all.' This inquisitiveness was grounds for cautious optimism. That she was unable to reach a coherent explanation did not change this prognosis, but I took it to be a positive sign that she was no longer as disposed to revert to confected rational explanations.

All of us are managing a varied array of inherent drives. Sometimes these drives are in competition with one another.

The tragedy for Michelle was that two powerful ingrained drives, which usually work in concert, were in contradiction. Her love for a man who could be abusive meant that her drive for intimacy ended up being pitched against her maternal drive to nurture her offspring. Rather than removing the conflict by once and for all leaving Pete, her view of reality had become altered to reduce the sense of conflict, allowing her to continue the relationship.

The first time Pete called her 'fat', Michelle had no way of knowing that this was the start of a pattern; before then he had seemed attentive and loving. When they first met, she felt an instant connection. He had made her feel special. They were soulmates. Why would she throw that away for one stray comment? For the first few months she saw each cruel insult in isolation. Due to her desperation for the relationship to work, it took time for her to recognise the pattern. She also did not see that her attitude towards herself was moving incrementally downwards, and by the time his behaviour was impossible to ignore Michelle had already accommodated to his critique. She now had a feeling that his put-downs were deserved. In this relationship, Michelle's sense of self had been recalibrated in a way that neutralised the contradiction of feeling in need of someone she also felt fearful of. This was an attempt at psychological survival in a persistently threatening habitat. But the effect was to cement her dependence on Pete. From her position of devalued self-worth, the idea of being unlovable, and therefore forever alone, seemed a more realistic prospect. Locked in this destructive cycle, she did not make relationship choices having objectively scrutinised the anticipated outcomes of those choices. As for us all, her feelings, which arose reflexively rather than from considered contemplation, were influential in decision-making. The difference in this domestically abusive scenario was that certain feelings, such as doubt, worthlessness and fear, prevailed so overwhelmingly.

From Michelle's position of emotional dependence on Pete, her appraisal of the risks to the children of witnessing the abuse was distorted. She was ready to accept his promises it would not happen again, however unrealistic those promises were, because it was what she wanted to believe.

Even though I had a better understanding of the contradictions in Michelle's life, I thought this was not the whole picture. When talking about the start of Pete's demeaning jibes, she said, 'It wasn't a surprise.' Did she mean that with hindsight she could see that there was something wrong? No, she clarified, it was that it felt familiar in 'a weird way'.

As with the battered woman syndrome description or the learned helplessness explanation, my exploration up to this point was confined to the relationship itself. I had not yet looked at the past Michelle had brought with her to the relationship. I was aware that women in an abusive relationship have often previously attracted the attention of other abusive men. I enquired about any earlier relationship problems. She explained that she had not had a 'proper' relationship before Pete. Until then she had lived at home with her parents. Her life had been, in her own words, sheltered. I looked further back. Speaking of her parents, she said 'they were overprotective'. Her choice of words implied caring over-concern, but I needed to dig beneath these words.

'What was life like at home?'

'Sort of normal . . . But, they were worried about my safety. I didn't go to friends' houses. I never had sleepovers . . . We had some holidays. Nothing out of the ordinary . . . School was good.'

'Did you have friends?'

'Oh yeah, in my first school, there was a little group of us. We were as thick as thieves.'

'Did you see them out of school?'

'No, not really.'

'What happened when you moved up to high school?'

'The group sort of split up. Well, really, it was more I dropped out.'

'Oh?'

'Yeah, it didn't really work for me. My father was quite strict.'

The approach Michelle took to introducing me to her early years seemed familiar. There were parallels to the way she started speaking about Pete. From the start of talking about her childhood, she offered explanations that sounded like excuses. At this stage, I didn't know whether her childhood problems extended beyond the excessive but loving attention of her parents. If they did, I could not tell whether her defences had been consciously and temporarily constructed for the purposes of this interview or whether they had a longer history. I must be especially careful burrowing beneath more well-established defences. We were not embarking on therapy; this was a stand-alone assessment and while coming away with a proper understanding was my goal and it would be in Michelle's interest, I should not leave her exposed to emotional forces that she was unable to manage.

'What about your mother?'

'She was pathetic . . . Sorry, that's not a very nice thing to say, but she always took his side. I'm more angry with her than him. She had no backbone.'

'Took his side? Can you say a bit more about that?'

'He was a mean man. He said I would never amount to much, but he never let me prove myself. When he wasn't there, she would say "Don't listen to your father", but when he said horrible things to me, she would sit quietly. She even nodded sometimes. It makes me sick to think about it.'

Michelle took a tissue from her bag to dab at the corners of her tear-filled eyes. Otherwise she held her composure, and carried on.

'I didn't know what I was supposed to do. No one would have me. I'd be on my own. These are the things he said. My spineless mother would stare at the ground. How could I prove myself to anyone if I couldn't even go out? I put on a brave face, but inside I felt a failure . . . I loved school because I could be myself there. I loved my friends. They took that away from me. I never resented my friends. It was me. I kept making excuses why I couldn't go out with them. They gave up in the end. I didn't tell them the real reason. I got good at lying. I think I sort of believed it myself.'

'It sounds like you've now got a good understanding of what was happening. Do you remember how you understood it at the time?'

'I was a child!' She tried to hide her irritation at my question. 'I didn't know anything. It was just the way things were.' As I was about to acknowledge it was not a fair thing to ask, I could see that she was straining to remember. '... They were the grown-ups. They had the answers. It must have been something I was doing. I know now there was nothing I could have done to change things, but then ...'

It is a mistake to assume that we experience our life only as a series of events. Instead, we see effects for which there must be causes. Humans have benefited from a particular refinement of the cause-and-effect detection processes. Our everyday view of the world is not a mechanical one in which one action is an inevitable consequence of another, in the way balls on a billiard table bounce off each other; we invest actors with attitudes and intentions that explain their actions. We are also able to hold these ideas in our mind even when the actor is not present. As a consequence, we can make social predictions about a greater number of individuals than our closest evolutionary relatives, such as chimpanzees, which rely on the immediate contact of grooming to understand members of their group. The mental gadgetry that enables us to conjure up theories about what is going on in someone else's mind to explain their behaviour has served us well in becoming the predominant species. However, if faced with effects that appear to be in contradiction to our beliefs about the world, we sometimes come up with spurious causal explanations.

If a young Michelle had rejected the idea that her parents had the authority to know and understand her world, then she would find herself to be psychologically on her own. How could Michelle maintain a belief that her parents were all-knowing while her father kept telling her she was a failure? The solution was to look inward for causes. Over time, constantly attributing responsibility to herself would have induced a more permanent sense of blameworthiness.

As an adult, she knew that she hadn't brought her parents' treatment on herself. When she put herself back in the mind of her younger self, she could tell that these alternative explanations would not have felt right at the time, but by the time she was old enough to appreciate their logic her idea of herself had already been shaped. I wondered whether she had made the connection to her relationship with Pete.

'Can you remind me, when was it that you met Pete?'

'Err, seventeen or maybe just turned eighteen . . . He worked in the local post-office depot. My father used to send me to pick up his post. Everything was hard copy in those days.' We had already discussed her father's job as a surveyor. In his mid-forties he became self-employed, which meant he spent more time at home. Talking about Pete, she said, 'He was a quite a bit older than me . . . He would chat to me whenever he was on duty. I knew he had a girlfriend, but there was nothing between us then. I just loved talking to someone else. I felt free. I'll never forget the day he asked me out. He said he had left his girlfriend and really liked me . . . A few months later someone told me that he was still with her. I don't know if it was true. Someone else said that he didn't finish with her, she chucked him out. I didn't care then. I ignored what people said. He was my escape route. Anything was better than home.' She did not want Pete to be like he was. But once it started, it reignited familiar expectations.

But what of the perpetrator here? Pete could be said to have exploited Michelle's vulnerability. Whether or not he understood the root of her vulnerability, surely he was aware that his dominance in the relationship rested on his aggressive potential. He couldn't have been blind to the power imbalance, which meant that all he needed to offer were occasional scraps of affection to satisfy Michelle's longing to be with him, or at least not to be alone. The abuser is no more likely than the victim to act in response to thought-through ideas. The abusive partner is also buffeted, not always knowingly, by intense and multi-directional emotional factors. When Pete promised he would stop, he probably also genuinely believed it. Working with perpetrators of domestic abuse, I often find that their dominating approach to partner relationships is driven by a fear of being unlovable and alone. Sadly, it often turns out that the conflicting emotional forces tormenting each member of the couple resonate together to bind them in domestic discord.

Six months or so after I filed my report, an email arrived from the instructing solicitor. The case was concluded, and she wanted to let me know the outcome. Michelle did stick to her promise to stay away from Pete and had shown a more positive attitude and less suspicion about the involvement of social services, but her drinking became worse. As a result, the social workers did not feel confident to return Michelle's children. As I read the summary, I speculated that Michelle was using alcohol in her battle to resist the draw of the relationship with Pete and to tolerate feelings of emptiness without her children or a partner.

I later found out that Michelle had managed to stop drinking altogether and that, following a gradual process of increased contact with her children, everyone involved agreed that the children could be reunited full time with their mother – though I will never know whether or not they stayed in her care.

7

Jodie

WHEN I ACCEPTED the commission to assess Jodie, I knew it would mean a round trip of several hundred miles to the prison, but I was curious to return to the first women's prison I ever visited. My visit there some twenty years ago had made a lasting impression.

I was a trainee in psychiatry then. In our junior training years, we were required to get experience in different branches of psychiatry before we decided on the career pathway we would follow. Every six or twelve months we would change placements. I had already worked on wards for elderly and adult-age patients, and then in a day hospital that patients living in the community would visit. After passing my general exams I became eligible for a post in a more specialised area, like forensic psychiatry. The placement at the county secure psychiatric unit was in high demand, so I was fortunate to work there. Most of my time was spent doing ward doctor duties: assessing patients who had just been admitted, reviewing patients who had already spent months and often years there, preparing reports for the ward rounds, taking bloods and so on. In my training up to that point these types of tasks had become second nature.

Once a week, I accompanied my supervising consultant, who ran a clinic at the prison for women. Earlier in my training I had visited a traditional Victorian prison that housed men, so I was expecting to find the prison surrounded by a wall impervious to eyes prying in or out. Instead the footpath from the car park to the prison entrance hugged a tall mesh fence. I also expected a fortified gatehouse. As it is a breach in the continuous boundary, the entry point of a prison is usually swollen to accommodate security measures. Movement through the area is controlled by a series of airlocks. There are spaces for searches and scanning. A secure room houses the officers who control the airlocks and dispense the keys. In contrast, I only noticed the way into this prison because of a huddle of people gathered by the fence. When I came closer, I could see that they were in a queue snaking in the towards the prison.

My consultant nodded in the direction of the entrance ahead of us and discreetly passed comment on the scene. It was clear from the mischievousness of the younger children, particularly when contrasted with the seriousness of the older ones and the adults, that they were oblivious to the significance of their situation. My mentor remarked on how profoundly sad he found the thought that many of these children's only direct contact with their mother would be in a supervised visiting area of a prison. While the prison was the thing keeping their mothers away from them, it was also the thing that would hold some of the fondest memories of their childhoods. For most people, a prison is sinister as much for what we don't know about it as what we do. For these children, prison would become as familiar as the shopping centre they visited at the weekend.

Returning years later I thought of that group of people by the fence. I thought about how much my approach to psychiatry had changed in the intervening time. Back then my medical student training and early junior doctor experience had encouraged a production-line approach to medicine. The mechanical style of assessment and diagnosis we had been taught, together with the pressure of the job and the effects of sleep deprivation from the regular on-calls without rest days, had the effect of stripping away the human element. It was as if there was no time to look up from the tasks and at the person. I now realise that I had become less a doctor and more an expensively trained hospital technician. If it were not for my consultant's comment as we approached the prison on that first occasion, I would have walked on by and been keenly focused on the forthcoming task of assessing and treating patients. Since then, I have come to realise that the person's mind cannot be examined in isolation from their wider existence, both now and in the past.

In preparation for my visit to see Jodie, I reminded myself of the precise wording of the Infanticide Act. The killing of an infant by its parent has not always been a criminal offence. In the medieval period it was a sin to be dealt with by the church. Through modern eyes the 1470 punishment of Joan Rose for killing her son would seem bizarre. Wearing clothes of coarse fabric and holding in one hand a half-pound candle and in the other the knife she used to kill her son or something similar, she was made to traipse slowly around the markets of several Kent towns. The ecclesiastical courts had accepted that paupers had to make an impossible choice between the life of a newborn and the survival of their existing family, and with increasing urbanisation came greater public awareness of infanticide. This awareness, together with concerns about the financial burden on the parish of illegitimate children, led to the introduction of specific laws.

In March 1802, Mary Voce was being held in a prison cell awaiting her execution the next morning. A Methodist preacher who sat and prayed with her through the night was witness to Mary's tearful confession to the killing of her own child. The preacher, Elizabeth Tomlinson, then travelled alongside Mary and an empty coffin in the cart that took them to the gallows.

A few days before, a jury sitting at a court session at Nottingham Lent Assizes had heard evidence of how Mary had poisoned her six-week-old baby daughter. The judge acknowledged that

Mary had showed genuine signs of distress, but he decreed that in the eyes of the law she was not insane. After just ten minutes, the jury declared that she was guilty of murder. She was removed to Nottingham Gaol.

When Mary arrived at the gallows, the executioner put a rope around her neck and placed a hood over her head. The floor opened beneath her and she dropped to her death. The custom was to leave the body for an hour, before it was given to surgeons for dissection.

Almost four decades after Mary Voce's death, Elizabeth told her young niece, Marian, about the execution. Although Marian was deeply moved by hearing her aunt's recollection of sitting and praying with the condemned woman, another fifteen years passed before she mentioned it to anyone. Then she happened to describe the episode to her lover, George Lewes. He pondered aloud whether the description of Mary Voce awaiting her own death could form the basis of a bigger story. Within a year Marian had started writing her first full-length novel. She identified the tale of Mary Voce as the germ for her book and the inspiration for the central character, Hetty Sorrel, the local beauty who was betrothed to the eponymous hero of the story, Adam. Realising she was pregnant from an illicit relationship with a local aristocrat, she became depressed and suicidal. She then went missing only to reappear in prison having been arrested for murdering her baby. The novel, *Adam Bede*, was published in 1859 under Marian's nom de plume George Eliot, a name that has become associated with some of the most enduring and socially insightful pieces of Victorian literature.

The real Mary Voce and the fictional Hetty Sorrel were convicted in an era when single mothers charged with infanticide faced particular disadvantage before the courts. Due to a law introduced in 1624, during the reign of James I, a grieving mother who delivered a stillbirth would have to prove their child was born dead. This is particularly striking for two reasons: firstly, the 'act to prevent the destroying and murdering of bastard children' turned on its head the presumption of innocence; and secondly, it could be difficult to prove that a child was born dead if there were no witnesses. The social prejudices of the time are revealed in the wording of the Act, which bemoans the 'many lewd Women that have been delivered of Bastard Children, to avoid their shame and to escape punishment, doe secretly bury, or conceale the Death of their children.' Even though the moralistic 1624 'bastardy act' was still in force at the time of the trials of Mary Voce and Hetty Sorrel, by then many jurors were so uncomfortable with the severity of the sentence that they would acquit the mother of murder rather than send them to their death. The harsh punishment completely reversed the desired effect of making an example of the offenders since juries were ignoring the law. In 1803, the year after Mary Voce was executed, the 1624 law was removed from the statute book, making it necessary for the prosecution to prove guilt rather than the defendant to prove innocence. This did not stop the continued stacking of the system against single mothers more generally, particularly those without financial means. Parish help was available, but on the condition that the unfortunate mothers submitted themselves to a workhouse and its prison-like conditions.

An alternative solution was to pay for the child to be brought up by others. Evelina Marmon was one of many Victorian women whose life was upended by the arrival of her baby daughter on 21 January 1896. The father would take no responsibility for the care of the child, and when Evelina could no longer hide her pregnancy, she was forced to leave her job as a barmaid in the Regency town of Cheltenham. Alone and without an income, her situation was hopeless.

Single mothers in Victorian Britain faced more than a financial struggle. The stigma of having an illegitimate child would have been all the greater in the insular farming community that Evelina had grown up in, and so returning to her parents' village would not have been an easy option. Added to that, the intense social shame would have extended to include her family. In order to stay in Cheltenham she would need to go back to work, but this would be impossible with a young dependant. This left her with no option but to consider adoption.

But in Victorian Britain, adoption was not a formal state-administered process. If Evelina could find a family to look after her daughter, she would have to come to a private arrangement with them. So Evelina placed a notice in the *Bristol Times and Mirror* asking for a respectable woman to care for her baby girl, Doris. Her hope was that this would be a temporary arrangement until her situation improved. As it happened, on the same page was an entry from a couple who wanted to adopt a healthy child. No doubt, Evelina would have been attracted to the description of the couple, who lived in a nice country home. She eagerly wrote a letter of enquiry and, equally promptly, received a reply. The letter was from a Mrs Harding, who explained that she and her husband were deeply fond of children and that they were churchgoers. She hoped to bring the child up as her own, she wrote, but she said it would be no problem for Evelina to come and visit. Mrs Harding told Evelina that she was planning to visit a friend in the area and would happily break her journey at Gloucester to meet Evelina and take over the care of Doris. The friend of Mrs Harding was in the Gloucestershire County Asylum, but Evelina did not know that Mrs Harding had herself been admitted to that very asylum four years earlier. It would later emerge that Mrs Harding had experienced a violent frenzy, during which she had complained of hearing voices and had cut her own throat.

Evelina wrote back urging Mrs Harding not to respond to any other enquiries. Just thirteen days after her notice had appeared in the *Bristol Times and Mirror*, Evelina was waiting in her lodgings for Mrs Harding's arrival. As was convention, Evelina was expected to pay for her child to be taken from her care, and although she tried to negotiate a more manageable regular payment, Mrs Harding would not budge and Evelina had no choice but to hand over £10. Delaying the eventual separation from her baby by a matter of hours, Evelina accompanied Mrs Harding on the train from Cheltenham to Gloucester, where she watched as Doris was taken on the train to Reading. She returned home alone.

A letter from Mrs Harding arrived to say that Doris was safe and well. Evelina wrote back asking for more details about her daughter, but did not receive a response. The next time Evelina heard about her daughter was eleven days after she had given her away, when she was called by the police to Reading. On arrival, she was escorted to the mortuary, where she saw a baby's corpse lying on a slab.

Exactly a week later she came face to face with the woman she had known as Mrs Harding. In the yard behind Reading police station, five women stood in a line. Amelia Dyer, who Evelina had known as Mrs Harding, was among them. Evelina broke down in tears.

The police investigation had begun when, on 30 March 1896, a bargeman who had been navigating a stretch of the Thames in Reading had fished a parcel from the water and found it to contain the body of a very young child. He immediately alerted the police. This was not Evelina's daughter; the bargeman's discovery was on the day before Evelina had entrusted her daughter to the woman from Reading. A local mail clerk had been able to make out an address and postage date on the parcel and reported that the recipient of the parcel had moved to a different address in Reading. The police devised an operation to uncover whether there were illegal activities at that address. A woman went to the house posing as a mother needing a home for her illegitimate child. The willingness of the occupant to enter into a discussion about an arrangement gave Detective Constable Anderson and Sergeant James enough grounds to question her and search the property.

Piecing witness accounts together, the police discovered the fate of baby Doris. After taking her from her mother, instead of returning home to Reading, Amelia travelled to the north London house where her adult daughter and son-in-law lived. She used tape to throttle Doris until her life was extinguished. Dyer's daughter took some clothes for her own daughter from a box Evelina had sent with her baby; the remainder of the box's contents were pawned. The following day Amelia went out and returned with another young child, whom she also throttled, to death. The two small bodies were stuffed into a carpet bag, which Dyer carried with her back to Reading. Late that night she dropped the bag, weighed down with pieces of brick, into the River Thames. These were two among several infant corpses dredged up from the riverbed. From the items in Dyer's house, the police deduced that she had been engaged in what was then known as baby farming.

Born in a small village near Bristol in the late 1830s, Amelia Elizabeth Dyer became the youngest of seven children following the death of her two youngest siblings. The daughter of a shoe-maker, Dyer endured a difficult childhood in which she was the main carer for her mentally ill mother. As an adult, she trained as a nurse and as a midwife, and it was at this time that she first heard about baby farming. Following the death of her husband, Dyer first opened a house of confinement in Bristol in the late 1860s. She charged a fee to take in unmarried women who could no longer hide their pregnancies, some of whom asked for their infants to be suffocated at birth to give the impression of still-birth. But Dyer also fostered infants for a weekly fee. A child to her was a commodity from which she could make money, and she could enhance her profits by cutting back on the cost of care. Consequently, children given over to her were neglected. She slowly starved the children, using daily doses of laudanum, which was known colloquially as 'the quietness'. If all humanity was removed from the analysis, the inevitable next step to maximise profit was disposing of the children altogether.

It is not known how many of the children Amelia Dyer took from their mothers died, but it is estimated to be in the hundreds. One explanation for Amelia Dyer's criminal behaviour is that her selfish interests were not balanced by a concern for others. Most people would not even contemplate such callousness. If in a darker moment they did, then the consolidation of the idea into an intention should be prevented by intensely disagreeable feelings that spontaneously appear. Critical to the human psyche is our ability not only to think, but also to feel, from the perspective of others. These millisecond-by-millisecond reactions to the anticipated effects on others of our actions serve to guide us to be mostly pro-social.

There are various reasons why this internal guide fails. Amelia Dyer may never have had the capacity to understand the emotional perspective of others – a Victorian example of what would come to be labelled as psychopathy. Alternatively, it could be that experiences in her life led to a dampening of the usual emotional response to the suffering of others. People who are repeatedly on the receiving end of someone else's aggression may find themselves switching off their concern with others' minds. It is not clear whether Amelia Dyer was exposed to trauma. It is not in doubt that she was incarcerated in mental asylums and she did report symptoms of psychosis, which were occasionally accompanied by extreme emotional disturbance. Uncovering the mental processes explaining someone's violent behaviour is dependent on listening to the way that person experiences the world.

Having been convicted of murder, Amelia Dyer was executed at Newgate on 10 June 1896. The following year, with the passage into law of the Infant Life Protection Act 1897, the local authority had to be notified of any child adoption. However, in the first few years of the new century, there were a number of other high-profile baby-farming trials, which gave force to questions about whether infants were sufficiently protected by the law. Around the same time, medical experts were calling for greater account to be taken of the potential effects of birth on the mental stability of mothers who killed their own child. There was a recognition of those rare cases where mothers, in a post-natal state of instability, are overcome by an irresistible urge to do something they would never normally countenance. Because they may have known what they were doing, they would not have fallen within the legal definition of insanity formulated immediately after Daniel M'Naghten's trial. Therefore, they faced the death penalty. The momentum building for a change in the law was stalled by the First World War, but then in 1922 the first Infanticide Act was passed. Under this Act, mothers suffering a significant post-natal alteration in the workings of their mind and who caused the death of their newborn could ask the court to consider a defence of infanticide. If accepted, then they were convicted of manslaughter rather than murder, though this depended on the court finding an imbalance of mind resulting from the effect of giving birth.

With this law, the term infanticide, which had until then been used to describe a crime, had also become the name of a defence to this crime. Although it was a positive step, testing the first version of the Infanticide Act in real-life cases exposed some weaknesses. In 1927, the Old Bailey heard how Mary O'Donoghue, who was in a dire state of poverty and malnutrition, had strangled her infant son with a napkin and stored his body in a box under her bed. His age of thirty-five days was beyond the court's interpretation of newly born, and therefore infanticide was not a defence that O'Donoghue could have presented to the court. In 1936, Brenda Hale cut the throat of her second child and her own. She survived; her three-week-old baby did not. She had first begun to experience symptoms of a mental illness several weeks after the birth of her first child, who survived. The same symptoms recurred soon after the arrival of her second child, but this time the child was to suffer a tragic fate, though again was not considered newly born. Lord Dawson, who had been the medical expert at Hale's trial and was the President of the Royal College of Physicians, introduced a bill in which the defence would be extended to twelve months after birth. At the second reading of the bill in the House of Lords in 1938, Lord Dawson said 'the intention of this Bill is to secure recognition in Parliament that under certain circumstances the killing of infants is provoked by illness and not always by criminal intent.' The 1938 Infanticide Act remains in force today.

Once I had rehearsed the specifics of this Act, I began studying carefully the papers setting out the prosecution's case against Jodie. She was a thirty-five-year-old professional musician whose husband's career as a journalist had just received a major boost with his promotion to lead an overseas bureau. He explained in his witness statement that he had returned for the birth of their first child, but as soon as Jodie was settled at home he had to leave again. Being in a different time zone made it difficult for him to stay in touch. Days would go by without phone contact and looking back he could see that he had missed the warning signs. Reading the transcript of the 999 call Jodie had made to report the offence, it was clear that there were grounds to question her state of mind at the time. She started the call by explaining that her three-month-old son was now safe. He was asleep for good. When the operator asked what she meant and whether she needed an ambulance, Jodie said, no everything was fine now, but she didn't know who were the right people to take away the body. I wondered whether saying her son was safe meant that he had been in danger – maybe he had a serious illness or she was protecting him from someone else. An alternative explanation for what she said was that she held a belief that he was in danger when, in reality, he was not. It is difficult to say much from reading the words alone.

I had been sent the audio recording of the call. Initially, Jodie sounded calm, almost relieved. Then she took on a bemused tone as if she couldn't really understand her own reasons for what she had done. Towards the end there were extended silences when she did not respond to the operator's questions and at other times I could not make sense of her mumbling. Finally, after ignoring the operator again, she said 'OK' for no obvious reason and put the phone down.

The recording added to the impression that Jodie was not in a good state of mind, but I needed to tread carefully. An audio recording or video footage of a defendant around the time of the offence is an invaluable real-time source that will feed into my analysis. Still, it is not a record of the person's mind. A pitfall in psychiatry is to jump to diagnostic conclusions quickly and then to shout about the confirmatory evidence and skip by the unsupportive evidence. The call happened after the offence and by then her state of mind may have been derailed by a realisation of what she had done.

Before Jodie had hung up, she had provided her name and address. When the police and ambulance team arrived, they found the door unlocked. Not knowing what they were going to be faced with, the police took the lead. They moved towards the sound of what they thought was a single voice in conversation, as if on a phone call. Entering the room, they found Jodie kneeling on the floor and leaning over the bed. She stopped talking, but did not look up. Her son was lying still on the bed. Noticing the body was drained of colour, the officers thought it was probably too late to save the infant, but because even the slimmest of chances should not missed, they needed to quickly make the space safe for the paramedics to assess the motionless boy for signs of life. In a firm tone, one of the officers told Jodie to look at them. She turned her head and although her eyes moved to the direction of the officers, her focus seemed elsewhere. In their own ways, both officers described in their witness statements how Jodie's face lacked emotion. They could not tell what she was feeling. She did not resist their commands to place her hands on the ground, to turn her body away from the bed, to move towards them and to stand up. As soon as she was escorted out of the room, two paramedics rushed to the boy. Very quickly they could tell that he had been dead for some time. Later the post-mortem would confirm that his life had been extinguished between eight and ten hours before Jodie had called emergency services. The cause of death was strangulation with a pair of tights.

I turned to Jodie's medical notes. There were letters from an audiology clinic, and ear nose and throat surgeons – Jodie had suffered hearing problems throughout her childhood and had undergone a number of operations. There had also been emergency department attendances. One letter documented her treatment for a broken forearm sustained by falling off a swing when she was six years old. There followed letters summarising her attendances at the fracture clinic. At the age of eight, her mother presented her to hospital again because she was sure she had swallowed a coin. Nothing was seen on the X-ray. When she was fourteen, she was brought in with severe abdominal pain. She was kept in overnight in case of appendicitis, but by the next day the pain had gone and she was discharged. Although there were no mental health service letters in this first section of the medical records, I read each side of every page. Very occasionally buried in a letter for a physical health problem is a reference to difficulties at home or a passing comment about the patient seeming unduly anxious, but I did not find anything of this sort in Jodie's notes.

The next section of the records was filled with antenatal charts and letters. No one had reason to be concerned about Jodie's mental health before Jack was born. The birth passed without medical complications; Jack appeared healthy. In the first week at home, Jodie told the community midwife about how she felt more emotional. She recognised that being apart from her husband made it more difficult, but her family were on hand to help. Her score on a screening questionnaire for post-natal depression was moderately high. An urgent appointment was made with her GP and she was prescribed antidepressant tablets. A week later she told the GP she was feeling a bit better. After that, in routine contact with her GP and the health visitor, she spoke about her worries for her son's health. At the time it wasn't thought to be out of the ordinary, as Jack had had difficulty feeding and he was not putting on as much weight as he should have done.

It was not until Jack would have been about six weeks old that there was a call from Jodie's father to the GP's surgery. He thought she was being, in his words, really weird. She had said to her sister, Rachel, that Jack was changing shape. When the family tried to pin her down on what she meant, she would reassure them it was just a turn of phrase. After a few days she would then make the same sort of comments about Jack again, mostly to her sister.

I flicked to the prosecution bundle to find a witness statement from Rachel. She regretted that she did not take it more seriously, that she did not 'connect the dots'. She had felt that Jodie had brief odd episodes, which cleared up when challenged, but when she was preparing the statement after the death of her nephew, she saw a very different picture. Rachel concluded now that when confronted by her family, Jodie tried to hide her worries. I would need to reserve final judgement until after my assessment, but the documentary evidence was pointing to a post-natal condition.

The risk of changes in mental functioning in the post-natal period has been recognised by physicians for millennia. Over two thousand years ago Hippocrates documented the case of a woman from a town on the coast of the Sea of Marmara – in the north-west corner of modern-day Turkey – who fell ill with a fever, insomnia and delirium after giving birth to twins. Her condition deteriorated, and she suffered convulsions and loss of her senses, until, seventeen days after her twins were born, she died. According to the Hippocratic school of teaching, if uterine fluid was not released following birth it would flow to the head, causing delirium, mania and even death. Although written in the third person, Margery Kempe's account of her own experience of going 'out of her mind' after childbirth is extraordinary, not least because it is taken from the first-known English autobiography, written in the fifteenth century. The richness of the subjective description is far more than anything that would appear in a present-day psychiatric characterisation of puerperal psychosis:

> [T]his creature went out of her mind and was wonderfully vexed and laboured with spirits for half a year, eight weeks and some odd days. And in this time she saw, as she thought, devils open their mouths, all inflamed with burning flames of fire as if they should have swallowed her in, sometimes menacing her, sometimes threatening her, sometimes pulling and hailing her both night and day...

Distilling her description into symptoms such as visual hallucinations or persecutory delusions takes away the true essence of her experience. Kempe went on to explain that she behaved in a way so outside her usual self because it was 'like spirits tempted her to say and do, so she said and did'.

By the middle of the twentieth century, physicians of the mind turned to their diagnostic manuals to explain psychiatric disorders. But there was a crisis of confidence emerging in the art of diagnosis – psychiatrists in different parts of the world used the same diagnosis in different ways. Global research studies in the 1960s and 1970s found that the same diagnostic labels were being used to describe dramatically different types of patient experience. It made psychiatrists look foolish in comparison to our physical health colleagues, who could be sure that when they spoke about, for example, appendicitis they were talking about the same thing whether they were in the United States, Europe or Asia. Psychiatrists were at a disadvantage because they did not know the thing that caused the symptoms – they did not have the equivalent of the inflamed appendix. (We still do not.) Psychiatrists' diagnostic manuals rely wholly on symptoms. For each diagnosis there is a list of symptoms and accompanying rules that dictate the combination of symptoms required to make the diagnosis. My psychiatric training told me that the words of the mentally ill were only important in so far as I could extract symptoms from their experience and then use the extracted symptoms to make a diagnosis.

We now know that around 13 per cent of women who have just given birth experience a mental disorder of some sort. However, most of these post-natal mental health problems pass without any lasting issues. Violence is an extreme exception.

This time I was on my own waiting at the entrance to the prison. Where years before there had been a rickety Portakabin set back a few yards behind the fence, there was now a grander building. After a minute or two standing alone by the fence, an officer came out of the new lodge and down the stairs towards the fence. He held a small bundle of keys on the end of a chain attached to his waist. 'Yes?' he asked sternly. Ready with my ID badge in my hand, I lifted it for him to see and said that I was here for a psychiatric assessment. He peered through the narrow gaps in the mesh fence to look at the badge. Once satisfied the picture was my likeness, he unlocked the entry door and directed me up to the lodge. From there I was escorted to the visits area of the prison, where I waited for Jodie, who had been moved on to the hospital wing of the prison.

I was engrossed in studying the papers when Jodie arrived, accompanied by a nurse. She looked lost. The nurse made to leave but she then realised that Jodie was not sure what to do and so gently encouraged her to sit down and speak to me. Jodie complied and smiled only with her mouth. I explained the purpose of my visit, but I could not be sure from her empty expression that she had digested what she had been told. I asked whether she could tell me what I had said and was surprised that she was able to do so.

With the discussion underway, she answered questions directly with little tonal modulation. She did not elaborate and if I paused to allow her to say more, she did not appear uncomfortable with the resulting silence. Her facial expression was unchanging and gave away nothing about how she was feeling. I did not sense she was tensely holding back; more that she was emotionally hollowed out. The lack of even subtle feedback was disorientating and it reminded me how dependent we are on the reciprocal exchange of minute signals for fluid interactions.

Over the next two hours, I learned from Jodie how her concern had always been to protect her son. What changed was the source of the danger. To begin with it was the usual parental preoccupations such as that he was safe from the cold when they were out. Then she became aware of something impending but she could not articulate exactly what. The closest she could get to putting it into words was a fear for her son's safety that nothing would allay. Not a fear in terms of worry; this was a thick doom-laden fog. When the reason for her fear became clear it only made her more frantic: her son's body was being taken over. Two screechy voices urged her to do something before it was too late; they told her that she was going to lose her son unless she acted quickly. Towards the end, she couldn't be sure whose side her family were on. They seemed to be pressurising her to talk and she spotted they would go quiet if she came into a room. With encouragement from the voices, she reached the conclusion that the way to save her son was to take the life out of his body. Jodie could not get the elements to cohere now, but back then they hung together in a way that left her feeling she had no option.

As I was escorted out of the prison, any thoughts I had about the role of Jodie's disordered mind on her criminal actions were overshadowed by more immediate concerns: she was in critical need of hospital treatment. Once in my car, I called my secretary to ask her to text me the number for the forensic hospital covering the area where Jodie was living. Patients in prison who may need help beyond what the prison doctors and nurses can offer remain the responsibility of the NHS services in the area they come from. I then called the solicitors to ask permission to make the referral. The reason I was asked to see Jodie was to prepare a report for the court, not to meddle in her treatment, but often my meeting with a defendant is the first time they have been psychiatrically assessed. Occasionally, forensic psychiatrists uncover a previously unidentified major psychiatric disorder.

I had no doubt that childbirth had led to a severe disturbance in the balance of Jodie's mind and that this had caused her to kill her son. The conclusions of my report were not contentious; the psychiatrist directed by the prosecution to examine Jodie agreed. An infanticide defence was accepted by the prosecution and the court saw no need to hold a trial. Moving straight to sentencing, Jodie was made the subject of a hospital order with restrictions, which meant that the forensic psychiatrist responsible for her care would have to seek the agreement of the Ministry of Justice before making any significant changes to the conditions she was detained under. There was a strong likelihood that she would recover and, eventually, once the psychiatric team were sure it was safe for her to do so, return to the community.

8

Narin

NARIN WAS A recently sentenced prisoner when she was referred to our team for a second opinion. At the time, I was running a specialist forensic service, which had been established to assist in the management of offenders who were identified as both personality disordered and dangerous. The prison psychiatrist believed that Narin needed treatment in hospital, but the team from the hospital disagreed.

When I first entered psychiatry, personality disorder and mental illness were seen as completely separate categories of mental disorder. According to the received wisdom of the time, mental illnesses were those conditions that developed suddenly and represented a change from how the person had been before. The typical pattern in, for example, the mental illness schizophrenia was a change from their usual self to an obviously bizarre state. But personality disorder is seen as an extreme position on a continuum with normality.

In all of us, different situations may elicit different reactions, but in the round there are some consistent threads across situations in the way we tend to think, feel and behave. These threads define who we are and how we are distinct from others. This is our personality. We may be known for certain foibles. Being a perfectionist and adopting painstaking attention to detail, for example, can enhance educational and occupational attainment, but in the extreme these tendencies may interfere with finishing a task and someone who has these traits such that they cause serious distress or dysfunction is at risk of receiving a diagnosis of obsessive-compulsive personality disorder. As with any personality traits, disordered or not, they begin to emerge in childhood and become more obvious in adolescence.

The prison psychiatrist explained in her letter to me that Narin had been diagnosed with personality disorder, and that they were finding her behaviour very difficult to manage. They could not guarantee her safety. She wanted my opinion on whether Narin needed to be transferred to a specialist unit. A week or so before I was due to visit Narin in prison, one of the junior members of my team presented the key information from Narin's reports at our weekly team meeting.

After suffering unexplained seizures, Narin's daughter, Jasmine, died aged four. In her short life, Jasmine had been seen in the accident and emergency department six times. Each time, Narin told the doctors that she had been feverish and had suffered fits, but the cause could not be found, and each time Jasmine recovered and was sent home. The post-mortem found an abnormality in the electrolyte blood levels. There were a number of possible causes: one was a physical health problem, though again, none could be found; a more sinister explanation was the deliberate administration of a noxious substance to her food – poisoning.

Investigations of Narin's background found that she had had her own health problems, but these were physical rather than psychological. Narin's school attendance had been marred by absence for a number of non-specific health issues, but her medical records did not mention any previous psychiatric treatment. To the accident and emergency staff who encountered Narin when caring for Jasmine, something seemed amiss. After Jasmine's death, they reported to the police some unusual behaviour, telling them that Narin would appear agitated during her admissions, but to some it seemed as though she was excited rather than anxious. In police interviews, inconsistencies emerged between the accounts Narin gave about Jasmine's illness and, when placed under pressure about the discrepancies, Narin broke down in tears and admitted that she had been tipping salt into Jasmine's drinks. Narin later withdrew this account, claiming it was made under pressure, but she was convicted for the murder of her daughter and sentenced to life imprisonment.

As we sat in the team meeting, my colleague told us about Narin's progress in prison. Soon after being remanded in custody, she came to the attention of the prison nurses. To begin with the problems were no more than the prison staff were used to. It was not unusual for an officer to hear a cell alarm, and when she realised it was the cell of a recently sentenced prisoner, she probably assumed the occupant was in a state of panic. For any first-time prisoner, adjusting to her new future would take time. She would also have to adjust to her new shrunken space. For first-time offenders, confinement is more than just physical. Every day each of us makes a multitude of tiny decisions, but these decisions are removed from the life of a prisoner. Narin would not have discretion about mealtimes, where she should be at any time of the day, when she could receive visitors, or what time the lights go out. She did not need to think about bills or the rent. She did not have to plan her time. This is unsettling to anyone at first but, gradually, she would be reprogrammed to make different decisions and deal with different challenges. As she acclimatised to her new environment, she would become even less equipped to survive outside an institution.

The officer responding to the cell alarm would have had to slide back the bolts securing the hatch on the door to pull the flap open. The scene was one she had seen many times before: Narin was perched on the edge of her bed clutching her right forearm with her left hand. Some blood had escaped from under her grip. The officer could not go in immediately; before opening a cell door she needed to be accompanied. When she returned to the wing office to ask for support, she also phoned the health-care department for a nurse to attend.

Even when Narin's cutting became a regular occurrence, it did not make her stand out within the prison. It is saddening that prisoners inflicting harm on themselves are not considered particularly unusual. Self-harm and suicidal behaviour is especially prevalent within women's prisons. While women account for only 5 per cent of people in English and Welsh prisons, they are responsible for between a quarter and a third of the acts of self-harm. But Narin had not harmed herself or even thought about harming herself before she came to prison, so it was a surprise that her behaviour quickly became such a problem. As well as cutting at her arm, she began tying material tightly around her neck. Ligaturing, as it is euphemistically known, is so commonplace that prison staff have training in the use of safety knifes to cut the material. The more the staff intervened, the more it seemed to encourage Narin. They felt it was like a game for her, but a very dangerous one. She would rip strips from her clothes that would not be immediately seen by the staff. The first they would know there was a problem was when Narin's cell alarm was activated.

There were signals that Narin wanted to be saved: she was the one who pressed the alarm button. When they intervened, she did not resist or fight back. It just didn't seem to make sense that she would go on to do the same thing again. As well as the increasing frequency of this behaviour, her actions were becoming more risky. The use of multiple loops of material and the tightness with which she wound them made immediate removal difficult. It reached a point when the prison staff felt they had no choice but to insist that she don unrippable clothes. The prison policy meant that for these clothes to be used she had to be transferred to the hospital wing.

Structurally, the hospital wing was similar to a standard prison wing, only a lot smaller. Off a narrow corridor were ten rooms. Nine were cells and the tenth was a cramped office. Whereas officers staffed the ordinary wings, here nurses were in charge. Within days of moving to the hospital wing, the cutting and self-strangulation reduced. Soon it was deemed safe to allow Narin to use her usual clothes. The plan had been for her to stay for a week longer to make sure she was safe before moving her back to the wing. But as it turned out, her return to the ordinary wing was expedited because Narin was an annoyance to other residents in the hospital wing. She did not seem to know what she was doing wrong, but the reports suggested that she was getting involved in other prisoners' problems and she acted as if she was one of the staff.

This would not normally lead to a referral for specialist treatment. Narin came to our attention on account of the escalating seriousness of the self-harm. She was caught in a cycle of self-harm on the wing followed by transfer to the hospital wing with a reduction in self-harm but a return of tensions with other residents required her to be moved again for her own safety.

In her file were the two psychiatric reports from her trial. One was prepared at the request of her solicitors, the other had been commissioned by the prosecutors. Some minor differences aside, the psychiatrists were in agreement. They concurred on diagnoses of borderline personality disorder and histrionic personality disorder. They also both mentioned a third condition: Munchausen syndrome by proxy.

The name 'Munchausen' derives from Baron Munchausen, a literary character based on a German aristocrat of the same name, who was notorious for his fantastical tales of his military exploits. *Baron Munchausen's Narrative of his Marvellous Travels and Campaigns in Russia* was published in 1785, and its author Rudolph Raspe – who had, in 1775, fled to England following accusations that he had defrauded his employer – could not have foreseen that his book would become a runaway publishing success, the basis of several films, and that his protagonist's name would be co-opted as a diagnosis for people like Narin.

In his 1951 *Lancet* article, Richard Asher, a London-based physician, became the first to describe the syndrome when he wrote about patients he had seen who shared a triad of features. They were disposed to tell fanciful stories about themselves, to present with spectacularly unlikely medical complaints and to travel to hospitals far and wide. Asher wrote that 'like the famous Baron von Munchausen, the persons affected have always travelled widely; and their stories, like those attributed to him, are both dramatic and untruthful.' He continued, '. . . accordingly, this syndrome is respectfully dedicated to the baron, and named after him'. Then in the 1970s a doctor working in the north of England saw how this pattern of illness fabrication and induction could be imposed by parents on their children. For this problem, Roy Meadow, professor of paediatrics in Leeds, introduced the diagnosis Munchausen syndrome by proxy. Eventually, the baron's name was dropped from the diagnosis and a more literally descriptive term was introduced: factitious disorder imposed on another.

When I first saw Narin I had to double-check her date of birth. Glancing down to my notes as she approached the interview booth, I confirmed to myself that she was in her mid-twenties. Everything about her looked younger. The way she awkwardly and self-consciously carried herself. The way she had scraped her hair tightly in a ponytail. Even her complexion seemed to be that of a teenage girl. As I introduced myself and the purpose of my visit, she giggled nervously as she would do often during the meeting.

Although she was eager to tell me her story, I had difficulty following it. Her narrative wasn't confused, I just couldn't keep track of all the information she was unloading. I usually prefer patients to illustrate problems with real examples, but Narin presented too many. She kept introducing new characters without explaining who they were or what her relationship with them was. She did not seem to have a sense of how difficult it would be for the listener to keep up. I caught myself leaning on my forehead and sighing. Interestingly, this did not interrupt her flow, and so I tested out other slight gestures and expressions of bemusement. These had no effect. Once it was clear that subtle signals were ineffective, I took to interrupting her to ask who these people were and how they were relevant to her account. She did not seem troubled by interruptions and obligingly provided the extra detail. This continued until it was obvious that we were going to seriously overrun. I told her so and she apologised, but then continued in the same vein. I found myself repeatedly cutting her off in mid-flow and attempting to move the discussion on.

From her digressive and over-inclusive responses, I noted that as a child Narin took on a caring role for her mother, who had difficulty getting round independently due to her obesity and poor health. Usually the section on my assessment of childhood illnesses is brief. If there was a serious illness, I would investigate further, otherwise I would proceed to questions about developmental milestones such as walking and talking. After listening to the briefing the week before about Narin's history, I had made a note to dedicate more time to her early health problems. Narin told me that she had always been given to tummy gripes and headaches. She often had not felt well enough to go to school. Nothing was formally diagnosed, and she did concede that she would sometimes over-egg the pains and occasionally even feign illness. I was intrigued about a possible link between her own physical ill-health in childhood and her actions to induce physical illness in her daughter in adulthood.

Human babies are more dependent on their parents than the offspring of most other species. A foal can walk independently within hours of birth. By contrast, it takes a human infant on average eleven months to be able to take faltering steps and in the order of another six months before they can walk confidently. But despite the clear vulnerabilities, the child's reliance on their parents reaps considerable benefits in the long run. We are born with the potential to develop adult minds, but they are not an inevitable consequence of our growing brain. The attentive parent responds not just to the physical needs of their child. They react soothingly to contain the child's discomfort. Alternatively, at times of cheer, the child is confronted with the parent's face and vocalisation that reflects their joy back to them in a magnified form. Through these regular interactions in the extended phase of dependency, the youngster develops the capacity to experience a repertoire of emotions.

When it came to Narin, I contemplated whether there had been a disruption in the development of her capacity to experience emotions. As she was growing up, her interactions with her mother often centred on health concerns. Taking on a parental role of caring for her mother meant she had to grow up early and suppress her own emotions before she had achieved a proper understanding of them. Did the combination of the focus on bodily rather than emotional experiences colour the way she felt emotions? Emotions are experienced in the body as well as the mind – a churning sensation in our stomach is a common feature of anxiety; an aversion to food may accompany intense sadness – so was it possible that as she was growing up Narin's experience of emotions became skewed towards the physical and away from the mental? In this scenario, changes in how she felt would have a strong bodily component. Physical sensations would also become an important currency for communicating feelings to others.

We moved on to her experiences of school. 'What about friends?' I asked.

In primary school it was fine, she told me. Then the bullying started.

'Can you say a bit more about that?'

'It was horrible.'

'Yes, it must have been . . . What actually happened?' I was interested to see where she would start. I did not want to lead her.

'People just didn't want to be seen with me. I think they thought I was weird.'

'Do you think you were?'

'I don't know. I didn't know what to say . . . When I told a joke no one laughed. But they laughed when I wasn't meaning to be funny.'

'Did they call you names?'

'I was big then as well.' She meant overweight. 'They used to call me fat-nose.' Her nose was not particularly oversized. As I was trying to formulate a tactful follow-up question, she began to explain. 'When I was in primary school, they would go' – without self-consciousness she gestured her hand extending away from her nose and made a drawn-out 'oo' sound with a rising pitch – 'long-nose turned into fat-nose.'

I thought I knew what she meant, but checked it out. 'Did you tell stories?'

'Yes, I made things up.'

'What sort of things.'

'All sorts. I went a whole term saying I had leukaemia. That was in high school.'

'Do you remember when you started making things up?'

'As long as I can remember. The teachers called it a vivid imagination. I would daydream about a different life.'

'Different from what?'

'From anything.'

Later, once I'd had a chance to think through the findings from my assessment, I thought saying 'anything' rather than 'everything' was telling. Maybe not actively escaping; more a preferred state of being.

Narin had already spoken about her home life. It was not overtly abusive, certainly not by the standards of the lives I often hear about. Her parents were still together. She did not remember them fighting. They did not abuse her or her sister. She did not think there was any favouritism. Her father was the more attentive one. She remembered her mother as a bit cold; not really interested in her. All the same, home was not an unhappy place.

When other children started to make fun of her telling stories, she did not stop. Her tales became more outlandish. Illness was a theme that ran through many of them.

'Did you find it difficult to connect?'

'Yes . . . What was it someone called me? I didn't know what it meant. One girl said I was "pompous". I still don't really know what it means.'

Narin struggled to form bonds with her high school peers. She did not suppress her attempts to attract her peers' attention despite the counter productiveness of her tactics. It was surely not a coincidence that during the time I spent with her, she neither followed the usual rules of interaction, nor modulated her over-inclusiveness when presented with feedback initially in the form of my subtle body language and then more overt interruptions and explanations.

By her account, the move up from primary to secondary school was when her relationship problems started. The sudden enlargement of the social group that comes with this move and the step-change in the educational demands are difficult enough. Secondary school years are also a phase of significant mental change. Transitioning from childhood to adolescence throws up new challenges. Bonds in early childhood develop through shared interests and activities; making and maintaining friendships as we move towards teenage years requires more refined social skills. As well as experiencing and learning how to master our own widening range of emotions, we need to temper our response to the feelings of others. It feels good to be invited into, or accepted by, a social group. Rejection is acutely painful; the noxious feelings that come with loneliness motivate continued attempts to connect. Our social success becomes heavily dependent on our reputation and in adolescence it is a favourable reputation with our peers that we crave the most. Narin carried on trying, but she was frustrated by her interactional clumsiness. Her reputation was being damaged by her own actions. But then a modern phenomenon came to her rescue.

Our core drives to connect with others and to manage our reputation can to some degree be satisfied by social media. The advantage for Narin was that in a digital world she had more control over her self-expression. Also, she did not have to deal with the immediacy of face-to-face interactions, which were too complicated for her. Predictably, her social media posts often announced health-related events such as an episode of illness or doctor's appointment. By favourable comparison to her experience in school, cruel comments from her web-based social circle were in the minority. Mostly, responses were sympathetic. She now felt that she belonged, but the connections were virtual and highly managed. She became even more avoidant of in-person interactions.

Once we had spoken about her childhood and adolescence, we started making our way through different domains of her adult life. True to form, Narin met her first boyfriend through a dating website and there was an extended virtual courtship. She recalled it with fondness. In her eyes, they were a good pair and got on well. She did not acknowledge the apparent contradiction between this global positive appraisal of the relationship and the specific examples she went on to describe in detail. She told him she thought he was lazy and that he didn't pay her enough attention. If he didn't get the message, she would yell at him. He didn't seem to mind that much, she thought. Reading his witness statement, I could see that he had a different opinion of the relationship. He thought it floundered almost as soon as they began spending time together. He acknowledged that despite his limited experience of relationships, he thought it odd that she was so openly intolerant from the beginning. After three months, he said they should probably take a break. He never heard from her again. In their occasional weekends together, Jasmine was conceived. Narin told me that she had always wanted to be a mother and that Jasmine's arrival made her feel whole. She told her family that Jasmine's father dumped her as soon as he found out she was pregnant but, in fact, he never knew of Jasmine's existence until he was approached by the police conducting the murder investigation.

A neighbour interviewed by the police had sometimes heard Narin shouting out. Narin admitted to me that she would lose her temper; she couldn't bear Jasmine's persistent crying. When Jasmine became upset, Narin's first thought was that she was hungry and if she did not take the bottle, in her mind, she was being stubborn. Narin's first social media post about an appointment with the health visitor elicited a burst of social media interest, and this eased the stress of caring for Jasmine. Narin had a low threshold for taking Jasmine to the hospital; these visits presented new photo opportunities in which Narin could prompt others to pay attention to her. It gave a boost to her feeling of connection to others. Some members of this virtual group, who became witnesses in the criminal proceedings, had noticed that Narin, rather than Jasmine, tended to be centre stage in these snaps.

Narin opened up to me about the occasions when she had taken Jasmine to hospital despite her not actually being unwell. She said that she had liked having the doctors and nurses fussing around her. These health professionals would have been motivated by their vocational duty to care for a sick child, but Narin experienced the hospital visits as occasions when she felt she belonged. Then, at a time when she was feeling particularly alone, Narin conceived the idea of adding something to Jasmine's drinks in order to make her sick and allow for more hospital visits. She told me that she didn't think it would cause lasting damage and, even when it was later explained to her by hospital doctors that her daughter's condition was serious, she had reassured herself that they had always been able to make Jasmine better. As she spoke to me, Narin would make incidental remarks about the positive effect on her mood of the extra medical interest in her daughter's unusual symptoms and the extended hospital stays.

I listened carefully to her account for any signs of feelings attached to the memories of her actions. Now and then she alluded to the newspaper reports, to damning headlines that had labelled her as a 'monster mum'. She brought up these reports to express her annoyance at the contents and rebuff their conclusions as unfounded. Narin's logic seemed to be that since she was a good mother most of the time it was unfair to blast her for the occasional lapse. The emotion she experienced was more in the form of outrage at the damage to her reputation than regret for the harm she had caused. It was very possible that her flawed logic and the minimal emotional reaction to the harming of her daughter were manifestations of the underlying deficits that allowed her to commit the offences in the first place.

In the days after meeting Narin, I mulled over the treatment options in preparation for the next team meeting. But before then there was a development. I took a call from the prison psychiatrist, who told me that Narin was in hospital. Outside of her normal pattern of suicidal behaviour, on this occasion she had not activated the cell alarm after tightly winding a jumper sleeve around her neck. They thought it might have been relevant that a few hours before she had taken a week's worth of tablets, which she had hidden in her cell. I was advised that, with the increasing recklessness of her behaviour, she was posing more of a danger to herself and that the prison doctors and nurses felt there was a high chance she could kill herself even if she did not mean to.

I shared with the team my belief that the ultimate decision was not whether she warranted treatment – this was not in doubt. It didn't matter if you preferred to use diagnoses or underlying processes to understand the history – either way, there were obvious and severe psychological problems that were leading to significant distress and harm to herself and others. The question was how we would persuade other decision-makers that treatment was necessary.

People whose suffering can be understood in terms of personality disorder provoke a reaction from psychiatric services that is different from any other mental disorder. No one questioned Jodie's need to be rescued from the prison by transfer to a healthcare system. Narin's diagnosis meant extra effort was going to be needed. When I began my psychiatric career, a diagnosis of personality disorder could lead to unashamed denial of access to help. In my years as a consultant, policy initiatives have encouraged an acceptance that personality disorder is not a reason for exclusion from mental health services. Ironically though, these initiatives have caused many clinicians to argue that specialist personality disorder services are required and therefore mainstream services are not suitable. The consequence is that the patient continues to be faced with rejection and obfuscation.

If mental health clinicians behave in this way, it is hardly surprising that the criminal justice system also responds quite differently to these two sorts of problems. A finding in court that Jodie's responsibility was diminished was almost inevitable. Even a hardened cynical psychiatrist who understood the mind in a way that more often favours the prosecution's side would be moved by Jodie's case. Predicting a negligible chance of success, Narin's legal team did not even attempt to persuade the court about diminished responsibility. This was despite the psychiatrists agreeing that she met the criteria for three psychiatric diagnoses, at least one of which, by definition, explained her actions.

Before transfer to a treatment service could be considered for Narin, we had to jump through a series of hoops that delayed any decision for almost six months. After more assessments, more report writing and more meetings, she was finally transferred to hospital. The proviso was that as soon as the risk to herself was reduced she should be returned to prison. Why were the responses to Jodie and Narin so very different? Could it be to do with differences in the underlying nature of their conditions? Jodie was clearly the unfortunate victim of anomalies in the workings of her mind. The irrational beliefs about the danger she and her son faced became such a dominant force that she chose a course of action that she wouldn't ever have come close to entertaining before. Her usual reserved but thoughtful and caring disposition was replaced with a distrustful, withdrawn and irritable temperament. But Narin was equally at the mercy of mental perturbations. That her experience of emotions was more physical than mental was not something she consciously brought on herself. Neither did she deliberately set out to scupper relationships or curb emotional responses to callous urges. Jodie and Narin were alike in acting under the dominant influence of unwelcome disordered psychological forces. Clinicians trying to justify their more forgiving attitude towards violence linked to mental illness can often be heard invoking the notion of conscious awareness. Narin would have been fully aware of her actions. This is not in dispute, but so would Jodie.

So if differences in both the nature of the underlying problems or in the degree of awareness melt away on analysis, why does the prejudice against personality-disordered patients persist? I believe the answer can be found in people's immediate reactions. During my visit to assess Jodie, the officer who escorted me within the prison asked me to remind him who I was seeing. It was friendly small talk, but when I told him his cheery manner abruptly changed. His face crumpled with concern. His resonant voice quietened. By contrast, an officer with whom I spoke while visiting Narin could not hide his disdain for her. 'There's nothing really wrong with her, you know. She's acting out, and when we react, she ups the ante. She knows what she's doing.' Revealingly, these were not the form of words a prison officer would spontaneously choose. Later, when I discussed Narin with the doctor and nurses on the health-care wing of the prison, it was clear that they were the source of the prison officer's phraseology. They had given clinical credibility to what in fact was a dismissive judgement.

Jodie's mental disorder – like Seb's – was obvious to everyone, even to those without psychiatric training. She stood outside our perception of normality and therefore our expectations of acceptable behaviour. As a consequence, the instinctive reaction of being appalled by violence is much more likely to be suppressed. By contrast, on casual meeting and putting aside the offence, Narin would not stand out as markedly unusual. The cause of her problems was hidden below the surface. An explanation that might counter our immediate negative feelings is not immediately available. There is an irony that the power of emotions on behaviour is illustrated not only by the offence Narin committed, but also by the unsympathetic attitudes towards Narin that were pervasive, including among health professionals.

9

Paul

A NARROW STREAM ran in a deep ditch next to the farmer's track. When a farm worker returned after the weekend to continue clearing the drainage ditch, he caught sight of what looked like rubbish caught in the undergrowth on the far bank. As he stood on the edge of the ditch and stretched to see better, a wave of nausea accompanied his realisation that it was not rubbish, but the exposed abdomen of a human body.

Isabel was twenty-seven. She had been missing for ten days. She was close to her parents and her sister, whose three-year old child she doted on. She was new to the area, but had been accepted into a tight group of female work colleagues who met up on a Friday or Saturday night. They preferred good food and wine rather than an evening at a rowdy club. Isabel had been joining them a bit less regularly since meeting her boyfriend a few months ago.

Eight months later, I found myself in the witness box of the Crown Court facing rigorous cross-examination about my evaluation of Isabel's killer.

'So, do you agree that the defendant was suffering from a medical condition?'

It was inevitable that my evidence would be unpicked. The tactics employed come in many different forms. I took from the quizzical tone adopted by Mr Eddison, the senior barrister for the defence, that I was likely to be subject to a direct attack. In my reply, I was careful with my choice of words. 'A recognised medical condition as it appears in the Coroners and Justice Act is, as I understand it, taken to mean a diagnosable medical condition . . .'

While I was still mid-sentence, Mr Eddison gave an exaggerated sigh while looking down at the papers on the lectern he was gripping. The signal was clear. I was not giving him a straight answer. Was he – as his posture and demeanour suggested – frustrated, or was he secretly pleased that my answer gave him a chance to feign frustration?

As an expert witness in a criminal trial, I am used to being cast in an unwanted role. In this case, the part I was being offered was that of the slippery psychiatrist whose verbose responses were overcomplicating what should be a straightforward issue. Reminding myself that the melodrama was being engineered allowed me to press on unperturbed. '. . . and I believe that Mr Campbell meets the criteria for a diagnosable medical condition, and so . . .'

My pause for breath was an opportunity for Mr Eddison to take the stage again. He knew from my report how I was going to answer his question. Showing the court that it had to be dragged from me added to the impression he wanted to create. 'I see, but what are you saying? Does he suffer from a medical condition or not?'

Earlier that same morning I had already been on my feet in the Crown Court witness box for an hour and a half. The prosecution lead barrister, Mr Oxley, took me through the main conclusions of my report. He asked me to read certain paragraphs, or to clarify a technical term, using my evidence to steadily build a case against the diminished responsibility of the defendant.

Using diagnosis to explain behaviour is uncontroversial to psychiatrists, and in my report, submitted some months before – and then again in my oral evidence – I had done just this. But this accepted method appears more contentious to lawyers when the 'patient' does not show any outward signs of mental disturbance. Observing Paul, the defendant in this case, would not cause even an experienced psychiatrist to question his sanity – outwardly he appeared to be of sound mind. And indeed, talking to him would confirm that he was not troubled by depression or anxiety any more than the transitory changes in mood that we all experience. In the company of others, Paul did not appear suspicious, and neither did he regale the listener with tales of persecution or unlikely happenings. He had been taken aback when I asked whether he had heard voices that others couldn't hear or whether he had been subject to apparitions. Paul had held down a job with no problem and his relationship with his partner seemed unremarkable.

But it was an intense and hidden passion that made Paul a candidate for a psychiatric diagnosis. His diagnosis fell within a category of mental disorders known as the paraphilic disorders. Derived from the Ancient Greek for love, 'philia' is used in a diagnostic context to mean sexual urge; the prefix 'para', in its original Greek form meaning 'beside', denotes abnormality.

The release of the first edition of *Les 120 Journées de Sodome* in 1904 almost went unnoticed. Only a few hundred copies were printed and the publisher – a German psychiatrist who assumed a pseudonym to avoid controversy – promoted the book as an impressive typology of sexual deviance. Paedophilia, rape, sodomy, torture and lethal mutilation among other types of sexual aggression were described through fictional characters holed up in a castle.

The novel had been crafted over a century before in unusual circumstances. In 1772, the authorities investigating the death of a prostitute at a Marseille house party suspected foul play. The host of the party, Donatien, fled the country and in his absence he and his valet were convicted of sodomy and attempted murder. A farcical cycle of arrests and escapes ended in 1777 when Donatien started an extended period of imprisonment. Eleven years later, the governor of the Bastille complained that unless this troublesome inmate was removed, the safe running of the institution would be jeopardised. By distributing notes and using an improvised loudhailer from his cell window, Donatien had stoked the crowds that had been gathering outside the prison into a dangerous fervour. What his jailers didn't know was that Donatien had occupied himself while in solitary confinement by documenting his own sexually depraved experiences and fantasies in the form of a novel written with materials smuggled to him. To avoid discovery and almost certain confiscation, Donatien wrote in miniature on sheets glued together to form a continuous roll that could be concealed in his cell wall.

On 3 July 1789, Donatien was removed from the Bastille and transferred to a mental asylum. When he was summarily extracted from his cell, he had no chance to retrieve his stash. Just over a week later, in that symbolic event in the early phase of the French Revolution, the Bastille was sacked. Although Donatien was ideologically on the side of the insurgents, the storming of the prison meant the loss of his major literary endeavour. In his own words, he 'shed tears of blood' daily for his lost manuscript. But Donatien was never to know that the scroll – designated a French national treasure in 2017 – had been rescued from its hiding place and sold on to an aristocratic family, where it remained largely hidden until it was first published in the early 1900s. Before then, though, Donatien had acquired a public reputation for his sexual perversions. Such was his infamy that the name by which he was known became the basis of a term to describe cruel sexual practices. The word 'sadism' originates from Donatien's inherited title, the Marquis de Sade.

A wide variety of stimuli can trigger sexual arousal in humans. Some stimuli have diagnostic importance. For example, becoming sexually aroused by watching an unsuspecting person undress or engage in sexual activity is the pivotal criterion for voyeuristic disorder. Those who gain sexual gratification by rubbing themselves against others exhibit the central feature of frotteuristic disorder. Sexual arousal in response to a non-living object such as shoes has attracted the diagnostic label fetishistic disorder.

According to the court rules I was Mr Oxley's witness, though this does not mean that I was helpful to the prosecution; it is that the opinion expressed in my report is helpful to them. This may sound like a distinction without a difference, but it illustrates a paradox of acting as an expert witness within our adversarial system. I should arrive at the same opinion and respond with the same answers irrespective of which side instructed me to prepare a report or called me to give evidence – I am neutral. Yet, from the meeting with the prosecution team that morning, all the signs are that I am on their side.

Indeed, soon after first arriving in the court building that morning, I was whisked into a side room for a discussion away from the ears of the defence. Ahead of the trial, Mr Oxley had insisted that I attend court before I gave evidence, in order to listen to the other psychiatrist's evidence, but – while I could see the usefulness of this – my hospital commitments meant that I could only spare one day that week for the trial, and so I missed the opportunity to listen to my colleague's evidence and required a briefing from Mr Oxley. This briefing might have given the impression of being in hock to the prosecution, as indeed might the position reserved for me in the court on a bench behind Mr Oxley. In the face of my friendly inclusion into the fold of one side or the other, I often need to explicitly retell myself that my stance as an expert witness must remain independent.

The initial verbal tussle between me and Mr Eddison was a feature of the tension inherent in the psychiatric expert witness's role. An expert witness must be as clear about what is not within his or her expertise as what is. My role is to assist the court to understand a psychiatric issue so that the case can be concluded justly. I am not there to act as a juror; the issue of guilt or innocence is definitely not one for me to comment on. If the jury is able to answer the questions without psychiatric expertise then I would not be called on to comment. Most importantly, I must be careful not to overstep the limits of my expertise.

'Yes, he does suffer from a medical condition,' I asserted.

'What is the medical condition he suffers from?' Mr Eddison continued.

'Sexual sadism disorder.'

'So, to be clear, on this point there is no difference between the opinions of you and Dr Stanlow.'

Making a psychiatric diagnosis is straightforward. It is a mechanical exercise involving the application of predefined rules. The defining criterion for this paraphilia is sexual arousal from the physical or psychological suffering of another person. When I met him the first time, Paul was not reticent about having been sexually aroused by the thought of – and even more so by directly witnessing – the suffering of others. The diagnosis also required him to have acted on these sexual urges with a non-consenting person. Paul had convictions for sexual assault and rape. From his description of these offences, it was clear he was motivated as much by subjugating his victims as by the sexualised nature of his violent actions. Aggressive domination and sex were intertwined in his mind. So what makes this a psychiatric condition?

Until the late nineteenth century, sexual deviance remained primarily an issue of morality, not medicine. Sigmund Freud is widely credited with placing sexual urges in the psychiatric spotlight. In his work with patients diagnosed with hysteria, Freud traced the origin of their symptoms to earlier sexual fantasies. He believed that the breakdown of defences built by patients to protect themselves from early sexual desires led to later hysterical symptoms. Freud's interest was the role of sexual seduction fantasies in psychiatric symptoms prevalent among the Viennese middle class, but he had surprisingly little to say about sexually deviant offending.

The landmark text that medicalised sexual deviance appeared when Freud had only just started his own medical practice in Vienna. In 1886, another psychiatrist working in Austria, Richard von Krafft-Ebing, published the first edition of a comprehensive study of sexual pathology. His book *Psychopathia Sexualis* introduced a system of categorisation illustrated by hundreds of case studies from across the globe. The term serial killer gained widespread usage in the latter part of the twentieth century, but Krafft-Ebing's work makes clear that serial killing is by no means a modern phenomenon. In one study in a later edition of the book, Krafft-Ebing described the characteristics of a series of eight homicides in the 1880s that have achieved enduring notoriety not for their brutality – indeed there were other case studies involving equal levels of barbarity, and in some a higher body count – but because the murderer was never found. In describing the killings of Jack the Ripper Krafft-Ebing notes, 'He does not seem to have had sexual intercourse with his victims, but very likely the murderous act and

223

subsequent mutilation of the corpse were the equivalents for the sexual act.' We will never know whether or not this was the case.

It was also Krafft-Ebing who co-opted the term 'sadism' to use as a medical description of 'the experience of sexual pleasurable sensations (including orgasm) produced by acts of cruelty, bodily punishment afflicted on one's own person or when witnessed in others, be they animals or human beings.' In the early days of psychiatric diagnoses, such sexual deviations were subsumed under the personality disorder category. Now paraphilic disorders are a stand-alone category.

Satisfied that I agreed with his expert on the diagnostic issue, Mr Eddison moved on as I expected to the next leg of the defence. 'Do you accept that there was an abnormality of mental functioning that arose from the defendant's medical condition?' The defence of diminished responsibility does not only rest on there being a recognised medical condition; there are a number of layers to this defence and a central one is that there is abnormality of mental functioning that arises from the medical condition.

I suppressed the urge to give a jargon-filled answer: 'Well, not really. We need to first resolve the ontological fallacy of diagnosis in psychiatry.'

Can abnormal mental functioning, as the law on diminished responsibility suggests, arise from a psychiatric condition? To put it another way, does having a particular diagnosis actually tell me what is wrong with the patient's mind?

A diagnosis in psychiatry is an abstract idea. It describes a group of symptoms from a predefined longer list of symptoms. The only thing we can really say that patients with a mental illness diagnosis have in common is the diagnostic list on which their symptoms appear. We cannot say that they all have the same pattern of brain disturbance, and the likelihood is that they don't. Diagnoses are not grouped together in diagnostic manuals because they have a type of brain disorder in common. The diagnosis *is* the list and nothing else. When I listen to some of my psychiatric colleagues, they give the impression that there is a specific thing called clinical depression that all patients with this diagnosis have in their brain and that causes them to feel depressed, in the same way that there is such a thing as high blood pressure or heart disease. This is the trickiness of psychiatry: there isn't a specific brain disturbance shared by everyone who is diagnosed with clinical depression. The diagnostic criteria that define clinical depression are real and the suffering of someone who meets those criteria is real, but the pretence is that the criteria are the manifestations of a known and singular brain disease: they are not.

Continuing my fantasised exchange with Mr Eddison, I could have explained that a list in itself is not something that has causal properties. Instead I shaped my thoughts in such a way as to give a straight and honest answer without provoking an existential crisis.

'Yes . . . sexual sadism disorder involves a disturbance of mental functioning.'

In the way most psychiatric diagnoses don't provide an explanation for what is happening in someone's mind, they also don't explain behaviour. But paraphilic diagnoses are in some respects an exception since the criteria explicitly connect something in the mind to behaviour. To give Paul this diagnosis, I had to be sure that he satisfied two statements on the Diagnostic and Statistical Manual of Mental Disorders list: he must have repeatedly been sexually aroused by the suffering of others and he must have acted on these urges; in combination these criteria describe something in his mind and the resulting behaviour. Daniel Dennett, the populariser of philosophy, has written about explanations that answer 'What for?' questions. They tell us the purpose of the behaviour. In Paul's case this was that in order to achieve sexual fulfilment he required the suffering of another. The more the suffering, the greater the fulfilment.

I continued, 'The disturbance, which is present in this case, is the link between sexual arousal and the suffering of others.'

'To recap, you agree that there is a recognised medical condition and a disturbance of mental functioning that arises from that medical condition.'

Not wanting to nitpick, I agreed with his summary. There was then a final critical issue to deal with. He took the sheet he had been holding and placed it down on one side of the lectern before turning to the other side to retrieve the next page of prompts. The usher used the lull to reach up to the ledge of the witness box and refill my glass of water, which I immediately sipped from.

The law says that a person's responsibility for a killing cannot be diminished only on account of there being a medical condition and a related disturbance of mental functioning. There has to be some connection between these things and the killer's actions. In law, this connection has to be via one of three specific types of mental dysfunction. There must have been an impairment of understanding, reasoning or self-control.

If my evaluation of the offence only produced answers to 'What for?' questions, it would not be especially helpful to the court in its deliberations about whether one or more of these impairments was present. Knowing only that Paul's objective was to achieve a sexual high and that this required his victim to suffer does not say anything about his understanding, reasoning, or self-control. I need to find a different type of explanation; one that answers the alternative type of question proposed by Dennett: 'How come?'

A description of the mental process leading to the behaviour will tell me 'how come'. Building this process narrative is a different task to making a diagnosis. It is more mentally taxing, but at the same time more rewarding. My objective is to generate a simulation of Paul's working mind. As this simulation starts to take form, I test it out. Would this imagined mind do the things that witnesses said he did? If not, then it needs to be revised.

Police officers investigating an offence take statements to build up an account of events leading up to and immediately after it. In common with the police, I am interested in what the defendant said and did. But there our interests diverge. The police officers need to make the case against their suspect. Does the evidence support the conclusion that he committed the offence? If so – and determining that is not a question for me – my job is to work out why; to answer both 'What for?' and 'How come?' with specific reference to Paul's mind, not just the prototypical mind of someone who is diagnosed with sexual sadism disorder.

Fortunately, witness statements are not just a bland description of the defendant's actions and words in the lead-up to the killing. Line by line, I sifted through each statement to extract sentences that described Paul's actions and demeanour. Patterns of behaviour that run through the statements are particularly helpful; they carry more weight in shaping my simulation of Paul's mind.

Two people on shift with Paul at the haulage depot on the day of the killing were obviously critical witnesses. If there was anything unusual about his behaviour, these colleagues should have spotted something. Was he distracted maybe, or edgy? Did they notice if he was clockwatching?

Due to the passage of time since the offence – he had been arrested two weeks later – Paul's colleagues couldn't be sure, but they did not recall that he was any different to his usual self. He didn't tend to hang around at the depot before his shift as a lorry driver started. But when he popped into the building, he was usually pleasant enough and as far as they could remember on that day he was no different. The police, though, were sure that Paul knew what he was going to do well before the offence. Extreme sadistic imagery had been found on the hard drive of his laptop.

The pathologist couldn't definitively determine the respective positioning of the victim and perpetrator from the pattern of bruising on the neck, but there were signs that they were facing each other.

The post-mortem report methodically described the evidence of a brutal sexual assault. However much I adopt an analytical approach to understanding violence, reading the pathologist's conclusions or the first-hand accounts of sexual violence victims – which I do in preparation for my assessments for the criminal courts – often causes me to recoil. I cannot just cleave off the father and husband parts of my identify. I am no less susceptible to an emotional reaction; which is commonly experienced as disgust. It is an involuntary and immediate response; not one that is born out of an analysis of the nature of the offence or of its consequences for the victim. This feeling drives the widespread desire to punish sexual offenders particularly harshly. The reactions are also the result of a mental process that explains society's positioning of boundaries between sexual behaviours that are viewed as acceptable and those that are condemned.

A mutually consensual sexual act can be intensely forceful. For some, force and inflicting pain are the necessary components of a sexually pleasurable experience. Consensual sadomasochism is sometimes cited as evidence of a level of immoral permissiveness. But whatever people's position on the morality of such behaviour, it does not provoke the same visceral reaction as rape or paedophilia. The repulsion is so intense that rapists and paedophiles are often dismissed as evil and their acts not worthy of explanation. My experience of working with sexual offenders in prisons and secure hospitals tells me that the extent to which their behaviour deviates from social norms indicates how powerful the mind-based forces are.

'I had not planned it,' Paul told me. For a second time, I quizzed him about the hours before the murder. His first account had left me sceptical. He had already told me that his favoured masturbatory fantasies contained scenes of torture to the point of unconsciousness, and I could not ignore the evidence that at least one of the previous rapes was preceded by considerable planning. But in talking about Isabel's death, he was consistent in his responses – he insisted that did not think about hurting her until they were having sex.

I was still left in some doubt. 'Can I check I've understood you? Before you went to Isabel's house you were not planning to kill her?' He agreed. I asked, 'Would you remind me how things changed?' A deliberately ambiguous question discourages a rehearsed response. It also means the initiative is with the patient; their choice of words interests me.

'You know what . . . I've thought about this . . . I'm not sure when I decided to do it.'

I noticed that he did not specifically refer to the offence. Using 'it' or some euphemism in place of a more specific descriptor is not uncommon. I take care not to interpretatively overreach. This may be merely random variation in the use of language. On the other hand, I must not miss clues about how his mind works. I made a mental note. Even if a pattern emerged, there would not be a single explanation. The offence is a reminder of his circumstances, and not overtly acknowledging what he has done could be a way of reducing the sorrow he felt for himself. Alternatively, Paul may, like most of us, experience an automatic and noxious wave of repulsion at the recalled real manifestation of such sexual violence. Could such a reaction occur in someone who has committed acts of sexual violence?

I wanted to encourage Paul to continue with his own musings. If possible, I preferred to not disrupt his narrative by introducing my own words. I nodded and looked up from my notes enquiringly.

'Maybe it was . . . I don't know . . . it could have been in the back of my mind before I got there?' He was uncertain, and posed the suggestion as a question, but I thought he was grasping at a more accurate approximation of his own internal state at the time.

I have sat through many discussions with colleagues about whether an offence was planned or impulsive, as if these are two mutually exclusive states of mind. They are not. The mental accompaniment of our actions is a mix of emotional vectors driving in varied directions with different levels of force.

'I know it doesn't make sense . . .' he continued. I am more sceptical of the explanation that from its first delivery is tidy, logical and internally coherent. I encouraged Paul to continue even if it didn't make sense to him. 'I think part of me knew this would happen . . . I didn't want to think about it with . . . I was pushing it back . . . When we were having sex, it was there. I couldn't stop it. It was all I wanted. That look . . . the fear in her eyes . . . when I saw it there was no way back . . . Did I say

I've been thinking about this?' I nodded. 'You know, now I look back, I think this was always going to happen. It was just a matter of time.'

I looked up imploringly again. This time, he seemed drained of emotion. He stared through me. I had delayed directing the discussion about the offence as long as I could, but I now realised that he would not be able to continue under his own initiative.

'Are you OK to continue?' I asked. He mouthed 'Yeah' as though there was not enough breath to utter the word out loud. I didn't want him to step back from the perspective he had reached. Paul seemed more insightful than before. Feeding back what he had said would take the pressure off him while keeping the ideas present, but I knew that I must not contaminate his reflections with my assumptions. Referring to my notes, I parroted what he had told me but with a genuine tone of questioning interest. Paul seemed to regain some focus.

For as long as he was aware of having sexual urges, Paul told me, he had been turned on by seeing or imagining others in pain or under threat. In adolescence this was just a necessary part of his climax fantasy. In early sexual encounters it was enough to imagine himself beating or tying up his sexual partners, but the urges remained secret: Paul's early sexual partners would not have known that a strong grip held a moment too long or fingers passing fleetingly around their neck enhanced his sadistic imagery and hence his sexual arousal. In this period, Paul was not causing harm to anyone, and he didn't question whether his fantasies were different from those of other people. Nonetheless, these urges were reinforced and refined by consistent association with the relief of his sexual needs. In his late teens, neither the fantasised sadism nor the increasingly extreme internet pornography he watched gave him the same satisfaction. He paid to inflict pain on sex workers, but this didn't satisfy him either; he came to realise that he needed the recipient of his sexualised violence to really be in fear or pain. Feigned emotion created a flat sexual experience. He disclosed that he had raped two sex workers before his first conviction. He did not know for sure why they did not report him to the police – though studies show that a majority of those working in the sex industry have been the victim of violence, most are reluctant to report these incidents to the police – but he felt he had licence to do the same again. The exchange of money led him to feel a sense of entitlement and allowed him to depersonalise the women. Then, at the age of twenty-three, Paul was arrested for rape of a sex worker who did take the risk of contacting the police. By plea bargaining, he agreed to plead guilty to the lesser charge of sexual assault and was sentenced to eighteen months in prison.

Paul was enrolled on a sex offender treatment programme. At first he was a passive attendee, but in time he could not help but become interested. He did not want to return to his former lifestyle. Alongside an unremarkable weekly routine of work, mid-week five-a-side football and weekends with his then-girlfriend, before his conviction Paul had a sordid parallel life in the red-light area of a city an hour's drive away. In his mind he was able to separate these two lives, but they crashed into one another when he was convicted, and he was left feeling dirty. The treatment programme offered an alternative.

At the time of his release Paul's resolve was strong. He stayed away from – he now used the terms he had learned on the course – triggers for reoffending, for seeking out that parallel life. But the problem was, Paul had also lost his other life – the one with friends, a girlfriend, a home and a job. Faced with isolation, it was almost inevitable that the habit would restart. The next rape charge stuck and this time he was sentenced to nine years' imprisonment.

Before the time of his third arrest, Paul had been out for two years, but the sadistic fantasies continued. He had only been at the haulage company for a few months when Isabel started working there, taking calls and doing the paperwork. On the evening of the offence, Paul had offered Isabel a lift home and, according to him, when they got to her house she invited him in for a drink; he claimed she said that her boyfriend was away and they weren't getting on. There was no way of verifying it, but Paul claimed that the sex was consensual. Isabel had been drinking – a fact that the post-mortem confirmed – but Paul was, he said, confident in his claim that she knew what she was doing. He did not particularly like drinking but had joined her with a couple of glasses of wine. 'I could not have planned it,' he repeated, as if a reason had just come to him. Paul went on to say that he did not know anything was going to happen until just before it did. He wondered out loud whether he saw fear first and then he throttled her, or whether he squeezed her neck to see fear; he wasn't sure. Whatever way it had started, once it did start, Paul was set on a singular course. He did not want to lose the feeling that came with looking into Isabel's panicked eyes.

At one level, what I am looking to establish in my assessment is a collection of chains of events – events in which Paul has played a part. In the chain of work-related events, for example, I am particularly interested in the relationships with a patient's colleagues and how that might have developed or changed. The timeline of this chain of events overlaps with the timeline of the partner relationship chain of events – shaped by meetings and break-ups, by romances or rejections. And then both of these overlap with the crime chain of events, in this case the sexual offence. There are patterns of behaviours unique to one chain and some that are common to several chains. For example, whereas some domestic abusers may only show overt aggression to partners, a pattern of arrogance is sometimes also apparent in their interactions at work and within their social group. The first time I speak to him, Paul tells me what has happened, what he has done, and through this I am able to plot various timelines in Paul's life in the lead-up to the murder. But to get at his state of mind, to understand what the driving factors behind the events were, I need to understand the causes for the events, and how they interact. What is the explanation for the part that Paul played in the event? Of course, I could explicitly ask Paul for the reasons behind each action, but I resist doing so. As with most people, even without knowing it, Paul's narrative will be littered with explanatory inferences, and these are often more revealing.

Later, sitting quietly in my study, I moved between leaning in close to the screen of my laptop and peering at the words Paul had used to stretching back in my chair and staring up, searching for meaning. In what circumstances are they activated? How are they experienced? How do they interconnect? What happens when they are in conflict? I am immersed in a construction of another person's mental world. It takes effort to hold on to the simulation, but gradually a picture of Paul's mental processes begins to take shape.

Every so often, though, my concentration is interrupted by the intrusion of my ordinary citizen self – the man who is a father, a husband, a friend. That self says, 'Paul knew what he was doing; he was satisfying himself in the most savage way.' In coming to an informed explanation for Paul's offences, I must include the role of emotional influences on decision-making. I am not just talking about Paul's decisions; I am as open to the influence of feelings on my decisions. What might be a carefully constructed psychiatric explanation can serve as an excuse in different hands. Excusing his actions feels wrong, but it does not make an explanation any less valid. The legitimacy of my contribution rests on applying an informed understanding of the mind. The ordinary citizen's perspective is, of course, wholly valid, but that is not the one I am being asked to provide.

The behavioural description of Paul's deviance was that sexual arousal was dependent on the suffering of the other. I now felt able to produce a more insightful account; one that tried to represent his mind at the time of the offence. This rested on the enhancement of sexual arousal by the feeling that arose in response to the signs that the other was fearful of him. He had started by superimposing this scenario in his imagination on non-sadistic sexual intercourse, and then paid for others to enact the scenario, though the feelings accompanying these sexual encounters did not have the same intensity that came with actually witnessing the other fearing for their life at his hands.

The term serial killer has been criticised because it is defined by the offender's opportunity to kill repeatedly rather than a type of mind that can kill repeatedly. It is behaviourally, rather than psychologically, defined. The term compulsive killer used in the academic literature more accurately describes the individual. Paul had the psychological characteristics of a compulsive killer and, if he were not incarcerated, he had the potential to kill serially.

Mentally cleaving off his sadistic activities from his parallel mundane existence reduced the need for Paul to acknowledge the consequences of his behaviour. The reporting of an offence, involvement of the police and activation of the criminal justice process meant that he could no longer keep these worlds separate. But some offenders go to greater lengths to maintain a boundary between different worlds.

In January 1983, Elisabeth, a sixteen-year-old girl who had been missing for three weeks, was returned by the police to her grateful parents. Aged eighteen, she disappeared again and when she didn't return, her mother was led to believe that she had run away to join a cult. In fact, for the next twenty-four years, Elisabeth lived within several feet of her mother. Elisabeth's last memory was helping her father carry a door to the basement, after which everything went black. She regained consciousness to the realisation that she was chained to the ground in darkness. Two years earlier, the police had unwittingly returned her to the predatory clutches of her father, who had been raping her since she was eleven. Regularly, over the next two and half decades of her confinement in the basement of the family home, Josef Fritzl would continue to force himself on his daughter.

Before I visited Austria to meet Dr Adelheid Kastner, I had not had access to the Fritzl case other than via the media reports. Journalistic revelations from high-profile trials had never particularly captured my interest. In part, I had been put off by my direct experience of how the facts can be distorted. From the messy mix of reality, the articles often magnify one element to produce a breathtaking, but one-dimensional, story.

I recall a case in which the supposed anti-Semitic credentials of the prisoner I had assessed became the headline feature. In fact, in the lead-up to his near-fatal use of a firearm, this previously reserved man had shifted between wildly contradictory ideologies. In fairness, the journalists did not have access to the full extent of the evidence that showed that several months before the offence there had been a step-change in his personality. A weakening of his powers of logicality and the increasing conspiratorial prism through which he saw the world were critical in explaining his involvement in the offence. It was correct that he had become more fascinated by extremist rantings on social media and that he was drawn to barbarically violent content; but the political or religious leanings of the group was of secondary interest. This was not someone who was by character inclined to fanaticism or whose vulnerability had been exploited by racist recruiters. Undoubtedly these are potential pathways to violent racism, but they were not the ones taken by my patient.

Journalists are not just disadvantaged by not having access to all the facts in these cases. The story available to them is usually one that has been massaged out of its original shape by the adversarial criminal trial process. The jury is not passively presented with an impartial account of the evidence so they can decide what happened. Snippets from the perspectives of a selected cast of witnesses are presented to tell a story: the case against the defendant. Equally the task of the defence is not to tell the court about the most likely series of events; their role is to undermine the credibility of the prosecution's story. Neither legal team is required to explain the behaviour. The way evidence is presented to the court does not help us understand the offence. The journalists then need to take what remains of the facts and distil a particular type of essence; one which is accessible and packs a punch.

I was reading the reports of the Fritzl case on a train out of Vienna in preparation for my meeting with Dr Kastner. She had received the commission to assess Josef Fritzl. As a fellow forensic psychiatrist, she had an expectation that she would be able to explain his actions.

When I am called to contribute to the criminal justice process, I know I will be asked about the index offence – the recent major offence. For the purposes of my assessment, the index offence is almost never an incident isolated in what it represents. Our risk manuals advise that we should assign a higher risk status to those patients who have a history of persistent offending and who have committed offences that differ in type, such as arson and fraud as well as violence. There is also meaning to be found from looking at the past offences. With the patient, I peer into his or her past in a search for related events. Laying these events side by side allows me to see common explanatory threads. It also helps me see how these events may be connected and how this connected narrative has led to the index offence.

Dr Kastner explained that as an eighteen-year-old, Fritzl developed a habit of masturbating behind women he had followed through a park. Exhibitionistic disorder involves exposing one's genitals to a non-consenting and unsuspecting person. Fritzl's actions were different. He wasn't exposing himself to the women – he did not want them to know what he was doing. Recalling her meetings with him, Dr Kastner noticed that what was important to him was the 'knowledge I know something they don't know, if only they knew'. She took from his account that the position he strove for was 'of course some sort of power'. Studies of sexual offenders have found that their offending is often motivated as much by a desire to achieve domination as by the anticipation of sexual relief.

A chance happening led to a change in the direction of Fritzl's offending. When one woman turned round and saw what he was doing, she chased him waving her umbrella. Fritzl decided he needed an alternative means of simultaneously achieving both sexual gratification and a position of power through knowledge over an unsuspecting female. On his route back from his work, he began listening at open windows. He learned which were bedroom windows and when couples were likely to be having sex. Lingering under these windows, he would masturbate while eavesdropping on the occupants' intimacy. Inevitably he took the opportunity to look in. Dr Kastner reflected that this was 'all with the feeling they don't know but I know'.

It was in this period that there was a worrying change in his offending. As he became more familiar with activities in some of the houses, he came to know when the husbands were away from home. Fritzl was among that minority of non-contact sexual offenders who make the transition to contact sexual offending. In his early thirties, he was arrested for a rape at knifepoint. Dr Kastner suspected that more than once he entered a property and raped the female occupant.

His imprisonment for rape led Fritzl to another review of his modus operandi. This reappraisal was not motivated by remorse for the harm he had inflicted on his victims, or an attempt to self-manage the risk that he manifestly presented. It was that he wanted to both rape and lead a normal life. By this time, he was married. His wife dutifully visited him in prison and she has said that he would never talk about why he was in prison. It is possible that under her husband's dominant influence she felt unable to question him. Whatever the reason, this complicity of silence would have left the contradiction between his two life plans unchallenged: one plan conformed to conventional aspirations of marriage, children, holidays and a successful business, the other was to create an opportunity to rape at will.

Frizl's solution was to keep a victim captive for his pleasure. Once he had imprisoned his daughter in the basement, he forced her to write a letter explaining that she had left to stay with a friend and they should not look for her. Over the twenty-four years of her imprisonment, Elisabeth bore seven of his children. Three were kept in the cellar, three were delivered upstairs – their appearance explained in written or recorded messages, purportedly from their absent mother, asking for her children to be looked after. A seventh child died soon after birth and Fritzl disposed of the body.

The way Fritzl's crimes came to light tells us something about the precise nature of his deviant urges. One of the basement children, Kerstin, now nineteen, became seriously unwell. Fritzl agreed for her to receive medical attention. He and Elisabeth carried Kerstin upstairs. Having spent almost two and a half decades underground, Elisabeth only had a moment outside before she was forced to return to her other children. Kerstin was taken by ambulance to hospital. Hospital staff were suspicious of Fritzl's explanation and a note he claimed was written by Kerstin's mother. They contacted the police. A week after Kerstin was taken to hospital, Fritzl acceded to Elisabeth's pleas to go to her daughter in hospital. The police arrested both Fritzl and Elisabeth. Only once the police had guaranteed that she would never see her father again did Elisabeth feel able to divulge how she had lived for the past twenty-four years. Fritzl was then charged with rape, incest, kidnapping, false imprisonment, slavery and the murder of an infant. He later pleaded guilty and was sentenced to life imprisonment.

Dr Kastner questioned why Fritzl didn't come up with a different solution to Kerstin's illness. 'It would have been much, much easier for him to close the door. He could have closed that door in the cellar and never gone back and nobody would ever have known anything about it. And when the daughter fell ill down there he could have gone out and closed the door and that was it.' Dr Kastner believed that this was an indication of some sort of moral compass, even if was seriously skewed. 'There are red lines, and killing somebody for Mr Fritzl as far as I know him was such a red line.' I think this interpretation is plausible. It can at least be assumed that the death of his victims was not part of his sexualised fantasies.

A strong desire to coercively dominate the victims of his sexual aggressive urges seems to have been a necessary element of the explanation for Fritzl's offending. Is it sufficient in itself to explain how he continued to offend in the way that he did against his daughter?

Dr Kastner's description of Fritzl included reflections that would not normally feature in a standard psychiatric report. She began with observations about how he made her feel. These were not the feelings provoked by an awareness of what he had done. She spoke about the more immediate aspects of her interaction with Fritzl. There was something of interest to her in the relationship between the two of them. She estimated having spent thirty-eight hours with him – I was envious of the time allocated to the assessment; in England, I am lucky if I have the opportunity to meet the defendant in a criminal case more than twice. But while the nature of the material discussed in the time Dr Kastner had with Fritzl was extraordinary, his persona was anything but. In Dr Kastner's words, he 'was extremely, extremely ordinary to me'. He had no problem recalling details. 'The structure of his life was very present for him.' What struck Dr Kastner was his style of delivery. 'To put it bluntly he was extremely boring. He was an extremely boring person.' Dr Kastner recalled that his way of expressing himself resembled someone reading the entries in a telephone directory. The effect was so profound that she found it soporific. On the basis of his actions, some had labelled him a psychopath. Dr Kastner's description confirmed my own experience that psychopathy cannot be diagnosed by just knowing about the offending behaviour. Being in a room with Fritzl would soon show that he did not possess even superficial charm, a diagnostic criterion for psychopathy.

Good storytelling does not just rely on a good story. It does not merely entail the transfer of facts verbally. To stimulate the imagination of the listener, the narrator intones, pauses, emotes, adjusts the pace, and reveals. Fritzl's style may have been a feature of a specific impairment with emotional expression; a limited capacity to infuse his spoken language with emotional tone. An isolated deficit of this type may not be particularly relevant to understanding his offending. Listening to Kastner's account pointed to something of more interest.

'He had no feelings concerning the child he once was,' Dr Kastner observed. The only consistent adult figure during Fritzl's boyhood was his mother, who was both neglectful and unpredictably aggressive towards him. Contrary to the commonly reported account that his father abandoned his son, Dr Kastner learned that Fritzl's mother would not allow contact. She was the product of one of many affairs between her father and household maids. The woman to whom Fritzl's grandfather was married could not have children. Fritzl's mother was left with a need to prove she was not barren. Fritzl was the evidence she sought, but thereafter he was a nuisance. From a young age, he was left on his own; when she was there, his mother would brutally beat him.

The effect of childhood trauma differs depending on its meaning to a victim. Dr Kastner had identified that it would have been difficult for Fritzl to take any meaning from what was happening to him. 'She punished him all the time and he didn't know for what, so it's a complete impossibility to know what you do to get what. She was the only person he could refer to, there was nobody else, no family, nobody else.' Unable to make sense of these experiences, he escaped them. There was no physical escape, so he sought a mental refuge. Dr Kastner explained that in his mind he transposed himself to a different reality. 'He read all day long. He totally immersed himself in another world. So you escape from the world that obviously was not so nice. And he was living in his books.'

Dr Kastner explained, 'when he went out from the cellar, he closed the door and he closed the door in his head'. She found that he had 'the absolute perfect ability to close a door in his head ... He was perfect in managing his thoughts.' In the twenty-four years, he never slipped up to give people reason to suspect his other life. 'Not because he was so clever. He wasn't so clever. He was average. He's not a genius. He's a totally average person that does things in a very planned and structured way. Not once – he told me – not once upstairs did he think about downstairs.'

As Dr Kastner was talking, I had the thought that Fritzl's skill in creating completely separate worlds had been crafted out of necessity when he was a child. I put this to Dr Kastner. She agreed. In her words, his childhood had served as 'some kind of training for separating two worlds'. I did not think there was enough to say either way whether his childhood experiences were the ultimate cause of his deviant sexual desires. But to me those experiences led to a way of thinking that allowed him to put his desires into unimaginably destructive practice. He was able to completely disconnect the two lives. He was also able to disconnect understanding from emotion. Dr Kastner found that 'he had complete cognitive understanding of what he had done and the emotion to what he had done was lacking completely'.

'We've heard Dr Stanlow's opinion that the defendant lacked self-control. May I remind you of his position?' Mr Eddison looked up towards the judge, checking that there would be no objection. The judge's expressionless fixation on his note-making was taken as permission to continue. 'If, at the time of the killing, the defendant was acting on a symptom of a mental disorder – which is the sexual urge – then it follows that his self-control was impaired. If this was a serious mental disorder, then the impairment was substantial.'

I was prepared to accept that Paul did not wish on himself a tendency to become sexually aroused by the suffering of others. I would also agree that once in the throes of a sexual encounter, the sadistic urges would become a more and more dominant force.

'It is important to distinguish between the urges and behaviour,' I explained to the court. 'There are factors outside the defendant's control that have led to the development of sadistic urges. On the other hand, he has made choices to act in ways to enhance his arousal. These choices have involved increasing harm to others. The alleged index offence is the culmination of a combination of the urges he has been afflicted with and the choices he has made. Whether this amounts to substantial impairment is a matter for the court to decide.'

Mr Eddison abruptly disagreed. I should, he told both me and the court, do more to help the jury. 'Do you think his self-control was impaired due to his mental disorder?' His frustrated tone now sounded unequivocally genuine.

I wanted to explain that scientific enquiry produces a model of the mind that doesn't match the law's model. The law implies that self-control is a process that we can retrospectively isolate. To answer the legal questions, we would also need to disaggregate the different components of impaired self-control and quantify the specific contribution from a mental disorder. But we cannot do these things and current neuroscientific findings suggest that this is just not the way the brain works. I attempt to deal with the mismatch between the legal and psychiatric models of the mind by taking the psychiatric evidence as far as possible towards the legal model without compromising the scientific basis of psychiatry.

'Yes, in the way I have explained, I do think that his self-control could be said to be impaired.'

'Was this impairment substantial?' Quite understandably, Mr Eddison wanted to pin me down on this issue.

'It depends what you mean by substantial, but as I understand this term, then no I don't think any impairment of self-control reached the substantial threshold.'

The following day, the jury agreed. The diminished responsibility defence was rejected, and Paul was convicted of murder.

10

Gary

THE PRISON OFFICER showed me into a room that was not really big enough for the desk and five bulky chairs that were pressed against the walls. A woman already seated looked up as I took a folder from my briefcase and sat down opposite her. The logo on her lanyard strap gave away her role.

'Hi, I'm Dr Nathan,' I said as I leaned over offering out my hand. In case I hadn't correctly remembered the name of the probation officer, I quietly mumbled, 'Is it Claire?' We had both submitted reports about the same inmate.

Claire and I had only just started sharing thoughts about the case when our conversation was interrupted by a third person. A solicitor introduced himself as Mr Goddard. The three of us were gathered together in this prison side room awaiting a hearing about Gary's future.

A formal system of licensed release was not introduced in England and Wales until 1967 with the establishment of the Parole Board. Derived from the French for 'word of honour', 'parole' is the permission for a prisoner to be released before their full sentence has been served. Gary's sentence was indeterminate and therefore had no fixed end, but having served five years, he was now eligible for parole. Once they had considered all the evidence, including from me and a number of professionals, the Parole Board would decide whether to allow Gary's release.

Gary had been referred to my prison clinic three years before this hearing by one of the nurses. In the assessment on his day of arrival at prison it became clear that he needed to be put through a detox programme. He had come off the streets with an addiction to heroin and methadone. His complaints of hearing voices were mostly dismissed as either lies or nothing to be concerned about. No one expressed a view as to which explanation was more likely, but they were sure that his report of voices was not a sign of a 'serious mental illness'. One of the nurses revealed how her judgement was influenced less by the outcome of a structured assessment and more by her emotional reaction to meeting him. 'He just doesn't leave me feeling "mental illness".' The consensus was that Gary was manipulating the system. He was, after all, someone who had made a living out of deceit and manipulation. And it didn't help him that he started complaining of voices at the same time as angrily objecting to the plan to take him off methadone.

One of the nurses, Sara, thought differently. Sara's colleagues saw her as a soft touch; too easily pushed around by the streetwise prisoners on the make. I saw her as someone who had managed to retain her compassion in a dispassionate system. Whereas other staff had written off Gary's changeable descriptions of the voices as too inconsistent to be taken seriously, Sara noticed that he continued to mention these aberrant experiences when there was nothing to be gained. He had now gone through the detox programme. Admittedly, he had stopped talking as much about the voices, though he later asked rhetorically why should he disclose something so personal if it was just going to be dismissed? Gary also later admitted he had hoped that by talking about the voices it would be a way of delaying the detox. That didn't change the fact that he was hearing voices at the time – just because someone has some devious motives for what they say doesn't always mean they are telling untruths.

Sara had knocked on the clinic room door during a gap in my list. 'I'm not sure, Taj, whether there is anything, but it really seems to bother him. He says he hears voices. Then he says it is more like a thought, but one he can't control. It tells him to attack and he sees horrible pictures in his head of what would be left if he violently attacked someone. I'd really appreciate it if you would just cast your eye over him.'

I was not fussy about who I saw in the clinic. I thought the nurses who were managing vast caseloads were in a good position to determine how my limited time should be used. 'Yes, no problem. Put him down for the next new patient slot.'

When, a number of weeks later, I saw Gary's name on my list I had forgotten my conversation with Sara. I did not even have time to look through his notes before his appointment time came up. I thought I could delay the start by five minutes to read the recent entries, but I was told that Gary had been pacing the holding cell and then growled through the hatch that if I did not see him there and then, he would go back to the wing. I went to fetch him myself. Calling him through and escorting him to the interview room would give me some scope to check out his attitude before the door closed on the two of us.

As I made my way to the holding area where prisoners were kept waiting for their appointments, a nurse who had had some dealings with Gary asked whether I wanted someone in with me during the interview. The presence of an extra person would probably be inhibiting and compromise the assessment, but I also had to think about my own safety. The room I was allocated was not ideal. It was a converted storage area and the desk was pushed against the wall furthest from the door. Unlike the purpose-built interview rooms, there was no viewing panel through which others could watch if necessary. Sometimes, as on this occasion, I would heave the desk closer to the exit. In so doing, I distanced myself from the wall-mounted panic button, but should it become necessary I preferred the option of making a speedy exit to the alternative of waiting for others to respond to the alarm. Instead of the nurse joining us in the assessment, I said I would leave the door ajar and asked her to keep an eye on the situation.

I unlocked and opened the door to the holding area and announced Gary's full name. Whereas most of the prisoners were huddled in groups of two or three whispering to each other, Gary was conspicuously alone. My sense was that it was mutual. He looked suspicious of the others and they seemed to be keeping an eye on, and a distance from, him. He came towards the doorway without meeting my eyes or even looking up. Once in the quiet of the corridor, I double-checked I'd got the right man. Gary did not answer my question, but I took from his continued movement along the corridor that he was confirming his identity and his consent to see me.

I noticed him hover for a moment at the threshold of the interview room. He was slightly shorter than me, but thicker set. His eyes flicked about the space. Seemingly satisfied it was safe to enter, he joined me standing by the desk. I gestured for him to sit down, but he stayed standing. He was uncomfortably close. 'What's this about?' he snapped.

Showing my apprehension would not be a good start to our first meeting. The culture that Gary was living in did not respect weakness. Witnessing signs of vulnerability in another could trigger processes outside his awareness, which would mean that this interaction would become defined as a combative one. At a more conscious level, he could feel annoyed that I was suggesting (by my apprehension) that a request for an explanation was a sign of potential aggression. If I were to explain it was more to do with his tone than the content of his speech, this would probably inflame his anger. At the same time as hiding my trepidation, I must not become noticeably authoritative.

As I began answering him, I extended one leg behind me and casually rocked my weight back on to it to put a bit more distance between us. Having not managed to look at the notes and having forgotten the conversation with Sara, I was as much in the dark about the reason for our meeting as him.

'One of the nurses thought that it may be helpful if we spoke,' I said.

I was relying on a generic statement that applied to almost all the prisoners I saw in the clinic. From his expression I could tell that I had not said enough for him to decide whether to stay or leave.

I continued, 'I've not had a chance to check the exact reason from the notes, but would you take a seat while I have a quick look?'

In another situation, the sudden sound of the chair scraping across the floor amplified in the echoey room would have made me flinch. In this situation, I was actively self-monitoring and so could resist the immediate urge long enough to realise there was no need to prepare to defend myself. He had kicked his chair back so that he could sit on it. I was caught off guard by his tacit consent to speak to me and, as I hesitated, he snarled, 'Go on then.'

If I had pulled myself right up to the computer, Gary, who was sitting against the side of the desk, would be at the limits of my peripheral vision. Instead, I angled the screen and swivelled my chair so that I was facing him across the corner of the desk between us. Scrolling through the electronic records, I kept an awareness of his shape and movements behind the left-hand side of the screen. I scanned the notes for a longer entry that would mark it out as more likely to have been one about his mental rather than physical health. My memory of the discussion with Sara was prompted almost as soon as I started reading her notes.

Despite Gary bringing the discussion to a premature close after about ten minutes and giving very little away, I thought our initial meeting was a success. He did not lose his temper, as I knew he was prone to do, and gave a qualified undertaking to see me again.

When it came to the morning of the next appointment, Sara came up to me sheepishly. 'You're down to see Gary this morning. I went to see him before heading home yesterday, just to check he was going to come across. He said he would see you, but only if you went to the wing to see him there.'

My first impulse was to say I wouldn't have time to go across to the wing today. The resulting delay leaving the prison would knock into the remainder of the day's appointments. I could argue that everything I knew about him suggested he had the capacity to decide such matters for himself and if he was not sufficiently motivated to walk the two hundred yards from his wing to the health-care department then he probably wasn't ready to accept help. But for Sara to check up on him yesterday, and to ask me to do something that she knew would disrupt the clinic, was unusual. I trusted her judgement that this was someone for whom extra effort would be necessary. I asked whether we could rearrange the other appointments that morning so I could go across to the wing at the end of the clinic.

I had to stand back some distance from the individual consultations over the next eight months to see evidence of progress, but it was there. Just before Gary was moved to a different prison, he was attending appointments fairly consistently and accepting treatment. If not the best-behaved prisoner, he was certainly getting into less trouble on the wing with both the officers and other inmates.

After almost two years, Gary's name appeared on my clinic list again. He had been returned to the prison where I worked in preparation for the parole hearing. In the first meeting following his return, it was almost as if we had never met before. I had to work hard to tease a few snippets of information from him. My sense was, he was checking whether I could still be trusted. He also knew I was going to be asked to prepare a report for the parole hearing. I could decline, citing the potential detrimental effects on our therapeutic relationship, but I kept an open mind about the possibility of doing a report and I asked him to do the same. It didn't take as long this time to get onto a better footing with him.

With the formal request for a report came the parole dossier. I already knew the main headlines about the offence and sentence, but now I had access to a comprehensive set of reports. There was the transcript of the judge's sentencing remarks, a list of his previous offences, and reports by the probation officer and the personal officer. The offence was a robbery of a corner shop. Gary had threatened the owner with a large kitchen knife. The type of sentence passed by the judge was one that had only recently been added to the statute books; although it was not a life sentence, it had no defined end point. Gary fell within the scope of this indeterminate sentence because when his previous offending was taken into account it was felt the public needed protecting from him, possibly indefinitely. He had applied for parole once before but his application was rejected. My report was to be submitted to his second parole hearing.

As I got into the preparation of my report, I started thinking through the details that needed to be factored in. How should

I translate an awareness of the risk factors, and the interplay between them, into a judgement about Gary's behaviour in the future? We have standardised procedures to do this, but our final judgement is also influenced by memories.

Forensic psychiatrists are supposed to be experts in violence risk assessment. There is no doubt we spend a lot of time thinking about risk. Most of the patients we assess and treat have demonstrated their potential for serious violence by the time we see them. Whether this experience serves us well to become experts in assessing risk depends on how we use it.

In a flash, people can form judgements about the likelihood of an event occurring. In-built mental shortcuts mean that we do not have to labour over data consciously. One shortcut allows us to estimate probability by using readily available memories. Our perception of what is likely to occur is influenced by the ease with which relevant examples come into our mind. The judgement about probability is based on the availability of the remembered examples, hence the term 'availability heuristic'.

The forensic psychiatric bias arises if we don't recognise that memories of cases in which there was an extreme act of violence are more available to us by virtue of the job we do. That we have seen more of these cases than our non-forensic psychiatric colleagues doesn't necessarily make us better at risk assessment. Yes, we are very experienced in assessing risk, but compared to a psychiatrist who sees a much greater turnover of patients, many of whom don't go on to commit serious violence, we are liable to overestimate risk. Countering this bias shouldn't mean that we ignore the memories available to us; there are valuable lessons in those cases, but they may not be instant lessons about probability. Working through the particulars of Gary's history, I was reminded of a case report I had previously studied. Due to the similarities with Gary, it lingered in my mind.

Michael was thirty-two years of age when he was released after serving five and a half years of an eight-year prison sentence for robbery of a theatre box office and another robbery, armed with an air pistol, of a building society. Even though at twenty-six he was a young adult when convicted of these offences, he was not new to the courts. Indeed, he was only eleven years old when first convicted for a dishonesty crime (taking someone else's property without their permission or under false pretences) – the same offence that would bring him back before the criminal courts eight times during his teens. There was then a change in the offending pattern. In his early twenties he began committing robberies and using violence, which culminated in the eight-year prison sentence.

During that sentence, he experienced some mental health symptoms for which he was prescribed psychiatric medication. The medication was continued after his release and he would attend appointments at a community psychiatric clinic. On occasion, Michael would talk about his aggressive urges. Alive to his criminal and violent past, the community psychiatrist sought a second opinion from a forensic psychiatrist.

As someone who abused drugs, Michael was receiving additional help from addiction specialists. He told one of the doctors that he was hearing voices encouraging him to be aggressive, but these voices were ameliorated by the prescribed medication or by heroin, which he continued to sometimes use.

He was not the easiest patient to help. There would be times when he didn't turn up for appointments. He would unexpectedly stop taking his medication even though it seemed to ease his suffering. He did not stop committing crime; there were convictions for burglary and possession of an air weapon. At one point he became more unstable and he was admitted to a forensic hospital. It was a pleasant surprise that while in hospital he did not live up to his dangerous reputation. One nurse even said that he was a model patient. After around six weeks in the unit he was discharged back to the care of the forensic psychiatric services.

The pattern of inconsistent compliance, drug abuse and occasional violent urges and threats continued. Even then there were some positives. At times, Michael looked well and he said that he felt supported. He did agree to take injectable medication and also agreed to an admission to hospital for opiate detoxification.

I often refer back to Michael's case, because in significant respects he resembled many patients who passed through my prison clinic. Substance misuse was certainly the norm among them, and they often also had a long history of criminality stretching back to childhood with some violent offences. They would not be seeing me if they did not experience psychiatric symptoms of some sort, but these symptoms could be amorphous and changeable. Aggressive urges were common. Sometimes they were accompanied by voices. The mix of drug and alcohol problems, criminality, aggression and out of the ordinary mental experiences did not set Michael apart from the many of hundreds of prisoners I have assessed.

In July 1997, Michael became an exception among mentally disordered offenders. A television documentary was aired about an unsolved crime twelve months earlier and one of the people watching was Michael's psychiatrist. He, and other staff members, independently came to the view that Michael fitted the suspect's description. The crime was a brutal attack on a mother and her two children as they walked with their dog along a quiet country lane. The mother and her six-year-old daughter died and the nine-year-old sister was left for dead with serious head injuries, but survived.

After receiving the information from the psychiatric team, the police arrested Michael. He was tried and convicted of two murders and attempted murder, for which he was sentenced to three life sentences.* His full name, Michael Stone, has entered psychiatric annals not just on account of the nature of the offence, but also because of the wholesale policy changes that followed his conviction.

In the immediate aftermath of his conviction there was understandable soul-searching and hand-wringing about how the offence occurred. A narrative of inevitability was presented to the public. For instance, the *Mirror* newspaper provided a neat account of a tragedy waiting to happen.

> Michael Stone was a walking timebomb. A crazy, vicious drug-taker with a record of crime, violence and instability . . . So many people knew how dangerous he was. He even knew it himself. He begged several times to be taken into care and was turned away. Why? Because he was too dangerous. Have you ever heard anything more absurd and calculated to lead to a tragedy? The police knew the full history of Stone's violence. Doctors and psychiatrists knew he was unstable to the point of insanity. Five days before the brutal attack on the Russells, a psychiatric nurse warned that he was 'in a killing mood'. All the warning signs were there. But no one did anything to control or stop him. Michael Stone was allowed to stay free. Free to attack the Russells, kill Lin and Megan, and leave Josie clinging to life. His conviction and imprisonment do not end this case. There are too many questions left about the failure to control Stone. We need to know WHY West Kent health authority behaved so hopelessly.

This was not just tabloid press hyperbole. *The Times*, usually more sober, also demanded to know 'why was Stone free to murder?' and highlighted that 'questions were being asked how the

---

* At the time of publication the Criminal Cases Review Commission was considering an application from Michael Stone to consider fresh evidence.

murderer, who had a long history of mental problems and violence, was refused a bed in a secure psychiatric hospital only days before the bloodshed' despite telling 'staff of his fantasies about killing children'.

Most of us have found ourselves identifying the image of a face within the grain of a piece of wood or in a cloud formation. This is called pareidolia; the process of seeing a formed picture in random lines and shapes. We experience it as a passive process. It seems to us that we just happen to notice the picture. In fact, our minds are actively scouting for shapes and patterns of significance. It is no accident that we commonly see certain images. We are heavily reliant on faces to understand ourselves and others.

Parents are not taught to use overly dramatic and repetitive facial expressions and noises when interacting with their infants, they just do it. Mostly, they are not thinking about why they act in this way. They do not need to – it is a reflex response. In part, the parent is motivated to mirror the child's emotional state. They exaggerate and hold the expression to get the youngster's attention and to mark the exchange as important. Through this interactive process, the prelinguistic infant is helped to understand his or her own feelings. It is not just an exercise of mirroring. When the child is distressed, the parent can help contain their offspring's emotions by using embellished soothing facial contortions and sounds.

The supreme power of the human mind to contemplate itself and the minds of others depends heavily on these exchanges during the early years of life. Noticing faces in our surroundings and monitoring shifts in expression remains an essential part of life into adulthood. Seeing someone facing us whose eyes widen as they direct their gaze over our shoulder is hard to ignore; it suggests to us that there may be someone or something behind us. A passing flicker of distress in a listener's eyes may lead us to change the subject before we are aware of what has happened. Quickly adjusting to the feelings of others and giving off our own signs is part of everyday interactions. It is what makes us such sophisticated social beings. Of all the stimuli we are bombarded with, faces are especially important. They are so important that it is better for us to be over-attentive. Sometimes seeing faces when they are not there is preferable to suffering the developmental and social penalties of failing to notice them. The general point is that we have evolved to interpret our environment in a way that may lead to false positives, such as the face-like image that appears to stand out from the wood grain or clouds. Dedicating attention to faces is just one example of how, as we search for pertinent patterns, we can occasionally impose order on randomness. The tendency to seek patterns where there are none, known as patternicity, does not just apply to making sense of our physical environment.

As well as stimuli constantly hitting our senses, our minds are presented with a never-ending mishmash of information about events that have occurred. To be able to predict and control what is going to happen we need to make sense of what has happened, and so our natural inclination is to construct a story. The commonest form of narrative places events in order from oldest to most recent. To turn a timeline into a story requires another ingredient — causal connection. The events that are more likely to feature in the story are those that explain other events in the sequence: events at the beginning of the story are causally connected to those in the middle, and events in the middle of the story are causally connected to the ending. We are especially gripped by stories that are constructed using embodied events, that is, those that involve people. The causal connections for these people-related events are the intentions and motives.

The early explanatory narratives for the extreme violence on that country lane in Kent start with a man whose previous criminal actions mark him out as someone who was motivated to be very dangerous. The middle part of the story is the psychiatrists' lack of motivation to act on the clear signs of increasing danger. Against this background, the ending of the story feels inevitable. We find a narrative of inevitability and preventability comforting; it helps us easily understand a complex situation. The story's persuasiveness not only rests on its ability to provide a simple explanation, it also directs us to the simple solution. If we lock up these obviously dangerous people then violence can be prevented.

Just because a story is constructed quickly without an opportunity to examine the evidence properly does not make it wrong. There are many cases when the initial suspicions of poor psychiatric practice turn out to be supported by a considered analysis of the facts. Is that always the case though?

An extensive inquiry led by a highly qualified panel forensically scrutinised every scrap of available information about Michael Stone and his contact with psychiatric services. The inquiry report, published in 2006, recognised the challenges of trying to help someone like him.

The task facing those caring for Mr Stone was daunting. No one could predict with much confidence from one contact to the next what he would say or how he would behave. It is understandable that there were differing views on the nature of Michael Stone's condition and how it should best be managed. The risk he seemed to present similarly fluctuated and the actual long-term risk he presented, to whom and in what circumstances, and what could be done to reduce it would have been impossible to assess with confidence . . . It is noteworthy that throughout the period under investigation, Mr Stone did receive very considerable input from all services involved. Whatever else may be said about the care offered to him, his case was never ignored.

The exhaustive analysis undertaken by the Stone inquiry demonstrates that it is possible to resist the seductive draw of overly simplistic narratives, but my experience is that this is the exception. Investigators who do not have the same amount of time, expertise and resources find it very difficult not to succumb to a biased way of thinking that is activated by the method of investigation.

I had finished the diagnostic section of my report on Gary. I concluded that he definitely met the criteria for a diagnosis of antisocial personality disorder. This is nothing more than saying he does the things many offenders do, but he does them a lot and he has done them for a long time: repeated offending starting in early adolescence, often doing things on the spur of the moment, and unemployment is enough to give someone this diagnosis. Not surprisingly, with diagnostic criteria like these, almost 50 per cent of prisoners share a diagnosis of antisocial personality disorder with Gary.

Mixed in with Gary's criminal behaviour was a problem he had with addictive drugs. This meant he could be given another diagnosis. Substance use disorder, as it is currently called, is also a problem for nearly half of all prisoners.

While voices and unusual thoughts of the sort described by Gary are less common, with a prevalence of 15 per cent of male prisoners, they are not rare. Among the patients in my clinic, those who have been selected on the basis of psychiatric problems, they are common. So, on the one hand Gary does not stand out from the hundreds of patients who have passed through my clinic and eventually back into the community who do not go on and kill. On the other hand, he has some striking similarities to Michael Stone. As a consequence, stories with frightful endings appear in my mind. I do not resist them. Allowing these horror stories to unfold has become an informal part of my assessment method. For instance, I imagine that after his release Gary stops attending the psychiatric clinic, increases his use of crack and becomes more tormented by his aggressive urges. This could very easily occur, I reflect. If it does, his situation could just as quickly improve. An empathic highly motivated community nurse could persuade him to restart his medication and to re-engage with the drug workers. He would emerge out of the unstable phase. In my fantasised scenario, by the time it comes to light that he has been shoplifting, the supervising team are pleased that the offending was not more serious and that contrary to expectations he was back working with them.

What about, I wonder, if on one occasion his re-engagement with the team is too late? If, before he gets back on his medication and off the drugs, the urges become impossible to resist? The nurse had noticed he was out of sorts and checks with the psychiatrist whether he should be readmitted to hospital. They decide that this episode does not look that different from the ones he has previously come round from. Just keep working with him, they agree. This time, though, turns out to be very different and he gives up trying to defy the urges to kill.

I envision the inquiry team narrowing their attention to two crucial missed opportunities. Forensically analysing the last relapse, the investigators identify differences with the previous relapse. There were, they conclude, clear signs of increasing risk. Putting myself in the position of the nurse and psychiatrist summoned by the investigators, I feel the anxiety and anger at having to defend a position that made sense before the incident, but no longer does. In my daydream, the other target of their attention is the decision to release Gary from prison. The homicidal urges were clearly a red flag, they conclude. He wasn't always compliant with his medication and he took drugs even when he was locked up in prison. How could I miss such obvious signs? It would be obvious to them, and also to me now I knew what was going to happen, that I should not have supported the release of someone as dangerous as Gary. Attempting to defend my decision by saying that he was not as dangerous then as he is now would sound feeble and defensive.

As far as politicians were concerned the way of preventing an offence of the type committed on that country lane in Kent was simple. Michael Stone should have been detained in hospital to protect the public. The reason he wasn't, they said, was the failure of psychiatrists to take their responsibilities seriously. Jack Straw, the Labour Home Secretary at the time, announced that it was 'time frankly that the psychiatric profession seriously examined their own practices and tried to modernise them in a way that they have so far failed to do'. There were two strands to the emerging narrative.

One was summarised by the *Mirror*'s description of Michael Stone as a 'walking timebomb'. He was so dangerous that the offence was inevitable. It was just a matter of time. From there, it was a small step to accepting that some individuals are so dangerous that detention solely to prevent a violent crime is justified. Even before the inquiry report was published, moves were afoot to ensure that dangerous offenders would be kept off our streets. This preventative detention approach is built on a zealous faith in the idea of dangerousness.

Bundled up with the belief in dangerousness was the complaint that psychiatrists had a discriminatory attitude to patients with personality disorder in comparison to those with mental illness. According to early renderings of the Michael Stone story, he did not receive the warranted level of input because he was identified as personality disordered as opposed to being considered mentally ill. There was certainly some truth in the analysis of psychiatrists' attitude to personality-disordered patients, summed up by the title of a 1988 research paper that appeared in the *British Journal of Psychiatry* – 'Personality Disorder: the patients psychiatrists dislike?' Things have changed now, but only because mental health professionals recognise that patients with personality disorder need help, even if there is still a reluctance to offer the person help within mainstream services. That attitudes have not softened is evidenced by a 2017 research study published with the title 'Personality Disorder: still the patients psychiatrists dislike'.

The irony of the policies introduced in the wake of Michael Stone's conviction was that they were not supported by evidence that came to light in the investigation. The psychiatrists involved in Stone's care did not dismiss the features of mental illness nor decline access to services on account of his personality disorder.

Regardless of the facts, a major policy framework was developed around a concept built in the image of Michael Stone's likeness. A pseudo-diagnosis was created to give credence to the idea of a definable category of men – and it was just men at the start. They had a dangerous and severe personality disorder. At huge cost, new high specification units were built in select prisons. These dangerous and severe personality disorder, or DSPD, units, as they came to be known, introduced complex processes to assess whether offenders met the criteria for entry, leading to lengthy waiting lists. The policymakers had to deal with the problem of those prisoners deemed to be dangerous and severely personality disordered who were approaching the end of their prison sentences. A new law was introduced that facilitated the transfer of these prisoners to newly developed special hospital units. The impression that detention instead of treatment was being prioritised was given by the transfer of offenders just before they were due to be released from the sentences that the courts had already decided fitted their crimes. By 2010, over £200 million had been spent on the new services. The investment had been concentrated on a very small number of highly secure placements with scant attention given to supporting the residents of the units in moving back into the community. The DSPD initiative turned out to be an extremely short-lived one. Due to mounting doubts about the approach, its effectiveness, and the cost, the idea of DSPD was swept aside eleven years after its introduction.

Faith and a large amount of money had been invested in the belief that it was possible to tell what Michael Stone was going to do before he did it. Such faith in being able to predict future violent behaviour long before it occurs rests on the assumption that dangerousness is fairly stable and not materially affected by circumstances. This assumption is not valid. The DSPD initiative may be no more, but the belief that violence can be predicted has been more difficult to shake off.

I imagined how it would be received by the investigation panel set up to look for the causes of Gary's possible future homicidal actions if I told them I wasn't sure how to assess the probability of Gary becoming violent. Possibly a quick call from the panel's chairperson to my medical director recommending I be put on gardening leave.

I am confident in assessing some probabilities. If I toss a coin I know there is a 50 per cent probability – or a 1 in 2 chance – of the coin landing with heads facing up; there are a fixed number of outcomes, each with an equal chance. And even if each outcome did not have an equally likely outcome – if the coin was weighted – I could have a stab at estimating the probability by running a few trials. The more trials, the more accurate my prediction becomes; yet predicting what Gary was going to do is not equivalent to the toss of a coin or the roll of a dice. There are innumerable futures at play that range somewhere between one where Gary commits no violence, through one where he is violent but not regularly violent or seriously violent, to a future in which Gary commits an act of very serious violence. And of these outcomes, I cannot be sure that each has an equal chance of occurring.

Although I cannot look at a person in isolation and define a probability of him carrying out a specific act, I could come up with another figure to express the likelihood of an offender reoffending in the future. Plenty of studies have followed the progress of patients discharged from secure hospitals or of prisoners released from prisons to track their rates of reoffending. Using the results of these studies, prediction measures have been compiled. To come up with a percentage likelihood of Gary committing an offence following release, I would consider each item of the measure and give it a score depending on whether, and to what degree, it applied in this case. The measure would then produce a percentage figure for a particular outcome, such as a violent offence in the next five years. If it were, say, 30 per cent then I could assume that of 100 prisoners with the same score on this measure, 30 would commit a violent offence in that time period. Or, 70 out of 100 would not. What I can't do is know whether among these offenders Gary would be in the minority group who go on to offend or the majority who do not.

Probability is not just a problematic concept in relation to predicting future events. The mishandling of probability has led expert witnesses to make serious misjudgements about the cause of past events. On 4 September 2001, baby Amber died at the Juliana Children's Hospital in the Netherlands. This tragic loss of life was attributed to natural causes. The following day, a nurse reported to her superior that she had suspicions about a colleague who had not only been there when Amber died, but who had also been present at the time of an unusually large number of resuscitations that had taken place in the hospital. Five child deaths that had previously been declared natural now looked suspicious. Lucia de Berk, a 41-year-old registered paediatric nurse, was present at all five deaths and many more resuscitations, which seemed more than a coincidence. The hospital managers quickly gathered together what information they could. Lucia was arrested and charged with murder and attempted murder of patients under her care.

The prosecutors called on an expert in statistics, Professor Henk Elffers, to examine the data and calculate the likelihood of Lucia's shift pattern matching the pattern of the suspicious medical events. The idea was that a very low likelihood of a random match would point to something untoward, suggesting that the probability of finding a match between Lucia's shift pattern and the suspicious medical events as equivalent to the probability that she was innocent. The calculated probability was 1 in 342 million. With such a minute probability that this was a random finding, the probability of the reverse – that she was guilty – must be high. Taking into account the statistical evidence, the court found Lucia de Berk guilty and she was sentenced to life imprisonment for seven murders and three attempted murders.

The prosecution's logic feels reasonable, but the flaw in its logic can be illustrated by another example of probability: imagine trying to persuade someone with a winning lottery ticket that because the likelihood of someone with his or her exact characteristics winning the lottery would have been so infinitesimally small, it's been decided that there must have been foul play and therefore the prize money will not be awarded after all. If we take the very low probability of a future rare event occurring (such as you being the person who goes on to win the lottery) at face value, then we must conclude that when this event occurs it was so improbable that it cannot have been purely down to chance –

and we know this is not the case: people do win the lottery. More considered use of the statistics in Lucia de Berk's case have produced a much higher probability of at least 1 in 49 for a random match. The case was reopened and a retrial held and, on 14 April 2010, seven years after she started her life sentence, Lucia de Berk was acquitted of the charges.

So, what went wrong here? It is important to understand that humans do not have an inherent ability to properly handle probability. Over the tens of thousands of years that our minds developed into their current form, the pressing decisions humans made did not involve analysing complex data sets and predicting distant events. Choices were simple and they had immediate life or death consequences. For prehistoric humans, not acting quickly could result in being killed by a predator or competitor. In such a situation, relying on memorable events to estimate probability – or using the availability heuristic – has advantages. In the face of danger, a memory of a previous brush with death encouraged us to take evasive action. Even if we overestimated the risk, being safe (or still alive) was better than being sorry (or dead). The availability heuristic is only one among many mental biases that skew our decision-making. Our natural programming encourages us to avoid costs, not to reach the truth.

Medical experts have also had trouble handling probability, with serious consequences. In December 1996, Christopher Clark died at just under three months old. The pathologist attributed bruises on Christopher's body to his mother's resuscitation attempts and concluded that this was a case of cot death, or sudden infant death syndrome. A year later the Clarks had a second son, Harry, and at eight weeks of age he also died. This time, the pathologist found evidence that he thought was indicative of deliberate shaking. In his opinion, the shaking was the cause of death, and so he revised his opinion about Christopher's death and concluded that both causes were unnatural. Sally Clark was arrested on suspicion of murder.

As well as relying on the evidence of the pathologist, the prosecution called a medical expert in child health, Professor Sir Roy Meadow, a well-known and respected paediatric clinician and academic. Professor Meadow gave evidence about the likelihood of these two deaths occurring from natural causes, asserting that the risk of a child dying as a result of cot death in a family such as the Clarks was 1 in 8,543. To come to the probability of two children dying as a result of cot deaths, he multiplied this figure by itself and, with dramatic flair, explained in court that the chances of both children in this type of family dying of natural causes were akin to four different horses with 80 to 1 odds winning the Grand National in four consecutive years – 1 in 73 million. Multiplying probabilities is a reasonable statistical manoeuvre to work out the probability of two unrelated events occurring. For example, given the probability of a tossed coin landing heads up is 1 in 2, the probability of this happening twice in a row is 1 in 4. But a prosecution case based on this figure is flawed in two ways. Firstly, the figure, even if it were correct, is the probability of a family with these characteristics having two cot deaths; it is not the probability that Sally is innocent. Secondly, and more fundamentally in the trial of Sally Clark, it was a mistake to multiply the probability of one cot death by itself. Having one cot death increases the likelihood of a second, therefore these are not unrelated events. Nevertheless, Sally Clark was found guilty.

The first appeal against conviction was dismissed, but on the second occasion, the Court of Appeal judges held that the statistical evidence should never have been presented to the jury in the way it was. This evidence was deemed to have been a decisive factor in the jury's deliberations. Sally Clark's convictions were overturned and she was released from prison.

It is quite rightly drummed into expert witnesses that we must not stray outside our area of expertise. Our input into court proceedings is justified because there is a matter about which a lay person cannot decide. We come to believe that we are not lay people because of our expertise, but we are prone to forget that while we have expert knowledge in one area, we are still vulnerable to lay-person styles of thinking in others. This can have profound consequences on the fate of a defendant and on the reputation of experts in court.

The first step for all of us is to understand the biases in our thinking. Aside from the heuristics and patternicity, there are many more processes that get in the way. In the same way that forensic psychiatrists must understand their own biases and limitations in looking into the future, investigators must understand and resist the assumptions that come from the false position they are in when looking into the past.

Many people have seen an optical illusion image, which is freely available on the internet, that is made up of what appear to be haphazard black blobs on a two-dimensional white background. When you first look at it, there is no pattern, but then, with persistence or help, the random splats seem to transform into a Dalmatian dog in the foreground of a three-dimensional landscape. Whenever we look back at the image the dog is there; we cannot turn our mind back to seeing randomness. In the same way, once we know about Michael Stone's offence, we can't un-know it. We also find it almost impossible to resist the retrospective ordering and linking of events in a way that leads to the ending we now know.

I was able to conceive a package of care and supervision for Gary that could mitigate the effects of the main risk factors. If the package was made available, I thought it probable that Gary could be managed safely in the community. Even though the chance of failure would, I thought, be very slim, the worst-case scenario vision still did not fade. There was a simple way to dispel it. Constructing an argument for why it was not safe to release Gary would be easy: I would emphasise his homicidal urges, the likelihood of non-compliance and the draw of drugs in the community. Playing it safe for everyone, including me, would mean arguing against Gary's release. I would safeguard my reputation and the reputation of my employing organisation. But this approach did not sit easy with me and I felt I should further explore the possibility of release.

An essential component of the package would be support and supervision by a mental health team in the community. With plenty of notice before the parole hearing, I wrote a letter of referral to the community psychiatrist who covered the area in which the probation hostel was located. My letter did not gloss over the complexity and the potential risks. Since I did not receive a response, I called the consultant's secretary, who told me that the doctor was busy in clinic, but would get back to me. He didn't. I persisted and we eventually spoke. He told me that, following discussion within their team, they did not feel Gary was appropriate for their service. There was no other service, I explained. After I politely applied some pressure, the doctor responded in a way that I believe revealed his main concern: 'It is not appropriate for us to carry this risk.' Whereas the cause of a person's actions lie within their own mind, when that person commits a serious offence the impression is given that the cause can be found in the minds of the professionals – in essence, the community psychiatrist feared that he would be blamed if Gary committed an act of violence. He was resolute that they would not take Gary on to their caseload. Being honest with myself, I could not criticise him; in his position, I probably wouldn't have either.

I made reference to this exchange in my report for the Parole Board and formulated a risk assessment. In the final draft, I explained that Gary had become used to aggressive thoughts randomly appearing in his head. He did not like them, and while they made him more irritable, he was sure that these thoughts alone would not lead him to become physically aggressive.

But sometimes Gary's experience was different. The thoughts would start to feel as if they were not his own. Then he would start to lose himself in bizarre flights of fantasy. Aggressive scenes would appear in his mind's eye. If he could not distract himself from them, they became captivating. An analysis of Gary's past behaviour indicated that the combination of alienated thoughts and aggressive images had made him more aggression-prone. He did not hear voices regularly and when he did they were not always a problem, but when they berated him and demanded he take violent action he found himself overreacting and, sometimes, resorting to the use of force.

I could not put a figure on the probability of Gary doing something much more serious than he had done before. What I could say was that if the elements that made up his violent mind were spotted early and addressed, then he could be generally less aggressive than he had been and, by extension, his aggression would be less likely to escalate further than it had done before.

Gary accepted that the antipsychotic medication sometimes helped. It did not completely get rid of the unwanted thoughts, images or voices, he just felt less bothered by them. The problem was he did not like how the medication changed him in other ways. The feeling of indifference that gave a welcome relief from the unpleasant internal experiences was a problem because it extended to everything. He hated that the medication made his appetite gargantuan and his waistline expand. From my perspective the medication seemed to be doing some good things. When Gary took it there were fewer prison adjudications for bad behaviour and he was able to sustain longer periods on the wing without finding himself on the segregation unit of the prison.

But I was not the one who had to take it, and I had worked out that he was much more likely to comply with the tablets if I did not oversell them.

Gary, of course, knew that street drugs did not help his mental health. At the same time, they gave him peace, even though it was short-lived. The drugs had an advantage over the medication: they came with an immediate pleasant hit. The rush from heroin bathed his body in a warm euphoria. Crack was quite different – the high was accompanied by confidence and increased alertness. When things were going his way, he did not actively seek out drugs. Despite the benefits, he could retain the memories of the problems that drugs had brought him. He could remember that he felt less in control of the thoughts, images and voices, that the paranoia would become all encompassing, that he got into debt. He knew that, when he took drugs, those family members and friends who were a positive influence kept their distance and that the people he mixed with were not friends. Relationships became transactional. Like his acquaintances, at the front of his mind was how to secure his next hit. But holding on to these memories was more difficult when under pressure.

I had asked Gary what he could think of doing when stress was building and was surprised that he acknowledged the link with professionals was important to him. But as things stood, there was no mental health team, and if he was released, the allocated probation officer would have no choice but to supervise Gary, with the help of the staff in the probation hostel.

Two and a half months later, I sat with the Parole Board, Gary's solicitor, probation officer and named prison officer, and a psychiatric nurse from the community team to discuss the possibility of Gary's release. Gary sat still with his head tilted forward, avoiding eye contact with anyone, while his solicitor set out the case for his release. The community psychiatric nurse explained that, though Gary needed the input of a more specialised team, since such a team did not exist her team had agreed to take him on. She was at pains to emphasise that working with Gary was not going to be straightforward, and I suspected that the community team's change of heart was not motivated by optimism about Gary benefiting from their input, but because they did not believe they could withstand the pressure of the Parole Board. Any hope I might have felt on hearing this news was snuffed out by the likely interpretation Gary would have made; I'm sure it was not intentional, but a message was conveyed loud and clear that this was not going to be a therapeutic relationship built on trust and hope. With his release approved, I could only hope that the chances would work in Gary's favour.

There was no reason anyone would give me feedback on Gary's progress following release. It was only because of a chance encounter with his probation officer that I happened to find out. Gary had been at the probation hostel for eight weeks when he was woken by two police officers knocking at his door. The officers had back-up waiting in the car park in case of difficulties, but it was not needed. Gary did not resist, but he proclaimed his innocence. And, indeed, he was innocent: Gary had not committed a crime, there had been no violence. Gary was being recalled to prison because his probation officer felt that Gary was not working well with the community psychiatric team.

This might always have been the outcome, but hearing what had happened I thought that Gary could not have failed to notice the ambivalence with which the psychiatric nurse spoke about him at the Parole Board hearing. Here was a man whose trust had to be carefully earned, and what was probably an attempt by the nurse to demonstrate to the Parole Board that she and her team were going over and above ordinary expectations was likely to have been heard by Gary as a reluctance to work with him and as pessimism about the success of doing so. It did not feel like the start of a trusting therapeutic relationship. I thought the psychi-atric team's uncontained fear of falling foul of an investigation that could not unsee its own narrative constructed post-incident had compromised the likelihood of successful risk management. In my experience, this is not an uncommon phenomenon when a patient with complex forensic needs comes into contact with mental health services.

Conclusion

O N 22 JULY 2011, Anders Breivik detonated a deadly bomb in Oslo that killed eight people, before immediately travelling to the island location of a youth summer camp where he shot dead sixty-nine more people. Following his arrest, Drs Torgeir Husby and Synne Sørheim, two senior Norwegian psychiatrists, were appointed by the court to assess him. They spent thirty-six hours with him over thirteen meetings in which they administered internationally recognised diagnostic assessment tools. To supplement their findings from the meetings with Breivik, they also interviewed his mother and studied the records of all the police interrogations. On the basis of this exceptionally comprehensive assessment, Breivik was given a diagnosis of paranoid schizophrenia. In support of their diagnosis, the psychiatrists reported that Breivik held delusions that he had been the ideological leader for the Knights Templar, and that he could become the new regent of Norway, whereupon he would take the name of Sigurd the Crusader the Second. The report was subsequently approved by the Norwegian Board of Forensic Medicine. Such a diagnosis, if accepted by the court, would mean that Breivik would not be held criminally accountable for the offences. The Oslo court decided to commission another assessment and the second team of psychiatrists, Drs Agnar Aspaas and Terje Tørrissen, came to a different conclusion. Although they found that Breivik had peculiar ideas, they rejected the diagnosis of schizophrenia, and instead thought the core problem was narcissistic personality disorder.

There is a common assumption, including among psychiatrists, that offenders whose violence can be explained as a direct consequence of schizophrenic symptoms have less moral responsibility for their actions than personality-disordered offenders who commit violence. It is usually held that schizophrenia is a condition that the undeserving patient is afflicted with. As a person with schizophrenia, Breivik would be seen to have succumbed to the bizarre paranoid and grandiose delusions; that is, to the symptoms of an illness. As a narcissistic, however, it would be assumed that he knowingly made in-character decisions that suited his own perverted purposes in full knowledge of the impact of his actions.

Undoubtedly, the violent offender who is labouring under the effects of threatening voices and paranoid delusions (which are symptoms of schizophrenia) does not wish those experiences on him or herself. By the same token, though, the offender whose general personality seems typified by a callous disregard for others does not consciously dampen his or her automatic responses to their suffering. Likewise, sexual violence does not occur because the perpetrator decides one day to suppress normal sexual urges and to replace them with deviant ones. Although on the surface the violent offender diagnosed with personality disorder, or one with an extreme sexual deviance, may not seem bizarre, they are no less affected by unusual mental processes. But, what about the other difference that is commonly highlighted – the person's awareness of their own actions?

An offender diagnosed with personality disorder is usually fully cognisant of their actions. The sexually violent offender may even mentally rehearse their offence before acting it out. But, in my experience, it is rare for someone who is violent while psychotic to be unaware of what they were doing. They often don't realise that the premise on which they act is false, but they still know what they did. Both 'types' of offenders make decisions and carry out actions as a result of a combination of processes that would be considered markedly out of the ordinary and which they have not brought on themselves.

This supposed dichotomy between the mental illness and personality disorder mirrors a colloquialism that sometimes crops up in my discussions with lawyers whose clients have been charged with a violent offence. The formal letter instructing me to undertake an assessment includes a list of legalistic questions, on occasion reduced in a conversation with the lawyer to the main issue of whether the detainee is 'mad or bad'. The former offers some hope to the accused. It opens the possibility of a legal defence against the charge. It may also allow for admission to hospital rather than detention in prison. Even if it does not provide a defence and there is no possibility of an admission to hospital, the presence of a diagnosed mental illness at the time of the offence can be used as mitigation to argue for the sentence to be less severe. The alternative, that they are 'bad', means that they deserve not only to feel the full force of the law but also society's condemnation.

When interviewed in 1993 on law and order, John Major, then prime minister of the United Kingdom, said he felt 'strongly that society needs to condemn a little more and understand a little less'. Surprising as it may seem, I agree that we need to condemn, or more accurately I should say I believe that we have a need to condemn. Giving in to that need provides an outlet for our immediate emotional reaction to the offence. It also signals something to others about our moral character. The condemnatory evil monster narrative, which is often evoked in popular commentaries about the subjects of my assessments, fulfils not just the need to condemn. It goes further by providing a type of explanation – satisfying that other tendency to generate a causal explanation for threatening events. Like many readily available and uncomplicated explanatory narratives it is self-contained and does not warrant further thought. The problem is located within the soul of the offender and so is not amenable to rational explanation, and we are reassured by the implication of the narrative that it separates us with clear blue water from the offender.

Whether or not we give in to the need to condemn we must recognise that condemnatory explanations do not encourage an understanding of the complex real-world causes of violence we must reach in order to find solutions. And applying these narratives involves inhibiting the very thing that we condemn violent offenders for failing to show: empathy. But empathy is not something that offenders lack and others have. For all of us, including most offenders, our empathic concern for others fluctuates depending on the circumstances. When we are overwhelmed with feelings of repulsion after learning the gory details of a violent crime, for example, our capacity to openly contemplate the possible mind-state of the offender is reduced.

When I stepped from the world of physical medicine into my chosen speciality of psychiatry almost three decades ago, I was persuaded by claims that we would soon have diagnostic investigations to match the physician's blood tests or scans. Neuroscience has certainly brought us a much more refined understanding of some mental processes that influence experience and behaviour, but there are no routine physical tests for the diagnoses most commonly made in forensic psychiatric practice.

Whether it is a paper-based assessment process or a physical investigation, the intention of those striving to find diagnostic tests has been to introduce objectivity into psychiatry; to translate the patient's experience into predefined entities or objects. These objects could take the form of symptoms (such as hallucinations and delusions) or diagnoses (such as schizophrenia or narcissistic personality disorder). Even more desirable in this search is to turn the patient's experience into measurable patterns of brain dysfunction. But, how can we start to do that when, as illustrated by Breivik's trial, extensively detailed assessments still do not produce consensus on something as apparently straightforward as choosing between two starkly different diagnoses? I believe the problem lies not in our inability to find the right way to be objective. It is that our desire for objectivity itself may be the problem. While the brain is a physical object just like any other part of the body, it is associated with something that sets it apart from the rest of the body, and that is the mind.

In my practice, I do search for the symptoms and make diagnoses; the legal system I work in is as dependent on diagnoses for decision-making as the mental health system. But the more I have tried to use the diagnostic system as a means of understanding, the more I have become aware of its limitations. It gives priority to certain mental experiences over others. These experiences have been chosen because at some point in history they were thought to be the key symptoms of the disorder. Still without an independent marker of the disorder we remain unsure whether that is correct. The voice that the person hears telling him to retaliate against his persecutors is not suspended in isolation from all other experiences in the way the term 'command auditory hallucination' would suggest. There is no reason why those experiences that have achieved symptom status are any more central to the explanation of behaviour than experiences that have not made it onto the list. So, I now resist the usual practice of editing out all those comments and reflections that do not feed the diagnostic method. And, having done so, I have come to see that this is where the real understanding can be found.

This is where I find evidence that the offender may have a distorted sense of the feeling of connectedness to his or her own actions and to things going on around them … Or that there may be difficulties making accurate inferences about the intentions of other people … Or that they are more comfortable in a group that values dominance over prestige … Or that their sense of who they are is particularly fragile in a way that makes them over sensitive to humiliation … Or that they don't get the same reflex emotional reactions to signs of changing emotions in others … I could go on. The evidence is not only in the meaning of the words my patients use; I must also pay close attention to the way they communicate, the way they interact, and the way I feel when I am with them.

Without the diagnostic framework to structure the information that we gather in our assessments, where do we look for help in understanding the behaviour of violent offenders? I believe we should start by turning our attention back on ourselves. The minds of most of those people who have been violent seem to me to be more similar to than different from the rest of us. They may hold a set of ideas and perceptions that outwardly seem irrational – sometimes the distinction from generally acceptable beliefs or everyday perceptual aberrations is quite clear – but just as often I am working in the grey area between outright bizarre experiences and eccentric but not abnormal ones. Some people who have been violent are liable to automatically react to certain stimuli in what appears to be an extreme way. But we are all liable to misinterpret the actions of others, just not to the same extent as many violent offenders. The difference between a person who has been violent and others is usually a matter of degree.

However in recognising that we have more in common with violent offenders than we would prefer to imagine, we need to take care not to just apply our day-to-day assumptions to observations of their behaviour. If it looks like someone is being manipulative, then we should first ask why are the strategies they use to get what they desire so much more crude and transparent than those we use. Instead of being driven by our annoyed reaction to the experience of being manipulated, and dismissing the person manipulating us, we should be motivated to listen even more; to try to understand, in their own words, what it is like to be them and to do the things they do. Accepting that violence is underpinned by some altered mental processes raises the question of what caused the alteration in the first place.

Human minds are extremely adaptable and they are at their most adaptable during our early years. In this period, we can benefit from the interactions with our carers and in these interactions we acquire the capacity to understand our minds and the minds of others. Our adaptability has a flip side. During the same phase children are especially vulnerable to neglect or mistreatment. Without attentive and emotionally responsive care, emotions can become confusing and frightening. The human mind tries to adapt to trauma. Disconnecting from our feelings may help us when those feelings are intensely negative. In other situations, it may be better for us to shut down our concern for someone who has malign intentions towards us. Alternatively, in the face of a potential threat, hypervigilance can be a good strategy, but complications arise if defensive adaptations are overused. Under persistent unpleasant or threatening conditions the adaptations can become the norm. Then the person is prone to feeling disconnected from emotion or to be hypervigilant to threat. Even in the case of psychopathy, which is thought to be underpinned by an inherent failure to experience the ordinary aversive emotional response to the suffering of others, early experiences may influence the way this impairment is manifest in later life.

Whatever the origins of someone's propensity to violence, their feelings about, and interactions with, others can be further shaped by events in later life. How *we* respond to a person on an individual, institutional or social level has an impact on them; it is up to us whether that impact is to reinforce the mental processes that contribute to the violence, or to lessen them. To decide how to reduce violence, if that is what we want to do, we need to be genuinely interested in people's minds. As we support continued research into the functioning of the brain, we should not leave the mind behind.

Acknowledgements

I WILL NEVER know all the influences that have shaped the forensic psychiatrist I have become, but certain people stand out in my memory. My brilliant biology teacher, Rex Dibley, fostered my interest in his subject and so prepared me for medical school. As a young psychiatric trainee, I worked with Professor Keith Rix, who sparked my fascination with forensic psychiatry and I am thankful for our continued collaborations to this day. I must mention Dr James Higgins, a towering figure in the early establishment of British forensic psychiatry. Alongside attempting to teach me bridge and sculling, and indulging our shared passion for jazz, Jim introduced me, with his verve for storytelling, to the many backstories behind the history of our speciality. I am so thankful to Dr Cameron Boyd, an early forensic psychiatric mentor, who was unwavering in his support for my twin track clinical and academic career. Amongst the many things I learnt from my academic supervisor, Professor Jonathan Hill, key to my practice was the importance of adopting a developmental perspective and thinking about the psychological processes that drive behaviour.

Learning is more than a formal educational process and for me it has also occurred implicitly in conversations with colleagues. Through many years as a forensic psychiatrist in Merseyside, I am most grateful to Dr Steve Noblett, Dr Jennie McCarthy, Dr Owain Haeney, Bernadette McEllin, Andy Brown and Nick Benefield, all of whom have indulged my varied clinical and academic ventures. I have the utmost admiration for those nurses and prison officers who maintain their compassion while working on the front line of forensic practice. I have learnt so much from them and from the many lawyers I have worked alongside. Only by sharing thoughts with others do novel ideas assume greater definition, and I must acknowledge the many junior doctors who have worked with me for allowing me to test out and refine my ideas.

This book started to become a reality with opportunity afforded by the John Murray and *Spectator* Essay Prize. For reading and reflecting on my essay on the origins of violence, thanks to Pip and Mark McNamee, Paul Clisby, and Innes Reid. In preparing this book, I am grateful to Dr Heidi Kastner for accommodating my visit to her clinic in Austria and offering her insights into the Josef Fritzl case, to David James Smith for sharing his approach to understanding and writing about violence, and to Dr John Clark for his expert forensic pathology advice. My gratitude also extends to Nicola Whitby, Emily Danson, Debbie Williams and Joy Keenan of the Probation Service for their readiness to discuss approaches to managing offenders and to introduce me to men on their caseload, to whom in turn I am thankful for meeting with me. This brings me to the thousands of men and women in prison, hospital and elsewhere who have shared their difficult experiences with me. I am indebted to them because they have taught me more than any lecture or textbook ever could. To preserve the confidentiality of my patients, I have changed details as necessary.

I have been superbly guided by the brilliant editor Kate Craigie on a transformative journey from an author of medico-legal and academic texts to one who can now say he has written a book for a wider audience. For casting his critical and incisive eye over each and every chapter, I must also thank Richard Arnold. And finally, I cannot exaggerate my gratitude to Lindsay for being an ever-present source of inspiration and support, and to my father for subtly instilling a culture of compassionate inquisitiveness throughout my whole life.

Select Bibliography

For the historical case studies, a wide range of material was accessed, but the following sources were particularly useful.

Bader, M., Tannock, R. & Hadjikhani, N., 'The Zappel-Philipp a historical example of ADHD Clinics', *ADHD Atten Def Hyp Disord* 10, 2018, pp.119–127.

Bowden, Paul, 'Graham Young (1947–90); the St Albans Poisoner: His Life and times', *Criminal Behaviour and Mental Health*, 6.S1, 1996, pp.17–24.

Capgras, J., & Reboul-Lachaux, J., 'L'Illusion des "sosies" dans un délire systématisé chronique', *History of Psychiatry*, 5(17), 1994, pp.119-133

Carrère, Emmanuel, *The Adversary: A True Story of Murder and Deception*, Metropolitan Books, 2000.

Chase, Alston, *A Mind for Murder: The Education of the Unabomber and the Origins of Modern Terrorism*, W & Norton and Company, 2003.

Claridge, Gordon, Ruth Pryor and Gwen Watkins, *Sound from the Bell Jar: Ten Psychotic Authors*, Malor Books, 1998.

England and Wales Court of Appeal (Criminal Division) Decisions, *R v Clark, EWCA Crim 1020*, 2003.

Helmholz, R. H, 'Infanticide in the province of canterbury during the fifteenth century', *History of Childhood Quarterly*, 2(3), 1975, p.379.

Hermiston, Roger, *Greatest Traitor: The Secret Lives of Agent George Blake*, Aurum Press, 2013.

Holden, Anthony, *The St Albans Poisoner: The Life and Crimes of Graham Young*, Corgi, 1995.

Kaczynski, David. *Every Last Tie: The Story of the Unabomber and His Family*, Duke University Press, 2016.

Lewin, Gregory, *A Report of Cases Determined on the Crown Side on the Northern Circuit commencing with The Summer Circuit of 1822 and ending with the Summer Circuit of 1833*, S Sweet, 1834.

Melle, I., 'The Breivik case and what psychiatrists can learn from it', *World Psychiatry*, 12(1), 2013, pp.16–21.

Meloy, J. Reid, Elmar Habermeyer, and Angela Guldimann, 'The warning behaviors of Anders Breivik', *Journal of Threat Assessment and Management*,

2.3-4, 2015.

Nadel, Jennifer, *Sara Thornton: The Story of a Woman Who Killed*, Victor Gollancz, 1993.

Orange, Richard, *The Mind of a Madman: Norway's Struggle to Understand Anders Breivik*, Kindle Single, 2012.

Pearman, Joanne, 'Bastards, Baby Farmers, and Social Control in Victorian Britain' (PhD thesis), Kent Academic Repository (https://kar.kent.ac.uk/62866/), 2017.

Rattle, Alison and Alison Vale, *The Woman who Murdered Babies for Money: The Story of Amelia Dyer*, André Deutsch, 2011.

South East Coast Strategic Health Authority, Kent County Council and Kent Probation Area, 'Report of the independent inquiry into the care and treatment of Michael Stone', 2006.

The Council of the Inns of Court and the Royal Statistical Society, 'Statistics and probability for advocates: Understanding the use of statistical evidence in courts and tribunals', 2017.

The Stationery Office. *Rillington Place*, 1999.